Trad Nation

Tes Slominski

TRAD NATION

Gender, Sexuality, and Race
in Irish Traditional Music

Wesleyan University Press   Middletown, Connecticut

Wesleyan University Press
Middletown, CT 06459
www.wesleyan.edu/wespress
© 2020 Tes Slominski
All rights reserved
Manufactured in the United States of America
Designed by Mindy Basinger Hill
Typeset in Minion Pro

The publisher gratefully acknowledges the support of the AMS 75 PAYS Endowment of the American Musicology Society, funded in part by the National Endowment for the Humanities and the Andrew W. Mellow Foundation.

Library of Congress Cataloging-in-Publication Data

Names: Slominski, Tes, author.

Title: Trad nation : gender, sexuality, and race in Irish traditional music / Tes Slominski.

Description: [First.] | Middletown : Wesleyan University Press, 2020. |

Series: Music/culture | Includes bibliographical references and index. |

Summary: "A growing number of LGBTQ, female, and non-white individuals have become established in Irish traditional music. This is the first book to examine diversity in Irish traditional music, highlighting the possibility of an expanded genre"— Provided by publisher.

Identifiers: LCCN 2019049821 (print) | LCCN 2019049822 (ebook) | ISBN 9780819579270 (hardcover) | ISBN 9780819579287 (paperback) | ISBN 9780819579294 (ebook)

Subjects: LCSH: Music—Social aspects—Ireland. | Homosexuality and music—Ireland. | Music and race—Ireland. | Women musicians—Ireland. | Nationalism in music.

Classification: LCC ML3917.I74 S56 2020 (print) | LCC ML3917.I74 (ebook) | DDC 781.62/9162008—dc23

LC record available at https://lccn.loc.gov/2019049821

LC ebook record available at https://lccn.loc.gov/2019049822

5 4 3 2 1

FOR GRANNY AND PA

CONTENTS

Acknowledgments ix

Introduction 1

ONE Mother Ireland and the Queen of Irish Fiddlers: Women Musicians and the Nation in Early Twentieth-Century Ireland 25

TWO The Not-So-Strange Disappearance of Treasa Ní Ailpín (Teresa Halpin): Class, Gender, and Musical Style in Early Twentieth-Century Ireland 64

THREE Biography, Musical Life, and Gender: Julia Clifford as a Woman Traditional Musician 98

FOUR Subjectivity, Flow, and "the Music Itself" 135

FIVE Playing Right and the Right to Play: (Dis)identification Tactics Among Queer Musicians and Musicians of Color 153

Notes 179

Bibliography 207

Index 225

ACKNOWLEDGMENTS

> My head starts to spin
> When I think where I've been
> Playin' twin to an old fiddle tune
> Bob Lucas, "The Road Is a Lover"

Since I discovered Irish traditional music at the age of seventeen, the tunes have taken me all kinds of places, from the mountains of Virginia, Sliabh Luachra in Ireland, and upstate New York to the flatter lands of New York City and southern Wisconsin. More people have offered tunes and friendship along the way than I can thank here, and the extent of my gratitude extends well beyond the limits of these few paragraphs.

This book would not have happened without the encouragement and generosity of mentors and friends—and it's often difficult to distinguish between the two categories, since I am delighted to count my mentors as friends and have learned so much from my peers. In the Irish traditional music scene, I especially thank Connie O'Connell, Donal O'Connor, Liz Carroll, Philippe Varlet, Jackie Daly, Matt Cranitch, Bernadette McCarthy, and Maurice O'Keeffe (RIP)—my playing would not be what it is if not for you all. Likewise, my musical life and this book would not be nearly as rich without the camaraderie and insights of friends like Sara Read, Niamh Parsons, Laura Parmentier, Deirdre Ní Chonghaile, Alan Ng, Don Meade, Susan McKeown, Lori Madden, Sophie Liebregts, Sasha Hsuczyk, Alicia Guinn, Aoife Granville, Augie Fairchild, Eibhlín de Paor, Jean Denney, Alex Davis, Patrick Cavanaugh, Myron Bretholz, and Crystal Bailey.

My gratitude to Suzanne Cusick is greater than a few short sentences can express. I am especially thankful for all the intellectual energy, moral support, laughter, faith, and productive ass kicking she has given me over the years, and

I am a better person and a better scholar for her friendship and mentoring. I am also grateful to my fabulous dissertation committee members, Jane Sugarman, Martin Daughtry, Lucy Delap, and Michael Beckerman, who gave vital feedback on this project in its earliest stages. I also greatly appreciate the input of Fred Maus, Zoe Sherinian, and Sean Williams, who have each moved seamlessly among the roles of reader, editor, and friend.

Sometimes friends offer support that encompasses and exceeds intellectual input, musical inspiration, and pure merriment. Rachel Mundy and Tomie Hahn have both encouraged me to step back, take a breath, think laterally, and engage in productive play—an approach that has shaped my work in subtle but important ways. Bonnie Gordon, Manuel Lerdau, and "the spawn" provided support of various kinds in the final stages of this project, including insightful conversations, merriment, and gelato breaks. I am also thankful to Elizabeth Keenan and Ryan Penagos for providing similar help and necessary fun in 2010 as I finished the dissertation that began this project.

My work has also benefited from many far-ranging conversations with Yvonne Wu, Lauren Weintraub Stoebel, Britt Scharringhausen, Gillian Rodger, Annie Randall, Monica Hairston O'Connell, Junko Oba, Gayle Murchison, Melanie Marshall, Maureen Mahon, Tamara Ketabgian, Lauron Kehrer, Ellen Joyce, Amy Jones, Kylie Quave Herrera, Nicol Hammond, Lillie Gordon, Denise Gill, and Susan Furukawa. Special thanks to Kylie, who helped name this book. I am also grateful to several of my Beloit College students for sharing their thoughts as students of Irish traditional music. They include Chris Thulien, Lucy Rosenmeier, Sadie Record (who also provided research assistance for this project), Sam Poyer, Sarah Newton, Rachel Homeniuk, Alyse Gowgiel, Renata Goetz, John Glennan, and Alex Cheong.

Several individuals and institutions have helped me greatly in their stewardship and sharing of materials and knowledge. *Míle buíochas* to Nicolas McAuliffe and Brenda Seebach for their generosity with private archival material, as well as to Anna Bale and Simon O'Leary at the National Folklore Collection at University College Dublin; Jack Roche at the Bruach na Carraige Teach Cheoil in Rockchapel, County Cork; Jeff Ksiazek at the Ward Irish Music Archives in Milwaukee, Wisconsin; and the staffs of the Irish Traditional Music Archive in Dublin, the National Library of Ireland, the British Library, New York University's Tamiment Archives, and the Boston Public Library. Without the material support of McCracken and Mainzer fellowships at New York University, a Woodrow Wilson Women's Studies Dissertation Completion Fellowship, an American Council of

Learned Societies Recent Doctoral Recipients fellowship, and a sabbatical from Beloit College, this book might not exist. I am also grateful to have received a subvention from the AMS 75 PAYS Endowment of the American Musicological Society, funded in part by the National Endowment for the Humanities and the Andrew W. Mellon Foundation. And for their feedback and help at various stages, I am grateful to Suzanna Tamminen; Music/Culture series editors Deborah Wong, Sherrie Tucker, and Jeremy Wallach; everyone at Wesleyan University Press; and the readers of the initial manuscript.

In addition to my trad and academic families, I thank my family of origin for providing the gift of education and the space to be a nerdy bookworm fiddle player, as well as instilling in me an obligation to explore the mysteries of the past and the complexities of the present. In particular, my mother has modeled resilience, attention to detail, careful management of resources, and above all the importance of close listening as an act of generosity—skills that have helped me make my way as a musician and scholar in an uncertain world.

Go raibh míle maith agaibh.

INTRODUCTION

Origins

We all have our origin stories, mythologized in countless retellings. Telling these stories can be an opportunity, an obligation, a burden. We tell our origin stories for a host of reasons in Irish traditional music, but the main one is to situate ourselves in "the tradition": to connect our lives and music making with the people and places who have most influenced us. Our origin stories account for our presence in the Irish traditional music scene and often tell of fathers, teachers, homes, heritages, and obsessions. For some of us, these stories are also an attempt to establish our right to musical space—a space that has not always been readily granted to Irish women instrumentalists and that remains a complicated place for queer and / or ethnically non-Irish musicians. As in nationalism, space, place, and territory remain enduring metaphors in Irish traditional music despite sound's way of reminding us that spatial, temporal, political, and intersubjective borders are permeable and dynamic.

Here is the version of my "trad origin story" that is most legible to the people who hear my American accent and last name and ask how I started playing Irish fiddle. "Your mother's Irish, right?" they suggest hopefully, looking for an easy way to place me. They seek family lines traceable like tidy ink on paper rather than the meandering dirt tracks of lived experience, muddy and sometimes hard to locate if you don't know exactly where to look—like the path down through the woods to the graves of my ancestors who fought in the War of 1812. My unmarked whiteness and visible traces of Scots-Irish heritage from my mother's side provide a fairly easy answer, enhanced by the legend that the family patriarch who came to Virginia from Scotland in the late eighteenth century paid his passage as the ship's fiddler. When necessary, I can augment this story by offering that my grandfather played old-time banjo and fiddle, even though I never heard him play because he had arthritis and hearing problems by the time I came along. I generally do not mention that although he seemed to enjoy hearing "Devil's Dream" and "Turkey in the Straw," he always asked me to play a particular Mozart minuet for him—that detail complicates the essentialized story of rural Southerners that most people seem to want to hear. After having established this vaguely Celtic lineage for myself, I mention that hearing Liz Carroll, Eileen Ivers, and Martin Hayes playing the reel "The Humours of Lissadell" on the National Public Radio radio show *Thistle and Shamrock* when I was seventeen set me off on the path of an obsession that has now lasted nearly three decades. I also make sure that people know I spent a great deal of time in Ireland during the late 1990s and lived there for a while in the early 2000s. In true genealogical fashion, I name my Irish musical mentors and compatriots—and since Irish traditional musicians (fondly, "traddies") are rarely separated by more than two degrees, this is usually an effective way to locate myself.

That is the easy story. Other stories are harder to tell. Do we ever really understand our own desire paths as we create them? Or are we like the man in the tale by the Danish writer Karen Blixen who is unaware that his nighttime footprints to and from a pond trace the figure of a stork?[1] Do our stories make sense only after the fact—or perhaps never?

FARMAGEDDON: A CHILDHOOD IN ARTIFACTS

Some stories gain coherence in hindsight. Others become more strange over time, fragmenting and losing coherence as they gain meaning. This story is the latter kind. If one place brought me to the fiddle, to history and ethnography, to myself, it was this place. And if one place complicates everything, it is this same place:

We are in the den of my grandparents' house. Let's say I am ten years old.

One bookcase with glass doors. Inside, the set of *Encyclopaedia Britannica* from 1959, complete with pages of color pictures of flags of the world. The Cokesbury hymnal and the red hymnal we never use except to find the "right" version of "He Lives." A veterinary manual from 1903, a book of Scottish tartans, *Christy*, and Granny's favorite cookbook with the writing on the spine worn off. These are the only books in the bookcase that matter to me at this age.

Pa's cabinet. Paper clips and rubber bands sorted by size and color. Fading letters from the Civil War whose words he is in the process of painstakingly tracing over with ballpoint pen to render more visible. A Bible. Hard candy. On top of the cabinet, the old manual typewriter, a wooden bowl of pecans and a nutcracker (the plain kind), and the pad of paper we use to communicate with him as his hearing deteriorates. The top page contains two lines so far: "two in the trap and one in the box" and "she died on Thursday."[2]

In the homemade pine chest (which is in the hall just outside the den): Pa's old homemade fiddle with banjo machine heads as tuning pegs, the bow convex and its hair held on (not very well) with some sort of brown putty. It's barely playable, but that doesn't stop me from trying.

The mantle: Masonic and Eastern Star plaques, outgoing mail, long-necked gourds hanging down. Above it, a Confederate cavalry sword looking down from its prideful place.

WHY THIS? WHY NOW?

What does this Southern Gothic cabinet of curiosities have to do with Irish traditional music, other than as an exercise in autobiographical archaeology? The rituals of customary genealogy do not yield the answers I seek, and others have done (or are doing) the work of tracing connections among American musics and their Irish, Scottish, and African roots.[3] Instead, I intend this book to look forward by looking back to the past and around at the present. I hope that my story-through-artifacts began to lead you to imagine the olio of pride, nostalgia, faith, love, *communitas*, yearning for connection with the past, and fear of decay and disappearance these items represent. Such feelings also suffuse my account of these objects, along with an overlay of shame. Like many Virginians, I come from a family that included slaveholders and Confederate soldiers, and I live in a society that does not yet collectively understand the need for reparations to the descendants of those whose lands it took and the people it once enslaved. My argument against ethnic nationalism comes in part from this perspective and in part from the study of Irish history, which exposes the illogic of a popular postcolonialism that has built for itself a house using the master's flawed tools of ethnic nationalism even as it has been quick to recount the wrongs of the colonizer. By presenting the stories of women; lesbian, gay, bisexual, transgender, and queer (LGBTQ+) musicians; and musicians of color in Irish traditional music, I hope to make the flaws in ethnic nationalism audible—with the goal of motivating us to find new tools for understanding music making and identity formation outside the parameters of embodied ethnicity that enclose national and cultural belonging.

Pride, nostalgia, faith, love, communitas, yearning for connection with the past, and fear of decay and disappearance—if I had begun with this litany of feelings and told you it was about rural Ireland, you would readily have believed me. Likewise, if I'd said it referred to Irish traditional music, it would have made immediate sense as a description of musicians' feelings toward "the music itself" and each other.[4] After all, the Irish trad scene hinges on community, from the aural transmission of instrumental dance tunes (mostly anonymous) to sessions (gatherings where musicians meet to play and socialize). Although professionalization has been part of Irish traditional music for centuries, most musicians play for the feelings of connection that participation in trad brings: connections with the past, the music, and each other. This is not the stereotypically Irish music of "Whiskey in the Jar" or "Danny Boy." Instead, this genre operates on a more subcultural level: "civilians" might occasionally encounter this music in pubs or tucked away in certain places on the airwaves or Internet, but trad is not about mass appeal—it is about relationships enacted through musicking.[5] In this book, I focus on instrumental music and point out that while many of the same questions about gender, sexuality, and race/ethnicity also apply to Ireland's singing traditions (which overlap with its instrumental traditions), the demographics and operation of the *sean-nós* (old-style) singing scene present other questions.[6]

Pride, nostalgia, faith, love, communitas, yearning for connection with the past, and fear of decay and disappearance—all of these things are true, and many of them are good. But feelings called by these same names also drive ethnic nationalism, whether the Irish nationalism of the early twentieth century that bought some kinds of freedom at the expense of others, or the white nationalism of the United States in the early twenty-first century that threatens the well-being and lives of people who do not match its limited ideal of heterosexual white masculinity. These Irish and American nationalisms consume the same fuel, and I hope that drawing this comparison will motivate readers to work actively to dismantle systems of ethnic nationalism that have upheld norms of Irishness based on race, class, gender, and sexuality since at least the late nineteenth century. This book seeks to discover these norms and how they have influenced history, historiography, and lived experience in Irish traditional music and among its musicians. Like the authors of "'Vote Yes for Common Sense Citizenship': Immigration and the Paradoxes at the Heart of Ireland's 'Céad Míle Fáilte,'" I call for "seeing Irishness as something constructed or performed; diverse, contingent, relation[al] and constantly in the process of formation."[7]

This book has two primary aims. First, I introduce musicians and topics that have not been discussed widely—or at all—in the existing literature on Irish traditional music. Second, I argue for the separation of Irish traditional music from Irish ethnic nationalism. As an American writing during an era of destructive nationalism, I believe that many of today's problems come from outdated investments in identity as an essential, inherent characteristic rather than as a construction that changes in response to encounters with other people, musics, and contexts. Such investments are not just American problems, and although the adjective "Irish" is attached to the material I introduce in this book, my argument for the separation of sounds and social practices from ethnicity applies well beyond Ireland and its diaspora.

This book is partially autoethnographic and is grounded in my own experience both as fiddler in the Irish vernacular music tradition and as a queer white woman brought up in the rural South of the United States. As I embarked on ethnographic research to better understand the experiences of today's women, queer musicians, and musicians of color in Irish traditional music, their stories resonated strikingly with those of Irish women musicians in the early twentieth century whose careers were driven by ideas about nationalism and ethnicity. A century later, similar ideas about nationalism and ethnicity continue to shape Irish traditional music and its reception, as well as the reception of musicians who differ from the white, ethnically Irish men who have historically constituted the most visible population of trad musicians. Extensive discussions of gender, sexuality, and race in Irish traditional music scholarship have been few and recent, and substantial public conversations within the scene about racism and (hetero)sexism are only slowly emerging.[8] This book arrives at a moment when frank conversations about inclusion and discrimination in many music communities mirror similar social and political conversations on local, state, and international levels. The stakes of these conversations are extremely high: maintaining the status quo of (hetero)sexism and racism within individual music scenes in the name of genetic heritage is no longer excusable in an era defined by the global threat of fascism founded on white ethnic nationalism. Thus, this work is unapologetically activist in its claim that ethnic nationalism is at the root of sexism, heterosexism, and racism in Irish traditional music performance and its reception.

Despite offering this critique of the foundational identity of Irish traditional music as "Irish," I have also attempted to translate the pleasures of playing trad into verbal language and to introduce readers to some of the affective aspects of participating in the Irish traditional music scene. Accounts of warmth and welcome, community, and belonging grace these pages, as well as the passion that traddies have for "the music itself." Indeed, I have chosen to use the more informal word "traddie" sometimes to remind readers of this sense of community even as I recount the hardships and violences that nonnormative musicians face. I pay special attention to subjectivity and the ways that playing trad "brings people to their senses," as the accordion player Joe Cooley so memorably said.[9] My motivation (like that of countless others) in writing this book is to ensure the continuity of the tradition—but instead of maintaining a conservative, preservationist mind-set, I argue that the best way to care for Irish traditional music is to call for its transformation. Instead of acting through the fear of change implicit in the concept of safeguarding that drove the tradition-innovation debates in trad scholarship in the 1990s and early 2000s, I suggest that attending to the experiences of women, queer, and nonwhite musicians issues an imperative to rethink the restrictions of a genre defined by ethnic nationalism and offers a way to amplify the qualities that draw musicians and listeners to trad.

Considering questions of ethnicity in the Irish traditional music scene illuminates the hypervigilant policing of whiteness in the United States and other so-called multicultural societies, where the "empty container" of diversity discourse works to protect white ethnic musics as "diversity."[10] Framing white ethnicities as diverse in relation to fantasies of unmarked Americanness (usually understood as white, Anglo-Saxon, and Protestant) allows these scenes to sidestep questions about whether ethnic heritage is the most important factor in who can (or should) play a genre. Using this logic, white supremacist / nationalist groups can then appropriate these genres to cloak their violent agendas and argue that white diversity is also at risk. Such arguments obscure other threats to vernacular genres (including neoliberal capitalism and conservative preservationism), as well as the overwhelming power differentials that diversity work seeks to address. Moreover, reinscribing genre boundaries based on ethnicity erases the complexities of musical and social practice and erases musicians who seem not to belong—and this kind of erasure has long troubled many genres, including American old-time music and Western art music.[11] This book provides a model for beginning to think through these issues.

Therefore, I begin with the assertion that it is not possible to fully understand Ireland or its traditional music without paying close attention to gender, sexuality, and race in connection with each other and with larger social, political, and intellectual currents in the places where Irish traditional music scenes exist. Three broad and widely applicable questions shape this work: First, what (and whom) do dominant systems of sex, gender, and ethnicity exclude? Second, how do societies rely on these systems and exclusions to reproduce national identity? And finally, how might we celebrate cultural traditions currently understood as national while dismantling the racisms and (hetero)sexisms that fuel ethnic nationalism? These questions are urgent for the overlapping audiences of this book, which include traditional musicians based in Ireland and those from outside Ireland, as well academics and cultural politicians based in North America, Ireland, and elsewhere.

This book begins to fill in some of the gaps in scholarship about women musicians of the past and, in doing so, introduces the cultural, magical, reproductive, and ethnic nationalisms that continue to shape the practice, discourse, and historiography of Irish traditional music. After tracing the reasons historians have withheld recognition from women musicians of the early twentieth century, I turn to subjectivity—of women musicians like Julia Clifford (1914–97); of present-day women, queer, and nonwhite musicians; and of "the music itself," which I use as a foil for understanding who counts as human in Irish traditional music. Finally, I discuss the epistemic and ontological violences toward women, queer musicians, and especially musicians of color that can emerge through musical aesthetics, social practices, and speech acts, and I investigate strategies nonnormative musicians use to make sense of their participation in the genre.

THE GENDERED, SEXED, AND RACED OPPRESSIONS OF ETHNIC NATIONALISM IN TWO FOUND OBJECTS

In Irish traditional music (and elsewhere), all forms of identity-based discrimination have roots in nationalist ideologies: which actions, sounds, and bodies produce the ideal nation, and thus count as "Irish"? As Kimberle Crenshaw articulated in her work on intersectionality, oppressions do not happen independently but overlap, and so gender, sexuality, and race are inextricable in determining who counts as a good [Irish or "Irish"] subject or an "authentic" traditional musician.[12] The connections among these categories were not invented in the early twenty-first century but emerged in the popular Irish press in the early twentieth century in both local and internationally syndicated material. In the following section, I use two items from 1913 issues of the *Kerryman* to provide historical background for some of the questions this book addresses. Though these items situate nationalist ideals and anxieties in the context of County Kerry, similar items were common in newspapers throughout Ireland:

> Ballylongford Echoes. By Clan-na-Gael. On Sunday night, November 9th, 1913, the Rev. M. O'Brien, CC [Catholic curate], Ballylongford, will deliver a lecture in aid of the Ballylongford Town Hall. A grand concert will follow. Anglo and Anglo-Irish songs, recitations and dialogues, Irish dancing, including four- and eight-hand reels, single reels and jigs, step dancing exhibitions by some of the foremost Feis prize winners in Munster, together with gramaphone [sic] selections conducted by the Rev. M. O'Brien. These are some of the night's attractions. Everything up-to-date National and attractive. No West British mongrel airs or Rag-time selections to be allowed on the stage. Something breathing the native airs of Kerry's mountains and valleys to be the principal features. It is to be hoped that the exponents of the "Turkey Trot" and other abuses will be conspicuous by their absence. Let the atmosphere be clear, clean, and healthy. The promoters are satisfied to do all in their power to please everybody, but under no circumstances will they allow any favouritism to interfere with their programme or alter it one iota. We want no songs from Dixie Land or the gutter productions of London back lanes or elsewhere. Let this be a timely warning.[13]

"Everything up-to-date National"—the vigorous energies of cultural nationalism in dancers' feet, musicians' hands, and from the pens of commentators like Clan-na-Gael. A "clear, clean, and healthy" atmosphere from the "native airs of Kerry's mountains and valleys," free from the moral dangers of immediately audible or visible foreign influence. If you wanted to make a case for the vitality and even the inevitability of an Irish nation in 1913, you would have emphasized the strength and right(eous)ness of your homeland and its music, dance, sport, and oratory. In working toward a culturally distinct "Irish Ireland," you would have eschewed foreign popular entertainments like the Turkey Trot and other "animal dances" that scandalized the United States, Britain, and Ireland in 1913. These dances would incite the censure of the Vatican in 1914 and presented a problem for a nationalist movement in the later stages of transformation from a nonsectarian movement into a Catholic one.[14] Moreover, "foreign" music and dance popularized through minstrelsy, variety, and vaudeville brought associations with blackness and the working classes—and along with them, notions of sexual license, weakened morals, and the woes of poverty Ireland's middle class was working so hard to escape. Irish cultural nationalism thus reinforced ethnic nationalism by using performance styles as shorthand for perceptions of ethnic and racial difference.

Ethnicity (and, by extension, race) is central to any discussion of Irish nationalism: by positioning the Irish in a subordinate position in an imagined hierarchy of races, the British justified their exploitation of Ireland's human and agricultural resources. This rationale for imperialism—which played out even more dramatically in other areas of the British Empire—was then available to Irish nationalists seeking independence. Like other European nations, Ireland mobilized the idea of ethnic difference (already embedded in British policies) in arguing for its right to independence. And as it has done for other white European immigrants, skin color eventually provided a ticket for Irish assimilation into the diaspora and, in the case of the United States, a way for the Irish to distinguish themselves from society's most disempowered members, black slaves. The Irish—initially cast as apes by the British—worked very hard to "become white" (and thus fully human) at home and in the diaspora, sometimes at the expense of people of color.[15]

In response to popular perceptions of large numbers of nonwhite immigrants to Ireland more recently, the 2004 "commonsense citizenship" referendum and subsequent amendment to the Irish Constitution changed the law from granting birthright citizenship to requiring that children claiming Irish citizenship have at least one Irish citizen parent. Framed as achieving compliance with European Union laws, the referendum responded to the popular perception that a growing number of "birth tourists" were exploiting Irish immigration law.[16] Despite a much higher number of white immigrants to Ireland, immigrants as a group are racialized as black and presumed to be refugees and asylum seekers.[17] Ireland, known as the "land of a hundred thousand welcomes," voted overwhelmingly in support of the referendum, which Una Crowley, Mary Gilmartin, and Rob Kitchin argue was "employed in such a way as to fix and essentialise Irishness, thus highlighting the threatening other, and to construct immigrants as suspect, untrustworthy, and deserving of Ireland's 'hospitality' only in limited, prescribed ways or not at all."[18] Consider this excerpt:

> That boy will do to depend on,
> I know that this is true—
> From lads in love with their mothers
> Our bravest heroes grew.
> Earth's grandest hearts have been loving ones,
> Since time and earth began;
> And the boy who kisses his mother
> Is every inch a man.[19]

Whether Irish or American, good nationalist sons love their mothers and nations with "grand hearts" and grow up to express their manliness through the

Introduction **9**

protection of both. In turn, loving mothers teach their sons the songs and stories of "our bravest heroes." In the fight for an independent Irish nation, everyone had to do his or her part, and these parts were strictly gendered "his" and "hers." In a bid to ensure social welfare, the 1937 constitution established that women's primary duties were in the home and "acknowledge[d] that the primary and natural educator of the child is the Family," which should provide for "the religious and moral, intellectual, physical and social education of their children."[20]

Reproductive heterosexuality—the production of ethnically Irish children—is at the center of these constitutional articles and the additional laws and social practices they have reinforced, such as the 2004 "commonsense citizenship" referendum and the 1932 marriage bar, which required women to resign from jobs in the civil service (including teaching posts) upon marriage. This set of laws was only fully repealed in 1973, while divorce would not become legal until 1995.[21] The fact that both sides of the 2015 Irish marriage equality referendum appealed to family shows just how embedded reproductive family structures are in Irish society, from the predictable "two men can't replace a mother's love" and "equality for children first" placards opposing same-sex marriage to the effective and heartfelt "Ring Your Granny" campaign in favor of marriage equality launched by students at Trinity College Dublin.[22]

ETHNIC NATIONALISM AND THE CONTROL OF BODIES AND DISCOURSES IN IRELAND (AND BEYOND)

These two tidbits from over a century ago demonstrate just how entangled gender, sexuality, and race/ethnicity are in Irish ethnic and cultural nationalism, which has at its heart the reproduction of bodies and practices understood as "Irish," whether at home or in the diaspora. Irish traditional music has long played a role in both delimiting and expanding who and what counts as "Irish" through its production of sound, discourse, and sociability. Trad is in constant dialogue with governmental, legal, and educational systems anywhere there are communities of players—it is both subject to and a component of the instruments of biopower, to use Michel Foucault's term for the forces that regulate the lives of populations on behalf of the state.[23] As the musicians' stories in these pages illustrate, nationalist and sonic subjectivities are inseparable, whether a musician hails from Dublin, Texas, or Tokyo, and the accumulation of ideas about gender, sexuality, and race/ethnicity from multiple sites shapes the experiences and reception of traddies of all kinds. Although this book does not discuss them extensively, issues of identity also concern ethnically Irish men: for example, while they enjoy the power that accrues to white masculinity, their sometimes uneasy positioning within ideas of modernity derives from Ireland's postcolonial relationship with Britain as well as with US cultural imperialism. Such relationships often play out in traditional music settings.

I begin from the premise that discrimination on the basis of race, sex, sexuality, or other identity characteristics is unacceptable in a scene that describes itself as open and welcoming—and that often lives up to that description. This ideal of openness does not always match the experiences of nonnormative musicians, however, and this book charts the racism, sexism, and heterosexism in the Irish trad scene that often goes undetected by those who are not subject to its aggressions and exclusions. I also begin with the claim that instrumental Irish traditional music has had an ambivalent relationship with ethnic nationalism since at least the late nineteenth century, and that the social and musical workings of this now-global scene already reflect more diverse outlooks, practices, and participants than trad's historic, discursive, and institutional relationships with ethnic nationalism might suggest. Connections with ethnic nationalism endure, however, and drive racism, sexism, and heterosexism within the scene. Perhaps more important, I assert that such seemingly innocuous manifestations of ethnic nationalism (like defining certain genres as "ethnic") normalize white supremacy and heteropatriarchy in an era when such doctrines threaten global human rights and social, political, and environmental integrity around the world.

Irish traditional music is not the only genre I could use to make this argument, and the work of Matthew Gelbart and Benjamin Teitelbaum informs my thinking, as do increasing reports of white nationalists' appropriation of Scottish, generic "Celtic," and—to a lesser extent—Irish sounds and symbolism in the United States.[24] From my perspective as an American who loves Irish traditional music and identifies as a traddie, this severing of trad and ethnic nationalism is urgent, both to protect the genre from being co-opted by right-wing extremists outside Ireland and to provide a model for redefining "ethnic" musics based on qualities other than genetic heritage, with its imperatives around so-called purity (often framed as "authenticity") and reproductive sexuality. This is not a decolonization project, exactly, but it is a reminder that decolonization is not possible without uncovering links among gender, sexuality, race/ethnicity, social class, and ability and redressing the power imbalances that are embedded in colonial and nationalist structures.

I have come to this argument for a postnationalist approach to Irish traditional music through nearly three decades of being besotted with trad and devoted to the chosen family I have met through my participation in it in the United States and Ireland. Like many of my interlocutors, I have often found the musicians in the Irish trad scene to be inclusive and community-minded, and as chapter 4 relates, the pleasures of playing trad can be exquisite. Thus, this book does not come from a feeling of rancor—quite the opposite. But most of my women, queer, and/or nonwhite interlocutors and I have chosen to participate in this realm of musicking despite recurrent negative experiences related to gender, sexuality, and/or race/ethnicity, and a few have distanced themselves from the scene because of such experiences. I tell these less happy stories at a moment of increased attention to the inequities that women, LGBTQ+ people, and people of color worldwide face. With that increased attention comes backlash, including physical violence, and this book would be very different had I finished it before the Black Lives Matter and Me Too movements emerged; before events in Ferguson, Missouri, Baltimore, Maryland, and Charlottesville, Virginia; and before right-wing nationalist politicians gained widespread public acceptance in Europe and the United States. At the time of this writing in 2018, traddies in the United States look wistfully to Ireland for its live-and-let-live mentality, but racism, sexism, and homophobia remain problems there as well, and immigrants—especially nonwhite newcomers—face significant barriers to employment (except in low-wage jobs) and discrimination inside and outside the workplace.[25] And while traddies from outside Ireland (especially white ones) may not always be targeted by Irish immigration and citizenship laws in the same ways as would-be residents, they are still vulnerable to social attitudes about gender, sexuality, and race in Ireland, as chapters below describe.

Taking the experiences of marginalized traddies seriously requires both a reassessment of current practice and a call for transformation. The Irish traditional music scene already has a significant number of women, queer, and nonwhite members, although scholarship, recordings, concert bookings, and forms of recognition such as TG4's Gradam Ceoil awards do not accurately reflect the scene's demographics even among ethnically Irish musicians. Within Ireland, more women and queer trad musicians are making their voices heard through the FairPlé initiative for gender equality in trad begun in 2018 and events like *géilís* ("gay" plus *céilí* [dance]) at Dublin Pride and other festivals, but the public face and "masters" of "the tradition" remain largely male, straight (or closeted), and white. At the time of this writing, no one has attempted to conduct a census of Irish traditional musicians, so we have no exact information about the demographics of the scene in Ireland or worldwide—although participants tend to perceive the overall scene as dominated by heterosexual white men.

Outside Ireland, the demographics of trad scenes depend on local population and include a significant and growing number of ethnically non-Irish players, especially in places without large numbers of Irish immigrants such as Japan, France, and Germany. Previous work, including accounts of non-Irish traditional musicians, assumes that ethnicity is central to the practice of Irish traditional music.[26] Helen O'Shea offers a necessary critique to the tethering of ethnicity to musicianship and approaches identity as "fluid and opportunistic, rather than unified and self-determined."[27] But in general, not being Irish implies a lack that must be accounted for—a lack that non-Irish musicians sometimes feel quite keenly. Mick Moloney describes how some traddies in the United States address this disjuncture between ethnicity and musical participation: "The discovery of Irish forbears may serve to rubber stamp a legitimate claim to participation in the culture or, for particular individuals, it may turn into a type of cultural crusade which can involve immersion in Irish history, language and literature and repeated visits to the home country to establish links with the 'real' Ireland."[28]

While genealogical research might allow some traddies born outside Irish or Irish diasporic communities to sidestep the "But are you IRISH?" question, many musicians do not have recourse to the validation of genetic heritage or the white skin that allows them to elude such interrogation, which can be intrusive and aggressive. My concern here is not with how individual traddies make sense of their ethnic backgrounds, but with the imperative that they must address them to explain their participation—especially in the diaspora, where being perceived to not "belong" in Irish music settings can lead to xenophobic commentary of the "go back to [Africa, China, and so on]" variety. Here, I remind white readers that as in Ireland, full cultural and sometimes political citizenship remains provisional for nonwhite members of society in Britain, Australia, and the United States in the 2010s.

The imperative to account for one's non-Irish (and especially nonwhite) ethnicity in trad contexts is problematic first because it implies that "Irishness" can only be jus sanguinis—and, as with the rhetoric in the 2004 Irish citizenship referendum, that it is simple "common sense" to base Irish citizenship or participation in Irish cultural forms on ethnicity (such arguments always require us to ask whose common sense is involved).[29] However prevalent it is worldwide, this method of determining citizenship denies the reality of an increasingly multicultural Ireland and ensures that trad as "Irish" will remain a closed system from which some of Ireland's residents will be metaphorically excluded, even if they participate: bodies excluded from citizenship have no logical place in a genre discursively defined by ethnic nationalism. This problem will be especially acute for ethnically non-Irish people residing in Ireland, who might reasonably expect to have a greater share in the culture of the nation. As chapter 5 discusses, many traddies from outside Ireland also endure constant questioning at home and sometimes in Ireland about their "right" to play Irish traditional music.

"THAT THE AGE OF NATIONALITY IS GONE": TRAD AS POSTNATIONALIST LIBERATION?

"That the Age of Nationality Is Gone" was the subject of a debate between members of the various Irish Universities at a largely attended meeting in University College, Dublin, last Saturday evening. The proceedings were conducted in the Irish language.... The debate was opened by Mr C. O'Brobein, U.C. Dublin, who contended that with a better understanding between the nations of the world nationality would die, and would be replaced by internationalism. Miss Mary Kelly, U.C. Cork, held that the universal use of the cinema would assist materially in establishing internationalism, which she said would end all wars. Mr McCarthy Willis, Trinity College, expressed the view that the increase of education would end nationality. Mr T. Guilfoyle, U.C. Galway, argued that some nations would completely die out, and that there would be one universal language and similar customs among all countries. Against the motion Mr M. O'Uardail, U.C. Galway, referred to Egypt and India as examples to show that nationality would always survive, and nationality could not die so long as the native music lived.[30]

Speaking in Irish, already an endangered language in 1925, university students heralded the end of the age of nationalism three years after the formation of the Irish Free State, although one Herderian holdout, Mr. O'Uardail, used the survival of "native music" to argue for the inevitability of nationalism. His argument that "native" culture sustains the nation echoed the rhetoric of the Gaelic League, Comhaltas Ceoltóirí Éireann, the Gaelic Athletic Association, and other institutions dedicated to preserving Irish culture. Proponents of this brand of cultural nationalism also sometimes fear that the "native music" will die if the nation perishes. In this book I disagree with both and instead argue that examining gender, sexuality, and race/ethnicity in Irish traditional music provides a powerful critique of ethnic nationalism and, in doing so, protects rather than endangers the genre. Furthermore, I suggest that in seeking ways to maintain its positive social and musical aspects while addressing sexism, heterosexism, and racism, the Irish trad scene can pilot alternatives to ethnic nationalism as a form of social organization. This argument is utopian in its call for transformation, and I hope that the trad scene will view its transnational present as an opportunity to rethink its nationalist past. Instead of reinscribing ethnicity or nationality as the normative container of Irish traditional music—or calling for the kind of uniform internationalism that some of the 1925 university students supported—I extend O'Shea's critique of static ethnicity-based musical identity to argue that ethnic nationalism has served its purpose for both Ireland and Irish traditional music, and that timeworn and damaging ideas about gender, sexuality, and race must not endure in the name of "tradition."[31]

Moreover, the Irish trad scene has the potential to model a postnationalist approach that is simultaneously local and transnational—cosmopolitan, even—without serving to justify the existence of the nation by restricting who can belong to it.[32] Here, recent developments in the United States provide a powerful negative example of a system that disregards the well-being of the majority of its citizens for the benefit of a small elite group and that blames its nonwhite, non-male, non-Christian, disabled, and nonheteronormative populations for a host of economic, social, and moral evils. With the diminution of local and regional identities (a capitalist problem), white Americans depend on national identity and patterns of consumption (including corporatized team sports) as a way to understand who we are. American cultural and political nationalism instills economic, terror-based, and demographic fears of the foreign and the nonwhite and uses reproductive sexuality, domestic femininity, and the inseparability of national identity and whiteness to shore up colonialist and imperialist logics of domination. While the motivations of Irish nationalism in the early twentieth century and American nationalism a hundred years later differ, they share some of the same instruments. Irish traditional music must not ignore these larger social and political currents.

Such currents emerge in recent Irish approaches to immigration. The authors of "'Vote Yes for Common Sense Citizenship'" identify the disjuncture between Ireland's self-image as progressive, tolerant, and open and its retention of antithetical attitudes like intolerance and provinciality in the name of "tradition."[33] Here, I read slightly against these authors' assertion to argue that Irish society and the transnational trad scene already contain the seeds of postnationalist transformation: while narrow definitions of "tradition" can occlude and exclude, "tradition" as a set of practices does not need to be confined or confining. Indeed, Irish traditional music has demonstrated its expansiveness for centuries, from the incorporation of musical elements from art and popular musics to its ever-widening reach worldwide. In 1992, Mick Moloney wrote, "For musicians with absolutely no Irish ancestry whatever, long term involvement in the music and culture is extremely rare."[34] In the past several decades, hundreds of musicians have demonstrated that this claim is outdated through their continuing participation in the scene, and for some, "Irish traditional musician" is a major part of their self-identification—more important, some say, than nationality, gender, or sexuality. This phenomenon challenges mainstream ideas about identity, ethnicity, and artistic affinity: when musicians with no Irish ethnic heritage refer to themselves as "Irish traditional musicians," does "Irish" apply to the music or the person? This slippage provides an excellent opportunity to question the relevance of ethnic nationalism to musicking and, by extension, to individual and group identity formation. It will take more minds than mine to fully think through removing ethnic nationalism from Irish traditional music, but I see several places where the trad scene has already laid the groundwork.

I argue that attention to connections—on transnational or global rather than national levels—should be central to institutional, scholarly, and community-based understandings of Irish traditional music. Some work, including Gearóid Ó hAllmhuráin's rich account of music making in County Clare, *Flowing Tides*, has acknowledged these connections, but inevitably our ears and minds are drawn back to the national as regularly as the tide comes in.[35] But I suggest that while the nation has been vital in the development of Irish traditional music, it is less important today in defining or directing the network of scenes worldwide. Instead, the genre has already organized itself around regional and local styles and scenes, and this transnational network of local, face-to-face scenes is multiply reinforced: players within a local scene often share connections with people in other scenes, and social media platforms afford individuals additional opportunities to get to know fellow traddies virtually. Shared repertoires and mutual friends smooth social interactions when traddies meet in person, and musicians frequently use the trad network to find housing, jobs, and friends in new locations. This kind of networking through music represents a form of chain migration that does not depend on ethnicity.[36] Compared with the organic and unrestricted flow of musicians, tunes, recordings, instruments, and news among trad scenes worldwide, Comhaltas Ceoltóirí Éireann's nationalist branch-county-province-nation organization seems artificial and has led to the strange practice of delineating "provinces" in Britain and North America.[37] At this point, no Japanese "province" exists, though musicians can qualify to compete in the All-Ireland Fleadh Cheoil na hÉireann through the Comhaltas branch in Tokyo. Time will tell whether Comhaltas—a notoriously conservative organization—will fully annex Japan into its expansionist concept of the nation in the same way it has enveloped areas of the Irish diaspora, or whether it will stop short of embracing Japan as "Irish."

In a genre where styles and repertoires remain firmly connected with particular places, the roots of musicians matter tremendously. A particular challenge in achieving a fully postnationalist manifestation of trad will be maintaining this foundational sense of people and place while expanding it beyond the restrictive frameworks of ethnic nationalism. Again, practice and discourse diverge: individual relationships among musicians often do operate "postnationally," but always with the looming reality of institutionally and discursively embedded ethnic nationalism. Legacies of colonialism and ambivalence about capitalism in the context of trad also generate anxieties around the presence of outsiders and what some perceive as an appropriation of local tunes and styles.[38] Appropriation as it relates to Irish traditional music is peripheral to my arguments, but the question of ownership of tunes and techniques becomes more complex in a postcolonial and postnationalist context and is perhaps the most tenacious barrier to the excision of ethnic nationalism from trad. As Anthony McCann argues, conventional capitalist definitions of intellectual property fail to adequately describe or prescribe the treatment of a repertoire of mostly anonymous tunes, and many traddies find the idea of "owning" a tune strange in such a collective, transhistorical practice.[39] With roots in Enlightenment Britain, copyright laws are the tools of the colonizer imposed on the colonized, and tunes (and the teaching of tunes) have become commodities to be traded, bought, and sold. Higher market values accrue to performances deemed more "authentic," where criteria include extramusical qualifications like the provenance of tunes and players. As long as trad musicians (rightly) seek compensation for their work in a capitalist system that treats ethnicity as added value, calling for the dissolution of ethnic nationalism will be fraught for economic reasons. A shorter-term tactic for moving away from ethnic nationalism might be to focus attention on the noncommercial aspects of the scene, such as amplifying practices of inclusion that already exist in trad as a way to identify so-called difference as value rather than threat. Ultimately, though, if the trad scene hopes to dismantle structures of discrimination, it will need to move beyond inclusion and toward transformation.

Some members of the Irish traditional music scene attempt to signal inclusion by claiming to focus on "the music itself" rather than on the identity of players—but the statement that nothing matters but the music has the opposite effect when used to silence conversations about discrimination in the trad scene, as I discuss in chapter 5. For nonnormative musicians, not talking about negative experiences around identity in the scene may ease assimilation, but my call for relinquishing ethnic nationalism as a way of organizing the trad scene is a call for transformation rather than assimilation. This call echoes that of black and indigenous scholars like Angela Davis, Hortense Spillers, Sylvia Wynter, Alexander Weheliye, and Vanessa Watts in asserting that nationalism, like liberal humanism, is racialized (and gendered and sexed).[40] Hierarchies are built into both national and humanist systems, in which some people are human and others are not quite human. Like other cultural forms of the white West, Irish traditional music is the inheritor of these systems and their ways of understanding the world.

As a genre that also emerged from a history of colonial domination (including the imposition of settler colonialism) and discrimination based on hierarchies of human, not-quite-human, and nonhuman, ethnically Irish traditional musicians have a special obligation to rethink the genre's relationships with ethnic nationalism and liberal humanism. I believe that trad has a head start in this process of transformation: in addition to the power of its diverse relationships built through collective music making, the idea of "the music itself" as a participant in musicking gestures toward a posthumanism in which humanness ceases to be the only way we can imagine organizing ourselves. If we can admit nonhuman actors like "the music itself" into the field of music-making, then discrimination against humans based on ethnicity/race, gender, sexuality, or other forms of difference becomes harder to rationalize—as indeed does discrimination of any sort. This idea of "the music itself" liberating humans from our fear of difference is admittedly optimistic in the extreme and puts a tremendous burden on the endeavor of musicking, but I suggest this possibility to jar readers from the complacency and hubris of thinking that humanism (much less nationalism) is the only framework through which we can consider music making or engage in meaningful action.

A CABINET OF METHODOLOGIES, OR THE FREEDOM OF REPURPOSED PARCHMENT[41]

In its dialogues between past and present and among musicians within and outside Ireland, this book represents a conversation among methodologies and disciplines. A catholic approach to archival research, ethnography, and critical theory seemed the best—and indeed the only ethical—way to ask and begin to answer the questions I wanted to ask. In some cases, new ideas emerged from seemingly disparate sources of information, theoretical frameworks, and lines of thinking. For example, I began the present-day portion of this research by interviewing musicians who live in the United States because as an American, I already knew where to start finding nonnormative traddies in that country. Although I was not initially planning to address ethnicity or race, it came up in almost every interview I conducted as inextricable from my interlocutors' other identities. In working to make sense of how the experiences of present-day, mostly American musicians might relate to those of Irish women musicians in the early twentieth century, ethnicity, nation, and belonging became central organizing tropes to consider how the ideologies of nationalism use gender, sexuality, and race/ethnicity to allocate labor, control bodies, and lend legitimacy to the state. Thus, my opportunistic ethnographic focus on musicians in the United States refocused my work on Irish women in the early twentieth century by enticing me to trace their common thread of ethnic nationalism.

In its earliest stages, this project was going to be an ethnographic account of the experiences of women traditional musicians in Ireland today. As I began research for an initial chapter on historical context, I discovered material on past women musicians that had languished unconsidered in archives—including information that corrects erroneous assumptions about women's public music making in the early twentieth century and establishes their influence on traditional music performance more generally, including on renowned male musicians like Michael Coleman. Suddenly, historiography and history became as urgent as ethnography: in the absence of published work on women's musical participation in the Irish nationalist movement of the early twentieth century, a less historicized work on gender in trad would risk inadvertently contributing to the fallacy of linear history that presumes that women's participation has increased steadily over time. A similar fallacy may operate for queer musicians and musicians of color—a line of inquiry worth pursuing in the future.

Historiography also provides an avenue for simultaneously reveling in and questioning the genealogical mind-set of Irish traditional music that, like the fantasy of a benevolent patriarchy, confines as much as it might comfort. Narratives of family connections among musicians and tunes trace out a world along heteropatriarchal lines: parents pass tunes down to children, and masters share their trade with students whose respect is filial. In most cases, the roots and branches of these musical family trees are male, as are most of the leaves. Because one's place as a "traditional" musician is predicated upon respect for the forefathers (and the few foremothers) of "the tradition," attempts to envision or validate alternative modes of transmission in Irish traditional music have been confounded in some of the ways that the literature scholar Janet Beizer identifies for feminist biography, in which the narrative tools of patriarchal genealogy are endlessly implicated in work that traces lineages of foremothers both metaphoric and biologic.[42] Trad discourse depends on wholesale subscription to the model of transmission as reproduction, wherein the genetic material of tunes and styles has a traceable lineage unless it is presented as magical or attributed to the genius of an inevitably male musician. Although lateral peer-to-peer transmission of tunes is the way most musicians learn repertoire, trad discourse privileges the metaphor of father/master-to-son/student transmission. Woman-to-woman transmission of tunes has been unacknowledged throughout most of trad's history, and the influence of foremothers is hidden compared with the eminently traceable lines and lessons of fathers and male teachers.

Uncomplicated genealogic thinking comforts us by suggesting that the past is always present yet unchanging, like the trunk of a family tree. Cultural politicians and Irish traditional musicians nurture this tree with metaphors of water or whiskey that reinforce the idea of reproduction and the (usually imaginary) purity of a family line. Musicians become human vessels, "tradition bearers" who carry cultural material unchanged, and "the pure drop" suggests that the music of the past is clear and untainted as long as it is protected from the contaminations of the present or the foreign.[43] Purity, of course, implies whiteness—especially in the context of a genre that has long defined itself in opposition to jazz, as I discuss in chapter 5. But the perceived constancy of the past masks the distillation processes that have refined the "pure drop" for today's delectation. Tracing each of these breweries and stills of tradition is work for another day, but the study of forgotten musicians, repertoires, and practices, however "traditional" they may have been, is effectively the study of what has *not* come down to us as the "pure drop." So, too, is attention to living musicians who exist outside the genre's norms of gender, sexuality, and/or race/ethnicity.

This book is an intervention in disciplinary conversations in music as well as an intervention in Irish traditional music history. Like some other work on vernacular and popular musics of the West, this project has always been "queer"—always a little off-kilter from the preoccupations and predilections of both musicology and ethnomusicology. This text challenges the unsustainable and unethical disciplinary "purities" historically associated with each field: musicology's uneasiness with performance rather than text and its focus on the "great works" of "great (white) men," and ethnomusicology's colonialist obsession with the non-Western subaltern. But luckily, reality is much more deliciously complex than such purities suggest, and therefore, instead of seeking disciplinary legibility in one field or the other, this text exercises the freedom of drawing from the perspectives, texts, and methodologies of both.[44]

Similarly, I imagine that the readers of this book will come from a variety of backgrounds, including traditional musicians and scholars inside and outside Ireland. I include details and sources that will speak to my fellow trad musicians, as well as discussions about disciplinarity directed toward my colleagues in academic music studies. Readers with a musicological bent will recognize this volume's obligatory yet useful musical analysis (albeit queered and trad-ified), while ethnomusicologists will identify the vignettes of encounter that characterize many ethnographies. I have tried to put the nuances of Irish traditional music performance into language that will resonate with readers unfamiliar with the genre, and I have glossed the ideas from critical theory I cite to render them intelligible to all readers. Though this book found its home in an academic press based in the United States, I hope that it will also reach readers and effect change beyond the rarified worlds of music's -ologies.

A FEW WORDS ABOUT WORDS

In choosing terminology, I have attempted to balance meaning and the flow of prose—and in some cases, to demonstrate the power dynamics I seek to elucidate. My choice to sometimes shorten "Irish traditional music" to "trad" is one example: in addition to its widespread use in the genre, "trad" reminds us that in Ireland, marking the music as "Irish" is unnecessary. Only outside Ireland is the adjective "Irish" useful to mark ethnicity, although "trad" often suffices within Irish traditional music subcultures outside Ireland, too. In the global trad scene, "non-Irish" becomes the marked term, since the stereotypical trad musician is Irish. Combined, "Irish" and "non-Irish" invoke one instability that characterizes post-*Riverdance* Irish culture: the historical view of the Irish as disempowered in contrast with the intense visibility and audibility of Celtic Tiger Ireland since the 1990s. Again following colloquial usage among some (but not all) musicians, I sometimes refer to those who play Irish traditional musicians today as "trad musicians" or "traddies" to declutter my prose and remove the ethnic adjective "Irish." (I generally do not refer to historical musicians with these colloquial terms, which are relatively recent additions as far as I have been able to determine.) I have used pseudonyms for all my interlocutors to protect those who wished to be anonymous. This choice was at odds with some of my interlocutors' wishes to escape the closet of anonymity, but safety concerns outweighed the benefits of full openness.

At times, I use "nonnormative" as shorthand for musicians who do not fit the dominant demographic of white, ethnically Irish, heterosexual men. I aggregate women, LGBTQ+ musicians, and musicians of color when it makes sense to do so, and I trust that readers will understand identity as intersectional—that a person might be a queer woman of color or a white gay Irish man, and oppressions and privileges will operate differently based on one's subject position and geographical location. Nomenclature for musicians of color and LGBTQ+ musicians has presented particular challenges, and again I have tried to balance meaning and readability. In general, I have preferred "musician of color" because it reinforces the subject position of "musician" and avoids centering whiteness, but in some contexts, I have used "nonwhite" to emphasize the effects of racism. Occasionally, "musician of color" proved too unwieldy, and I chose to prioritize the accessibility of prose. In most cases, I have chosen the problematic but less identifying term "Asian American" rather than identifying individual musicians by ethnicity to protect their anonymity. Despite critiques of the term "queer" for its associations with middle-class whiteness and its tendencies to obscure the differences among those named "queer," I have generally chosen to use it because it makes space for nonnormative sexualities not included in the "alphabet soup" of LGBTQ+ and because it is more accessible for reading out loud than a lengthy acronym.[45] Finally, in a move toward nonbinary use of language, I have chosen to use the "singular they" throughout this work whenever possible.

CHAPTER SYNOPSES

The chapters in this book focus on the effects of ethnic nationalism as they relate to gender, sexuality, and race in different eras and in the transnational circulation of Irish traditional music and musicians, especially between Ireland and the United States. In telling larger stories about how trad musicians have navigated questions of identity since the early twentieth century—and how traditional music scholars have often sidestepped these same questions—I also tell stories about how musicians and listeners interact with sound. In the case of the flute player Mary Kilcar (chapter 1), producing overheard sounds led to an interaction that provides what may be the only trace of her existence as a musician, while the timbre of vibrato contributed to the erasure of the fiddler Treasa Ní Ailpín from the historical record of Irish traditional music. My present-day interlocutors discuss the epistemological and social ruptures that can occur when "Irish" sounds emerge from bodies that do not fit stereotypes of normative Irishness, as well as the joys of sounding together. Such experiences both separate and connect musicians, and I maintain that attention to these separations and disjunctures has the potential to lead us to even more satisfying connections.

Chapter 1 begins with an explication of the relationships between gender and nationalism—and, by extension, sexuality and race—in the Irish nationalist movement of the early twentieth century. By exploring personifications of the nation as mother or maiden as a way to create space for publicly active women traditional musicians, I illuminate the role of gender and reproductive sexuality in producing and enculturating a properly "Irish" citizenry. I argue that women musicians' legibility as mothers or maidens enabled them to perform publicly in an era that asserted women's domesticity, and I provide previously forgotten historical information on several of these musicians, including Bridget Kenny, May McCarthy, Mollie Morrissey, and Mary Kilcar.

Chapter 2 discusses the Limerick fiddler Treasa Ní Ailpín's early life and music to make audible the connections among gender, class, national identity, and "authentic" performance practice that have led to her disappearance from oral and written histories of Irish traditional music. These connections are based on nationalist ideals of Irish traditional music as masculine, organic, and untaught, in opposition to the feminized refinements of "foreign" classical music education. By examining elements of performance practice and style, I pose larger questions about how determinations of authenticity change over time—how they become attached to certain techniques, and how those techniques carry the residue of gendered and racialized associations. I demonstrate that "authenticity" is a dynamic, slippery attribute and that, like "Irishness," it is a construction closely linked with discursive power.

Through a retelling of the Sliabh Luachra fiddler Julia Clifford's life, chapter 3 considers the role of biography in telling the lives of nonnormative musicians. It explores questions of subjectivity through tracing Clifford's navigation of gender norms as a woman economic migrant in Britain in the mid-twentieth century. In this chapter, I investigate the circumstances that led to Clifford's inclusion in the canon of Irish traditional music and contemplate what it might mean to put gender and musicianship on equal footing to claim an identity as a woman traditional musician.

Chapter 4 begins by connecting magical nationalism (mobilizing the supernatural to demonstrate Irish exceptionalism) with musicians' reverence for "the music itself." This reverence, I argue, comes in part from the joys of reaching trad flow during performance. Through ethnographic accounts, I demonstrate that (hetero)sexism and racism disproportionately prevent women, queer musicians, and musicians of color from entering flow states. I then take a playful approach to the term "the music itself": instead of arguing for or against the primacy of text (or performance-as-text), I ask how treating "the music itself" as an actor might shift how we interact with fellow musicians within the trad scene.

In chapter 5, I investigate the role of aesthetics, including understatement and silence, in shaping behaviors and discourse around gender, sexuality, and race/ethnicity. Through the words of my interlocutors, I relate some of the challenges that musicians of color and queer musicians face, as well as their tactics for dealing with state-induced and quotidian racisms and (hetero)sexisms born of ethnic nationalist mind-sets and policies. I address the problems of attrition and the limits of assimilation, and I close with a discussion of the transformations that nonnormative musicians wish to see in the transnational Irish traditional music scene.

ONE

Mother Ireland and the Queen of Irish Fiddlers
Women Musicians and the Nation in Early Twentieth-Century Ireland

INTRODUCTION

And yet if you took the hero out of the story, what was left? What female figure was there to identify with? . . . The heroine, as such, was utterly passive. She was Ireland or Hibernia. She was stamped, as a rubbed-away mark, on silver or gold; a compromised regal figure on a throne. Or she was a nineteenth-century image of girlhood, on a frontispiece or in a book of engravings. She was invoked, addressed, remembered, loved, regretted. And, most important, died for. She was a mother or a virgin. Her hair was swept or tied back, like the prow of a ship. Her flesh was wood or ink or marble. And she had no speaking part.[1]

In this quotation, the Irish poet Eavan Boland (b. 1944) describes her dawning awareness that the heroic stories of Irish nationalist struggles left little room for women activists or commentators. She continues: "To the male principle was reserved the right not simply of action but of expression as well. I was ready to weep or sing or recite in the cause of Ireland. To do any of that, however . . . I would have to give up the body and spirit of a woman."[2] Boland thus identifies a primary problem for women activists in the early twentieth century, who sometimes negotiated gender stereotypes by embracing androgyny, but who more often participated in nationalist struggles by working within accepted categories of femininity established by personifications of the Irish nation as a woman in poetry, song, and rhetoric. For women traditional musicians who were publicly active in the early 1900s, such strategies of symbolic identification were vital.

Although this chapter focuses on the activities and social positions of women, it would not be possible to discuss the gendered aspects of nationalism without also addressing both sexuality and race / ethnicity, since the basic premise of ethnic nationalism is the reproduction of "appropriate" citizens. This reproduction requires normatively white and ethnically Irish citizens to engage in sanctioned procreative activities, which in turn requires the maintenance of social mores, religious doctrines, and legal codes to uphold "correct" sexual behaviors. Gendered anxieties around Irish whiteness based on British colonial discourse shaped ideas about both gender and race and produced complicated relationships between Ireland and India, its fellow colonial subject, as well as between Irish immigrants and enslaved African peoples in the Americas. While I do not extensively chart the relationships between Ireland and India or Irish attitudes toward blackness here, these topics bear further study, especially in relation to music and sound.

This chapter first examines the construction of the Irish nation as a woman and discusses Mother Ireland / Hibernia and India's Bharat Mata ("Mother India") in relation to their shared colonizer, England's Britannia. Personifications of the Irish nation as a woman required that Irish men behave in certain ways toward the feminized nation and the nonmetaphorical women within it. I then outline poetic representations of the Irish nation between the late eighteenth and early twentieth centuries to introduce the images of Mother Ireland, the Shan Van Vocht, and Erin / Hibernia that were ubiquitous by the early twentieth century. Using work on the cultural politics of emotion, I argue that the affective power of these representations was as influential as the visual and moral parameters that they established for living women.

The cultural meanings of personifications of Mother Ireland, Erin, and their counterparts determined how women's public nationalist activity would fit within, reproduce, and sometimes challenge discourses of nation and home. The next section of this chapter examines the Gaelic League and the Irish Ireland movement to trace the gendered aspects of cultural nationalism encoded in their missions and policies. Then I briefly describe the ways some women's organizations in the early twentieth century used gender stereotypes as justification for nationalist—and sometimes militant—action. Such rationales for women's political activity resonate with discourses around women's public nationalist musical activity in the same era.

THE ROAD TO INDEPENDENCE: A VERY BRIEF HISTORY

Ireland's relationship with England is at the center of its modern history and is encoded in Irish popular memory through such events as English settlers' seventeenth-century "plantation" of Ireland, Oliver Cromwell's invasion and bloody conquest of it in the mid-seventeenth century, the institution of penal laws in 1691, and the 1800 Acts of Union, which made Ireland part of the United Kingdom of Great Britain and were instituted in response to the Rebellion of 1798.[3] In the nineteenth century, attempts to win Irish sovereignty through rebellion or parliamentary process included the Young Ireland movement in the 1840s and a series of Home Rule bills that ultimately led to the partition of Ireland in 1920. As a result of such nationalist political, cultural, and military activity, including the 1916 Easter Rising and the 1921 Irish War of Independence, the Irish Free State was formed in 1922 after a brief civil war.[4]

The Irish historical gaze also looks beyond its own shores—for military help, as it looked to France during the Rebellion of 1798; and for homes for millions of emigrants, including those who left Ireland during and after the Great Famine of the 1840s and those who went to England, the United States, and elsewhere during the economically bleak years of the mid-twentieth century. Among those who left were Francis O'Neill (1848–1936), a Cork native who moved to Chicago and published the tune collections that now define the core repertoire of Irish traditional music, and Lucy Farr (1911–2003), a Galway fiddler who emigrated to England and became one of the few Irish women musicians of her generation to become known beyond her immediate circle. Farr's memories of her musical childhood in Ireland provide material about the flute player Mary Kilcar (dates unknown), whose story will emerge later in this chapter.

The circulation of musicians and musical texts among Ireland, England, and the United States is integral to any study of Irish traditional music, and these exchanges have helped define the style, repertoire, and social practice of the music. Individuals like O'Neill and Farr are remembered for their individual musical contributions, but they also occupy a historiographically rich space as Irish commentators on music within and outside Ireland. Following the idea of the Italian feminist philosopher Adriana Cavarero that a narrator bestows upon his or her protagonist the gift of drawing the shape of that protagonist's life, I contend that O'Neill's and Farr's diasporic positions allow them to tell the stories of several early twentieth-century women musicians in a way that traces larger patterns among nationalism, representation, and gender.[5] These patterns also tell us about symbolic understandings of race/ethnicity and sexuality. To see the shapes of these musicians' lives, however, we must first understand the landscape behind them, a background of personifications of nation-as-woman and conservative social mores that influenced individual and collective expectations about the behavior and representation of women.

GENDERING THE NATION ON BOTH SIDES OF THE IMPERIAL GAZE

Since the early 1990s, scholars have examined the circulation of power between and within nations and between men and women inside the nation. The sociologist Nira Yuval-Davis has enumerated the ways in which women participate in nationalist activity: by biological reproduction, cultural production and transmission, symbolic identification with the nation, and participation in nationalist struggles.[6] These categories are inseparable, and the work of cultural production and transmission done by Irish women musicians in the early twentieth century is meaningful only when understood in connection with the multiple personifications of the Irish nation and in dialogue with histories of women engaged in the fight for Irish independence in public and at home. We must also consider the interplay of gendered symbolism and political action between Ireland and the nations closest to it geographically or conceptually: France, the United States, India, and Britain. These nations inspired its fight for independence, received its immigrants, and shared its colonial past on either side of the imperial gaze.

Metaphors of land as woman abound, with her body fruitful, nurturing, beloved, or in need of protection from those who would ravish her. This feminization of land changes with the viewer's position: within the would-be national territory, the land is a bountiful (or barren) mother or a protected virgin; while in the eyes of the colonizer, the land is naked, a maiden to be deflowered. The multivalent metaphor of land-as-woman can reflect both gazes and is thus useful for powerful and emerging nations alike. The representation of England as Britannia, for example, is not fixed synchronically or diachronically: although she first appears on second-century Roman coins as "a captive . . . fallen before the might of the Roman Empire," her fortunes eventually improve.[7] By the nineteenth century, Britannia has become a warrior, a protector, and the wife who cleans up the home and empire for her male counterpart, John Bull. In Victorian times, she appears as the militant but mute saleswoman for whitening, brightening products like toothpaste and metal polish that sought to "civilize" so-called savages from Africa, Ireland, and elsewhere; and she appears as Hibernia / Erin's stern maternal protector in cartoons in the popular press.[8] France's Marianne also appears variously as a reformulation of feminized Liberty, a harlot, Everywoman, and as a goddess of revolution.[9]

For Ireland and India, both in Britannia's imperial embrace, female personifications of nation were also changeable. Like Britannia, nineteenth-century versions of Mother Ireland and Bharat Mata derived from ancient historical or mythological figures with variable characteristics and identities. Bharat Mata was first mentioned in the *Ramayana*, and by the time she came to personify India in the late nineteenth century, she represented a wide array of feminine archetypes, including "a glorious figure of abundance, the powerful mother Kali and Durga, a destructive 'shakti' . . . [and] an enslaved, all-suffering figure, a tearful victim and a frail widow."[10] In Ireland, the ancient goddess Ériu is alternately portrayed as a warrior queen, mother, and raven.[11] Her eponymous connection with Ireland (Éire) foreshadows the later popularity of multiple female metaphors for the Irish nation organized around tropes of the ravished, sorrowful, and enslaved maiden or the grieving, beloved old woman. Speaking from poems, songs, and plays, by the late eighteenth century these maidens and mothers customarily called for the sons, fathers, and husbands of Ireland to rescue and protect them.[12]

In history's usually heteronormative backward glance, metaphors of nation-as-woman are further complicated by metaphorically gendered relationships between colonizing and colonized countries and by the feminization of men othered by imperial projects. Anne McClintock writes that the colonizer's "discovery" of the woman-continent is always late, and whether the colonizer envisions the land as virgin or mother, the colonial imagination must account for—and deal with—the native men who got there first.[13] North America's native men are portrayed as cannibals, Indian men are depicted as dangerously lustful,[14] and Irish men are drawn as childlike apes or effeminate bards.[15] From England's point of view, Hibernia is too good for the Hibernians, from whom she must be protected—even though these same Hibernians also understand themselves as her protectors.[16] Luke Gibbons argues that "recourse to female imagery . . . turns the colonial stereotype against itself, positing an alternative 'feminized' public sphere (imagined as the nation) against the official patriarchal order of the state."[17] Although the notion of an "alternative 'feminized' public sphere" is evocative, I contend that maintenance of the nation-as-woman metaphor was necessary because Irish men were feminized in the relationship between England and Ireland: imagery of the nation-as-woman does not challenge colonial domination, but it allows the disempowered native man to contain the femininity assigned to him.[18] Representing the nation as a helpless woman—as Mother Ireland or the maidenly Erin—gave Irish nationalist men symbolic and actual power over the land, as well as over real women.

IRELAND-AS-WOMAN IN POETRY AND SONG IN THE LONG NINETEENTH CENTURY

In Ireland, opportunities for women musicians in the early twentieth century were intimately tied to familiar connections between women and the domestic sphere. Personifications of the nation as Mother Ireland, Cathleen Ní Houlihan, and other figures helped direct the fight for independence but further prescribed the behavior of actual women. The geographer Gerry Kearns asserts that "the circulation of allegorical women in national narratives overshadows their flesh-and-blood cousins" and presents women as passive symbols of picturesque sacrifice rather than as humans capable of action.[19] By the early twentieth century, literary, artistic, and musical representations of these allegorical women were plentiful. An exegesis of songs that represent Ireland as a woman would span the repertoire of songs from the Rebellion of 1798 to the fight for Irish independence in the early twentieth century, and such a project might also examine the circulation of music and metaphors of mother-as-home in the Irish diaspora through Tin Pan Alley songs and British street ballads.[20] Thus, a brief examination of some exemplary treatments of Ireland-as-woman grounds my discussion of Irish women instrumental musicians in the early twentieth century.

THE SHAN VAN VOCHT

O the French are in the bay,
They'll be here by break of day,
And the Orange will decay,
Says the *shan van vocht*.

Yes! Ireland SHALL be free,
From the centre to the sea;
Then hurra for Liberty!
Says the *shan van vocht*.[21]

"The Shan Van Vocht" ("The poor old woman") portrays Ireland as a *cailleach*— a mythological pan-Celtic figure of creation and destruction, a visionary and untameable crone. In the song, the Shan Van Vocht incites Irish rebels to action by predicting victory in the ultimately doomed Rebellion of 1798.[22] The song's catchy melody and easily adapted lyrics proved popular, and several versions were in circulation by the early 1840s. In 1882, A. M. Sullivan remarked that he "never knew an Irish election poet that did not invoke the 'Shan Van Vocht.'"[23] The ballad scholar Georges Denis Zimmermann argues that it and other street songs represented the beliefs and aspirations of working-class Irish people. Although this generalization is suspiciously broad, it locates the personification of Ireland-as-woman in both oral and written traditions.[24]

The song also retains a political message and feminine personification of Ireland similar to that of the *aisling* (vision or dream) genre, in which Ireland appears as a human woman. Most aisling poems establish a pastoral setting in which the male narrator falls asleep and, in a dream, meets a supernatural *spéirbhean* (literally, "sky-woman")—usually a breathtakingly beautiful maiden, but sometimes a stately queen or an old woman. She identifies herself as Ireland incarnate, laments her fate, and calls for or foretells liberation. At this happy news, the sleeping man awakes to find nothing changed in the waking world: independence was only a dream. An adaptation of the aisling form, "The Shan Van Vocht" departs from it by omitting the dream from which the dreamer must wake, thereby enabling nineteenth-century singers to retain the original lyrics of "The Shan Van Vocht" or adapt them to address immediate political circumstances without replicating the formulaic delay of victory. But despite the Shan Van Vocht's prophetic powers, preoccupation with military action, and welcome declaration of imminent triumph, she remains imaginary—the idea and the ideal that spurs Irish men into action, but no more.

Mother Ireland

If the Shan Van Vocht is an otherworldly figure, Mother Ireland is much closer to home—in fact, Mother Ireland *is* home. This metaphor of motherland is common among emerging nations, which invariably cast the nation's men in the roles of hero, protector, and dutiful son. This filial nationalism relies on constant reimaginings of personal and political history, as Julie Mostov's description of nationalism in the former Yugoslavia implies: "The national space

(Motherland) must be protected by new heroes, willing to join in the nation's age-old battle against the forces of evil."[25] Ireland and India also share this long-standing spiritualization and use of the motherland metaphor in defining and building a nation. Charu Gupta writes: "Mother as map as nation also served to define a loyal political citizenry, devoted in the service of the nation. . . . These dutiful children were largely articulated as the male Hindu sons of the nation, who were promoted as constituting an ideal Indian."[26] About Ireland, Richard Kearney writes that "it might be argued that the transposition of Irish women into desexualized, quasi-divine mothers corresponded in some manner to the ideological transposition of Ireland from a fatherland (the term *an t-athardha* was often used to denote Ireland in much bardic poetry up to the seventeenth century) into idioms connoting a motherland."[27] This transposition, Kearney argues, occurred when political sovereignty began to seem inaccessible and intangible—just like the figure of the Virgin Mary.

Juxtaposing the Shan Van Vocht and Mother Ireland allows us to explore the role of love in the construction of Ireland as a motherland—a construction that many Irish women readily took up, but whose authors were almost exclusively male.[28] In "The Shan Van Vocht," the woman's voice fills the song, but as quoted speech from a presumably male narrator. The song did not prescribe desired or ideal behaviors for real women, and the Shan Van Vocht does not seek, expect, or inspire love for herself, but for Ireland. She is merely the messenger who calls men to arms, and the problem that Dipesh Chakrabarty identifies for modern nationalisms remains:

> It does not take much effort to see that a photographic realism or a dedicated naturalism could never answer all the needs of vision that modern nationalisms create. For the problem, from a nationalist point of view, is this: if the nation, the people, or the country were not just to be observed, described, and critiqued but loved as well, what would guarantee that they were indeed worth loving unless one also saw in them something that was already lovable?[29]

The Shan Van Vocht, with her clear connection with the cailleach, is not "already lovable" and occupies an ambivalent position between veneration and revulsion.[30] Therefore, she is less effective as an instrument that inspires nationalist devotion, however powerful her message.

The metaphor of Mother Ireland, in contrast, assumes and requires that her sons love her, and because they love her, they must fight to protect her. Reverence for the Blessed Mother Mary and for mortal mothers connects love and protection of the familial home with love and defense of the nation: "Love . . . reproduces the collective as ideal through producing a particular kind of subject whose allegiance to the ideal makes it an ideal in the first place."[31] Sara Ahmed's additive phrasing here performs the erasure of the nation as the object of love in favor of the loving subject whose agency produces the lovable—who then must be loved. Love for Mother Ireland and love for the Virgin Mary become inextricable, and to render these two loves sensible, the proper nationalist must also love his own mother. In addition, because the metaphor of Mother Ireland depends on the idealization of a son's love for his mother, Mother Ireland, and the Virgin Mary, the metaphor in turn defines what is lovable in the idealized yet real woman, whether she is mother or lover, as Ahmed points out: "Love becomes a sign of respectable femininity, and of maternal qualities narrated as the capacity to touch and be touched by others. The reproduction of femininity is tied up with the reproduction of the national ideal through the work of love."[32]

Just as the nationalist son loves his mother, so must the nationalist mother love her son. To do otherwise jeopardizes "respectable femininity" and the national project and threatens the reciprocity implicit in maternity and belief in an ever-loving Virgin Mother. In "A Mother Speaks," written two days before his execution in 1916, the revolutionary Pádraig Pearse likens his mother to Mary, thus completing the circle of reciprocal love between metaphoric, holy, and real mothers and their nationalist sons:

> Dear Mary, that didst see thy first-born Son
> Go forth to die amid the scorn of men
> For whom He died,
> Receive my first-born son into thy arms,
> Who also hath gone out to die for men,
> And keep him by thee till I come to him.
> Dear Mary, I have shared thy sorrow,
> And soon shall share thy joy.[33]

The fight for Irish independence thus receives divine sanction, and Irish mothers' losses are made glorious by being likened to the sorrows of Mater Dolorosa, the long-suffering Virgin Mother.

Songs reinforced mother-son love as an organizing principle of Irish nationalism, and popular culture in the early twentieth century relentlessly presented images of the idealized mother for consumption in Ireland and its diaspora. Instrumental and vocal music circulated in both directions, and emigrants often shipped sheet music and sound recordings to their relatives at home. Tin Pan Alley participated in the idealization of the Irish mother in songs like "Mother Machree" (1910):

> There's a spot in my heart which no colleen may own.
> There's a depth in my soul never sounded or known.
> There's a place in my memory, my life, that you fill.
> No other can take it, no one ever will.
> [Chorus:] Sure, I love the dear silver that shines in your hair,
> And the brow that's all furrowed and wrinkled with care.
> I kiss the dear fingers so toilworn for me.
> Oh, God bless you and keep you, Mother Machree.[34]

The actual and symbolic connection between women and the domestic sphere aligns with the lived experience of emigration. To the ideal immigrant son, mother and country become synonyms for home, and the Anglicization of *mo chroí* (my heart) transforms the son's love into a functional surname, "Machree."[35] Like the love-created collective that Ahmed describes, Mother Machree is defined entirely by her son's love. In turn, the ubiquity of the Mother Ireland metaphor ensures that mothers in literary works can never escape a symbolic connection with Ireland, and that Irish women are tied to the work of reproducing ethnically Irish sons.[36]

"Dark Rosaleen" and "Kathaleen Ny-Houlahan": Two Maidens

The personification of Ireland as a mother inspired the protective love of a son, and its personification as a maiden, the passion and single-mindedness of a lover. The aisling genre allowed the adaptation of love songs and poems into expressions of fervent nationalism. Popular opinion assumes that writers of rebellious songs coded incendiary notions in metaphor and allegory, but Zimmermann argues that poets and songwriters usually used these literary devices in the service of art, not concealment.[37] By the early twentieth century hundreds of songs and poems had portrayed Ireland as a woman, and some, like "Roisín Dubh" ("Dark-haired little rose," an inspiration for "Dark Rosaleen"), had been read allegorically often enough by the late nineteenth century that nonnationalist interpretations were impossible for Irish readers of newspapers like the *Nation* (1842–1900) and of poetry by Thomas Osborne Davis (1814–45) and James Clarence Mangan (1803–49).[38]

Like the metaphor of Mother Ireland, the personification of Ireland as a maiden requires the gaze of a male protagonist who strives to protect or liberate the woman-nation he loves. And as in the case of the metaphor of Mother Ireland, the connection works because the man fighting for his nation can also envision the girls of his own village. In turn, these maidens are bound to maintain the qualities deemed worth fighting for: youth, beauty, regal grace, and virgin "purity" in an ethnically Irish body. Mangan's versions of "Dark Rosaleen" and "Kathaleen Ny-Houlahan" both celebrate these qualities.[39] In "My Dark Rosaleen," the speaker pledges himself to action on behalf of his "virgin flower," with her "bright face" and "holy delicate white hands":

> Woe and pain, pain and woe,
> Are my lot, night and noon,
> To see your bright face clouded so,
> Like to the mournful moon.
> But yet will I rear your throne
> Again in golden sheen;
> 'Tis you shall reign, shall reign alone,
> My Dark Rosaleen!
> My own Rosaleen!
>
> Over dews, over sands,
> Will I fly for your weal:
> Your holy delicate white hands
> Shall girdle me with steel.
> At home in your emerald bowers,
> From morning's dawn till e'en,
> You'll pray for me, my flower of flowers,
> My Dark Rosaleen!
> My fond Rosaleen!
> You'll think of me thro' daylight hours,
> My virgin flower, my flower of flowers,
> My Dark Rosaleen![40]

A reader might also liken Rosaleen to the Virgin Mary: earlier in the poem, the speaker addresses her as his "saint of saints" and mentions her "holy white hand" and her virginity. Although the rose often symbolizes England, an unsuitable association for expressions of Irish patriotism, it can also represent Ireland

and imminent freedom, and it is iconographically connected with the Virgin Mary.[41] "Kathaleen Ny-Houlahan" also supports an interpretation linking beloved woman, beloved country, and Mary:[42]

> Long they pine in weary woe, the nobles of our land,
> Long they wander to and fro, proscribed, alas! and banned;
> Feastless, houseless, altarless, they bear the exile's brand;
> But their hope is in the coming-to of Kathaleen Ny-Houlahan!
> Think her not a ghastly hag too hideous to be seen,
> Call her not unseemly names, our matchless Kathaleen!
> Young she is, and fair she is, and would be crowned a queen,
> Were the king's son at home here with Kathaleen Ny-Houlahan!
> Sweet and mild would look her face, O none so sweet and mild,
> Could she crush the foes by whom her beauty is reviled;
> Woolen plaids would grace herself, and robes of silk her child,
> If the king's son were living here with Kathaleen Ny-Houlahan!
>
> He who over sands and waves led Israel along,
> He who fed with heavenly bread that chosen tribe and throng,
> He who stood by Moses when his foes were fierce and strong,—
> May He show forth His might in saving Kathaleen Ny-Houlahan![43]

As the literature scholar Catherine Innes points out, Mangan "dilute[d] and etherealize[d]" the sexual imagery present in earlier versions of both poems. She asserts that the spiritualization of Erin in the nineteenth century was deeply related to the "increasingly puritanical and asexual ideal of women by the Irish Catholic Church."[44] The Virgin Mary became the conduit through whom Irish men understood the nation and Irish women understood ideal behavior. But as Marina Warner argues, the paradox of virgin conception means that mortal women exist in a state of constant and inevitable failure, never able to reach perfection: "Mary establishes the child as the destiny of woman, but escapes the sexual intercourse necessary for all other women to fulfill this destiny."[45] Social and economic conditions in Ireland in the nineteenth and early twentieth centuries further complicated such contradictions between purity and reproduction, helplessness and self-help—contradictions absent in nationalist poetry and rhetoric but inescapable in everyday life. Ideas about race and ethnicity based on Britain's other colonial encounters also drove this idealization of white womanhood. Thus, patriotic readings of "Dark Rosaleen" and other works depended on an understanding of the woman-nation as pure and helpless, her need of rescue expressed through her youth, size, delicacy, and mild manners. These qualities appear again in early twentieth-century descriptions of Irish women musicians.

DOMESTICATING NATIONALISM: WOMEN IN EARLY TWENTIETH-CENTURY IRELAND

Living the Ideal—or Not

The Irish historian Rosemary Owens writes that veneration of the Virgin Mary in early twentieth-century Irish life "placed women on such an ideological pedestal that no middle ground for ordinary, struggling women remained. . . . The only salvation . . . lay in realising the ideal by becoming either mother or virgin, wife or nun."[46] However, women in early twentieth-century Ireland found the idealized transformation from youthful virginity to devoted motherhood difficult for economic and social reasons, and most women remained single or married later in life. In the decades after the Great Famine of the 1840s, the numbers of single women in Ireland rose steadily. Most historians attribute this rise to farm consolidation and subsequent changes in inheritance patterns, as well as to increasing emigration and difficulties raising dowries. Between 1851 and 1901, unmarried women and widows outnumbered their married counterparts: in 1901, approximately 44 percent of Ireland's adult female population was single, while only 26 percent was married.[47] Yet marriage and staying in Ireland remained the ideal, if not the reality—a sentiment stridently asserted by a New York priest named Father Joseph Guinan in 1903: "How blessed would have been the lot of an Irish girl, the poor betrayed victim of hellish agencies of vice, had she remained at home and passed her days in the poverty, aye and wretchedness, of a mud wall cabin—a wife and mother, mayhap—her path in life smoothened by the blessed influences of religion and domestic peace until it ended at a green old age."[48] Despite the "blessings" of home, 89,409 women emigrated from Ireland between 1871 and 1911.[49]

The women who remained home often did pass their days in poverty, and more women than men entered workhouses after the 1850s. According to the historian Maria Luddy, women in Ireland were more susceptible to economic hardship than men because they lacked employment opportunities outside the home, fair pay, and official support systems to deal with spousal desertion, pregnancy, child raising, ill health, and old age.[50] Single women were especially vulnerable. Some entered religious orders, and the number of convents and nuns rose drastically in the nineteenth century: in 1800, there were only 120 Irish nuns in 11 convents, but by 1901, 95 convents housed over 8,000 nuns.[51] Although convent life offered women the symbolic success of remaining chaste and becoming brides of Christ, only dowried women could become choir sisters—the educated nuns who performed the prayers and teaching particular to their order. Women without dowries became lay sisters and performed the menial work of the convent, and even they were usually expected to provide some money to contribute to their upkeep. The church, then, was not a solution for Ireland's poorest women.[52] Other single women lived with married siblings, a position that often provided more security, and one in which they contributed significantly to the family economy. The Galway fiddle player Lucy Farr (1911–2003) often spoke of the four maiden aunts who lived with her family during most of her childhood. While living with Lucy's family, two of the aunts clothed the family, and another, who remained unmarried, tended to the housework while Lucy's mother worked in the fields after Lucy's father's death in 1932.[53] Lucy immigrated to London in 1936 and married there.[54]

For many Irish women in the early twentieth century, lived reality bore a troubled relationship to the idealized domestic sphere wherein the sons of Mother Ireland courted maidenly Kathleens. For women in the workhouse or lay sisters in convents, "home" and "housework" had institutionally specific meanings different from the tasks carried out by married women in their own homes. Single women who lived with family members contributed to a family-based domestic economy, but their labor disappeared beneath the idealized image of married mothers who ran the household while their husbands worked the land or for wages. For some women, especially the relatives of prosperous farmers, single life may have been vastly preferable to married life. Even so, their position outside the mother/colleen ideal rendered them invisible to the nationalist public sphere, however familiar they were in Irish society. The broken connection between the idealized home and single women, poor women inside and outside workhouses, and itinerant Traveller women[55] meant that these women's relationships with the domestic sphere were not the ones nationalists fought to protect. These women were symbolically nonexistent and often materially disadvantaged.

Women and Activism

This idealization of woman and home meant that publicly active nationalist and suffragist women risked censure for transgressing appropriate gender roles. Furthermore, the relationship between these two causes was tense, and the larger nationalist movement considered suffragists a distraction from the "real" fight for independence.[56] Most male nationalists agreed that Ireland did need all her children, but many men were personally ambivalent and collectively divided about the forms that women's nationalist action should take. Most found women's military participation unacceptable and preferred women to fill the supporting roles of rearing and teaching children to be good Irish citizens, and of raising funds for men's nationalist organizations.[57] Therefore, most Irish women nationalists—unlike suffragists—were not considered transgressive because their public activity was primarily tied to the domestic sphere. Except for a few women who engaged in military action, Mother Ireland's nationalist daughters contributed to the cause through private familial action and domestically inflected public activism.

During the past several decades, historians have studied the institutions and activities through which Irish women contributed to the fight for Irish independence, and upper-class nationalist luminaries like Constance Markievicz and Maud Gonne have received much biographical attention. Despite the historical attention paid to a few women activists, the work of others has been downplayed, as in the literal erasure of Elizabeth O'Farrell from a famous photograph of Pádraig Pearse's surrender after the 1916 rising.[58] A brief look at women's nationalist work demonstrates the influence that discourses of woman-as-nation had on the activities and reception of real women—including women musicians—in the period 1893–1922. Three institutions illuminate the connections between the symbolic representations of women and the activities of real women: the Gaelic League and the related Irish Ireland cultural nationalist movement that began in the 1890s; the women's group Inghinidhe na hÉireann (Daughters of Erin), organized in 1900; and Cumann na mBan (Irishwomen's Council), founded in 1914.

By the late nineteenth century, several Irish home rule bills had failed in the English Parliament, and many nationalists decided to direct their energies toward first achieving cultural independence from England.[59] Douglas Hyde's influential 1892 lecture, "The Necessity for De-Anglicizing Ireland," questioned the legitimacy of a patriotic Anglophobia that hypocritically shunned the words and works of Irish Gaelic and whose adherents "protest[ed] as a matter of sentiment that they hate the country which at every hand's turn they rush to imitate."[60] A year after this speech, Hyde and several other men founded the Gaelic League to further the nationalist project through the use and teaching of the Irish language. In 1897, it sponsored the first annual Oireachtas, an event modeled on the Welsh Eisteddfod that hosted song competitions and an evening concert along with its literary activities.[61] In practice, then, the Gaelic League promoted a broader cultural nationalism than its roots in language revival suggest.

This cultural nationalism found voice in the Irish Ireland movement founded by the journalist David P. Moran in 1905, which called for the adoption of select traditions of Catholic Irish speakers in the rural West.[62] While some criticized the religious sectarianism implicit in Moran's articulation of an "Irish Ireland," nationalists agreed that a cultural approach to nationalism was worthwhile.[63] This view extended beyond the urban Irish intelligentsia, and many members of the rural lower middle class participated in the movement.[64] Like the Gaelic League, the Irish Ireland movement was strong in Ireland's West, and statements like this from the *Clare Champion* were common in early twentieth-century local newspapers:

> All that is now required to make the *feis* [festival] an unqualified success is that the people of Clare should show by their attendance that they fittingly cherish the most beautiful heritage of their race, the language which carries them back to the day's [sic] of Erin's glory and power, and which inspires them with new faith and fervour in the struggle to create an Irish Ireland which will be free, in manners, customs and language, as well as in Government from English influence or rule.[65]

Although the urban Gaelic League mind-set was often at odds with that of rural native speakers, the Irish Ireland movement provided a popular and galvanizing political outlet for mass participation in the fight for Irish independence.[66]

Unlike most other nationalist organizations of the late nineteenth and early twentieth centuries, the Gaelic League admitted woman members, and the Irish Ireland movement developed a clear sense of women's roles in creating an independent Ireland. Indeed, several women served on the league's executive committee at a time when women rarely held leadership positions in organizations that also included men. Women members' dedication to the language revival was noteworthy, as Timothy McMahon points out:

Reports from throughout the country indicate that women made up significant pluralities—if not outright majorities—of those regularly attending the branches over time. As early as September 1899, the Limerick branch reported that the "ladies easily outnumber the men two to one." In Lisdoonvarna later that fall the majority of those who enrolled in the branch were women, while in June 1900 an account from County Monaghan stated that the women students in Castleblayney were "much more serious, earnest, and persevering in the cultivation of Irish than the young men of the town."[67]

The participation, faithful attendance, and earnest study of women league members fit squarely within the view that women's responsibilities included transmitting traditional knowledge through the Irish language, storytelling, and song, as well as bolstering economic independence by purchasing Irish-made household goods.

Under the pseudonym "Máire," one writer articulated the responsibilities of nationalist Irish women in "Irishwomen's Work," published in the *United Irishman* in 1899.[68] This columnist embraced the prevailing notion of gendered spheres of activity but affirmed that women could do nationalist work within the domestic realm. "Irishwomen's Work" addresses the mothers and maidens of Ireland and offers suggestions for both that sidestep the question of civic equality. Máire urges mothers to teach patriotism to their sons and asks maidens to eschew the "growing fashion for dandies and dandyism" associated with Anglicized Irishmen in favor of the homespun charms of young men rooted in the Gaelic tradition. She uses feminine personifications of the nation to assert that women could contribute to the fight for Irish independence and cites "the sacred ties of Mother and Motherland." By addressing mothers and maidens, she reinforces the categories of symbolically legitimated Irish womanhood and excludes other kinds of women, just as the call for housewives to consume Irish-made products erases the labor of the women who often produced those goods.[69]

This domestication of women's nationalist activity reinforced the image of the ideal Irish mother who sang patriotic songs to her children, taught them the Irish language, told stories of ancient Irish heroes, and bought only Irish linen—or, alternatively, of the fresh-faced young virgin who industriously applied herself to learning home economics and Irish and allowed only salt-of-the-earth Irish Irelanders to court her.[70] In this formulation and in the reality that it constructed, neither mother nor maiden considered herself what we today would call "feminist." To many nationalists, progressive political activism—including the fight for women's suffrage—was damned by its connections with political developments in England, and the social conservatism that maintained separate gendered domains became "Irish" by contrast.[71] Women musicians, then, could potentially occupy two contradictory positions: within the home, singing, lilting, and playing Irish songs and tunes were patriotic activities; but outside the home, public speaking challenged the separation of spheres, and public traditional music performance at fairs and market days was almost exclusively the province of men.[72] Women activists and musicians often negotiated this challenge to social mores by maintaining discursive and actual connections with the domestic sphere.

The stated goals of the second organization, Inghinidhe na hÉireann (Daughters of Erin), upheld the roles for women put forth by the Irish Ireland movement:

> The re-establishment of the complete independence of Ireland.
>
> To encourage the study of Gaelic, of Irish literature, History, Music and Art, especially among the young, by organizing the teaching of classes for the above subjects.
>
> To support and popularise Irish manufacture.
>
> To discourage the reading and circulation of low English literature, the singing of English songs, the attending of vulgar English entertainments at the theatres and music hall, and to combat in every way English influence, which is doing so much injury to the artistic taste and refinement of the Irish people.
>
> To form a fund called the National Purposes Fund, for the furtherance of the above objects.[73]

The difference was that Inghinidhe na hÉireann sponsored public action instead of adhering quietly to the guidelines for private behavior promoted by Máire and others. As a public organization, Inghinidhe na hÉireann challenged the gendering of civic and domestic spaces, but most of its actions fit women's domestic roles as mothers, teachers, nurses, and bearers of traditional cultural material. By maintaining these roles, its work was a logical continuation of several political advances achieved by propertied women in the late 1890s: the right to vote in some local elections and to serve on district councils, and the right to act as Poor Law guardians.[74] Inghinidhe na hÉireann's work, though domesticated, occurred entirely in the public sphere and cast the naturalized work of women as an integral contribution to the nationalist cause.

In addition to working for the social welfare of Ireland's poor and attempting to discourage Irish men from enlisting in the British Army, Inghinidhe na hÉireann combined philanthropy with cultural nationalist activism. Formed in 1900 to organize a "children's treat" as a nationalist alternative to the celebration of Queen Victoria's visit, the organization also conducted free classes in Irish music, history, and language; staged *tableaux vivants* portraying Irish legends, and organized monthly céilís.[75] Male nationalists lauded Inghinidhe na hÉireann's activities, and its concentration on typically "womanly" activities enabled the group to function unchallenged—even though, as the historian Margaret Ward writes, a member of the organization undertook her work "in the role of political activist, and not as wife and mother."[76] This distinction between mother and activist echoes Inghinidhe na hÉireann founding member Maud Gonne's description of herself as Ireland's daughter, and the name of the organization placed members of the group in the same relationship to Mother Ireland that her nationalist sons enjoyed. Inghinidhe na hÉireann, then, resisted the elision of real women and ideal symbols, although it did not posit an alternative to the maiden / Kathleen personification.

Cumann na mBan provided a different though still domestically conceived challenge to the gendered separation of spheres. The organization initially raised funds for the Irish Volunteers, a nationalist militia. Agnes O'Farrelly, Cumann na mBan's first president, articulated this purpose as vital to the safety of hearth and home: "Each rifle we put in [the hands of the men] will represent to us a bolt fastened behind the door of some Irish home to keep out the hostile stranger. Each cartridge will be a watchdog to fight for the sanctity of the hearth."[77] As with Inghinidhe na hÉireann, which became a branch of Cumann na mBan in 1915, tensions between feminist and nationalist goals played out within the ranks of the organization: although Cumann na mBan later sought autonomy from the men's Volunteers, it put Irish independence before women's political equality. But unlike Inghinidhe na hÉireann, and contradicting earlier statements of purpose, some branches of Cumann na mBan did prepare for armed conflict and held first aid classes, foot drills, and arms smuggling exercises and practiced loading and firing rifles.[78] Cumann na mBan thus publicly and officially placed the instruments of warfare into the hands of some women. The Gaelic League and Irish Ireland movement likewise publicly and officially allowed a few women access to an instrument of musical technology previously reserved for men: the *uilleann* (or union) pipes.[79]

Next, I demonstrate that symbolic representations of the nation as a woman established the boundaries of intelligibility within which women traditional musicians in the early twentieth century did—or did not—operate: for women musicians who fit the visual, behavioral, and demographic norms reinforced by personifications of Ireland as maiden or mother, the nationalist movement created unique opportunities for nationally recognized performance, but for women musicians who did not fit these norms, public or semipublic music making was difficult or impossible.

PLAYING WITHIN AND OUTSIDE THE HOME AND THE IDEAL: WOMEN TRADITIONAL MUSICIANS

Introduction

Feminist scholars since the 1960s have worked diligently to return women to historical narratives and to explain their erstwhile invisibility as a function of gendered power dynamics past and present.[80] However, visibility is not sufficient, and interpretation is vital, as the historian Joan Scott writes: "When the questions of why these facts [have] been ignored and how they [are] now to be understood [are] raised, history [becomes] more than the search for facts."[81] While this book returns some women musicians to visibility and audibility, this is primarily a historiographical project: I ask how we might understand the vast differences between the public activity of women traditional musicians and the popular remembrance of them within the Irish traditional music scene today.

I begin by identifying a set of interlocking categories that describe women traditional musicians active in the period 1890–1970. First, a few—including Elizabeth Crotty, Bridget Kenny, Nell Galvin, Julia Clifford, Lucy Farr, and Aggie Whyte—were nationally or internationally visible and tend to be remembered as extraordinary rather than exemplary. The assumption that these women musicians, however skilled, were exceptional helps erase less famous women musicians from popular historical memory. The discourse of Irish traditional music throughout the twentieth century has enlisted this exceptionalism for two contradictory purposes: to refute claims that the Irish traditional music scene was (or still is) irascibly sexist and to imply that these more famous women were the only skilled women traditional musicians publicly active before 1970. This second pitfall is insidious, particularly for work that attempts to right the omission of women in the history of Irish traditional music. The tendency to focus on these women is understandable, however: information about them is more accessible, and several of them made commercial recordings.

Second, evidence shows that many women musicians were visible at one time but have since been forgotten outside their families and immediate communities. This category includes Mollie Morrissey and May McCarthy, as well as Peggy Hegarty, Joan Hanafin, Bridgie Kelleher, Maire Fitzgerald, and many more. Some of these women are easier to trace because they appear in Francis O'Neill's *Irish Minstrels and Musicians* (discussed below), one of the few published volumes that profiles individual musicians active before 1920. Most, however, were better known in their own communities and did not make any commercial recordings, although some appear on archival field recordings. Thanks to interested musicians outside academia and scholars like Gearóid Ó hAllmhuráin, whose fine-grained history of traditional music in County Clare is sensitive to the inclusion of women, more of these players are gradually becoming known, even if sometimes only by name.[82]

Third, I contend that in addition to these better-known women musicians, an unknown and possibly significant number of women musicians occupied social positions that rendered them illegible and therefore invisible to the musical public sphere, like the Galway spinster and flute player Mary Kilcar. A related category includes women musicians like the banjo player and singer Margaret Barry, a well-known performer in Cork and London who remains on the fringes of traditional music's historical memory because of her uncommon declamatory style and her origins in the marginalized itinerant Traveller community.

A fourth and often overlapping category involves second-degree visibility and includes women musicians primarily remembered as tradition bearers—mothers like Molly Morrissey (no relation to the piper Mollie Morrissey) and Margaret O'Callaghan, who gave songs and tunes to their sons.[83] Many of these women rarely played outside their homes, but motherhood allowed them to pass on the tradition in time-honored and politically supported ways. Today their names most often appear in connection with their sons.

Encoded in these categories is an intentionally essentialized assumption that traditional music's historical gaze still belongs to male musicians. With rare exceptions, Irish traditional music's texts are all written by men, and the brain trust of the tradition still consists of its "gentlemen scholars." Nearly all the accounts and recordings we have of pre-1970 women musicians come from male authors, interviewers, and collectors. Although this imbalance is slowly being redressed, the dearth of female commentators and collectors reveals as much about the situation of women in all areas of Irish life in the mid-twentieth century as it does about the enduringly homosocial traditional music scene.

In the first part of this chapter, I examined feminized representations of the

Irish nation and traced some of the ways early twentieth-century Irish women negotiated political activity through or despite these representations. Using biographical profiles from Francis O'Neill's *Irish Minstrels and Musicians*, I first argue that similarities between personifications of the Irish nation and representations of women musicians enabled these women to perform as good nationalists rather than as threats to the social order. I then contrast these publicly sanctioned women musicians with Mary Kilcar, a nearly forgotten flute player from Galway whose social position as a spinster rendered her illegible as a tradition bearer and thereby helped ensure her exclusion from the semipublic sphere of local musical events, as well as from the national stage.

O'Neill's Irish Minstrels and Musicians: *Mothers and Maidens on Stage*

Captain Francis O'Neill (1848–1936) is most famous for his collections of dance tunes, including *The Dance Music of Ireland: 1001 Gems*, which many musicians still call "the book" or "the Bible." Born in County Cork, O'Neill immigrated to the United States, joined the Chicago police department in 1873, and began collecting and publishing tunes in the early 1900s.[84] Therefore, he was not in Ireland during the height of the nationalist movement. What, then, might this famous but distant collector offer as a commentator on traditional music, nationalism, and the place of women musicians in both?

First, O'Neill's reputation as a tune collector helped popularize his other works, including *Irish Minstrels and Musicians*, a collection of biographical profiles first published in 1913.[85] As a collector, he inherited a rich tradition of music scholarship that had reached fever pitch in Ireland in the nineteenth century—first with collections by Edward Bunting and Thomas Moore before 1850, and then with publications by Patrick Weston Joyce, William Bradbury Ryan, and George Petrie in the latter half of the century. Connections with antiquarian studies elevated the status of folk music scholarship during this time, and O'Neill's collections were favorably received as resources for repertoire and examples of the single-minded devotion to traditional music that even now marks the "serious" traditional musician. The success and continuing availability of O'Neill's tune collections has ensured an enduring audience for his other books—an audience not shared by the traditional music scholarship of his contemporaries Henry Grattan Flood and Richard Henebry. O'Neill's influence on the repertoire and discourse of Irish traditional music means that *Irish Minstrels and Musicians* bestows upon its profiled musicians a public memory not otherwise available: they are remembered in internationally circulated print, while most of the musicians of either sex who weren't mentioned have either been forgotten or are remembered only within their families or localities.[86] For example, knowledge of the early twentieth-century musicians May McCarthy, Mollie Morrissey, and Bridget Kenny is almost entirely dependent on the ways O'Neill and his sources depict them.[87]

Second, O'Neill's residence in Chicago and his active participation in the already transnational Irish traditional music scene gave him critical distance from viewing Irish traditional music solely as an instrument of cultural and political nationalism. He treats traditional music as an art form in its own right, even though he also allows his belief in the power of Irish cultural nationalism to shape his treatments of the harp and pipes. The information and writing style of some of his biographies also derive from articles by nationalist-leaning newspaper reporters in Ireland and its diaspora, and descriptions of the women musicians in *Irish Minstrels and Musicians* resonate with images of the ideal Irish woman and with feminized personifications of the nation in the popular press.

Finally, *Irish Minstrels and Musicians* allows us to explore the relationships between nationalist discourse and women's music making. How did nationalist discourse affect opportunities for women to play in public? How was women's public performance rationalized or recast as nationalist activity? Here, O'Neill and his newspaper sources supply a sense of the historical present and provide material for uncovering contemporary attitudes about women musicians unshaped by the revisions of oral history. Although *Irish Minstrels and Musicians* and the newspaper articles that describe Kenny, Morrissey, and McCarthy leave no evidence about what these musicians may have thought about their musicianship or the rhetorics of cultural nationalism, these sources present vital clues about how and why they might have performed publicly, and how and why they might have been encouraged to do so despite an overwhelming social conservatism that asserted that a women's proper place was in the home.

Mrs. Kenny's Excellent Adventure: From One Public to Another

Of the women traditional musicians publicly active in the early twentieth century, Bridget Kenny remains the best known. The daughter of the piper John McDonough, Kenny grew up in Galway in the mid-nineteenth century. O'Neill writes at length about her domestic situation and emphasizes her ability to bear children and instill in them a knowledge of Irish traditional music:

> Devotion to art does not appear to have unfavorably affected the size of Mrs. Kenny's family, for we are informed she is the prolific mother of thirteen children. Neither did the artistic temperament on both sides mar the domestic peace of the Kenny home, and, though the goddess of plenty slighted them in the distribution of her favors, have they not wealth in health and the parentage of a house full of rosy-cheeked sons and daughters, several of whom bid fair to rival their mother, "The Queen of Irish Fiddlers," in the world of music.[88]

Although we can only guess at Kenny's political views, O'Neill portrays her as a proper Irish mother who provides her children with a love of music and nation along with their porridge, which though thin is surely Irish.

In keeping with the role of traditional music and its newly formed institutions in the practice of cultural nationalism, O'Neill also emphasizes Kenny's success in music competitions: "The Gaelic Revival brought Mrs. Kenny into the limelight, and after she had outclassed all competitors as a traditional violinist at the annual Feiseanna, winning first prize year after year, she was proclaimed 'The Queen of Irish Fiddlers.'" Yet he is indignant on her behalf for what he perceives as underappreciation: "This remarkable woman's talents ought to have been regarded as a national asset. Yet it does not appear that any effort was made to take advantage of the opportunities presented by her discovery, by the establishment of a school in which the much-vaunted traditional style of rendering Irish music would be taught and perpetuated."[89]

Newspaper accounts suggest that the nationalist movement did recognize and use Kenny's talents in venues outside her home community, however. For example, she received top billing at a festival sponsored by the Gaelic League and the Limerick Irish Pipers' Club in Kilkee, County Clare, in September 1903, and advertisements in the *Clare Champion* assured readers that "the best Gaelic talent has been secured for this year's Festival."[90] The existence and success of this concert relied on the importance of music in the expression of cultural nationalism. Because the philosophies of the Irish Ireland movement situated the teaching of traditional music in the domestic sphere and therefore with women, Kenny's public concert appearances could be seen as an extension of the activities she was encouraged to perform in the home. Likewise, Irish Ireland discourse about the role of women as tradition bearers gave Kenny opportunities for performing that would almost certainly not have been available to her otherwise as a woman.

By emphasizing her poverty and her occupation as a street musician, O'Neill's sketch raises questions about social class, the nationalist movement, and musical practice—and ethnicity. First, how did Kenny become the respected "Queen of Irish Fiddlers"? We know from surviving wax cylinder recordings that she was a tremendous musician, and we can guess that her origins in a musical family lent her playing and her persona an air of "authenticity" useful to the nationalist movement. But it is also possible that Kenny had roots in the Traveller community, another group marginalized by nationalist discourse: her maiden name, McDonough, is a common Traveller surname in the province of Connaught, and she was born in Galway, a county in that province.[91] Travellers are a long-standing nomadic population resident in Ireland, and to a lesser extent in Scotland and England. Various popular legends about their origins exist, including some stories that link them with the Roma of Eastern Europe, but this connection is largely discounted. Despite their romanticization as a "pure" and "ancient" Irish people, anti-Traveller sentiment has been widespread for at least the past century.[92] Despite the Travellers' stereotypical musical skill and the power of myth, the Gaelic revival and the nationalist movement were almost entirely the domain of settled folk: Travellers, like women, were not the citizens whose independence was fought for, and as a group they enjoyed even less access to the public sphere than did middle- and upper-class women.[93] If Kenny did indeed come from a Traveller family, the nationalist movement did not broadcast that information—and if she did, such origins could also help explain her disappearance from the collective memory of the nonitinerant traditional music scene.

By mentioning Kenny's occupation as a street musician, however, O'Neill's account also leads to an important point about the differences between "public" and "the public sphere": "In no country save Ireland, would a violinist of such demonstrated ability as the subject of this sketch remain unappreciated and practically unnoticed, while obliged by necessity to contribute to the support of a large family by playing for a precarious pittance along the highways and byways of Dublin for a generation or more."[94] Poverty directed Kenny toward the street, where she could be seen and heard—but not where she would automatically be noticed or accepted by the nationalist public sphere (the realm where decision making and directed action took place).[95] The nationalist movement's disregard for music performance outside concert settings also surfaces in the absence of contemporary published accounts of music making in commercial and semipublic spaces: although numerous oral histories mention traditional music at markets, fairs, pattern days (discussed below), and similar events, such musicking is missing from the written record except when a hapless musician runs afoul of the law.[96] For Kenny, an urban busker and a woman, participation in the nationalist public sphere was remarkable—yet O'Neill's profile remains the only widely available account we have of this "Queen of Irish Fiddlers." Her daughters Christina Sheridan and Josephine Whelan, who recorded at least one 78 rpm disk with the Siamsa Gaedheal Ceilidh Band, remain similarly unknown and uncelebrated today.[97]

Mama, ~~Don't~~ Let Your Daughters Grow Up to Be Pipers

On the very rare occasions when musicians today mention Kenny, they call her a "fiddler"—a remarkably automatic attribution of traditionality, given the early twentieth-century tendency to use "fiddler" and "violinist" interchangeably (see the discussion of "fiddle" versus "violin" in chapter 2).[98] The vehement distaste for the term "violinist" in today's traditional music circles sometimes leads to confused readings of earlier sources—a topic I address in chapter 2. But the Irish traditional fiddle and the violin are the same instrument, and if traditional styles were associated with rural people and attitudes in the nineteenth century, the instrument itself does not seem to have carried these associations. The instrument's integral role in art music as well as folk styles also meant that it was much less likely to become iconically Irish.

The uilleann pipes, however, have been considered ineluctably Irish since at least the late eighteenth century, and unlike the fiddle / violin, the pipes evoked poverty and debauchery during the nineteenth century.[99] By the time O'Neill published *Irish Minstrels and Musicians* in 1913, the dominant narrative held that pipers—whether common men or gentlemen—had once been respected members of society, but that the occupation and its practitioners had fallen into disrepute. "Kelly the Piper," a famous story by Mrs. S. C. Hall, illustrates the relationship between a piper and his Anglo-Irish "betters." First published in 1829, the story presents Kelly as a ne'er-do-well drunkard who earns a meager living by playing at the local "pattern" (or patron's) day, a celebration featuring music and dancing.[100] The squalid laziness of Kelly and his family contrasts with the industry and wealth of the Anglo-Irish "quality," and the skill of the piper, though considerable, is nonetheless inextricable from his poverty and, ultimately, his Irishness. The story seems to have been widely available in the latter half of the nineteenth century, and O'Neill includes it as a source for *Irish Minstrels and Musicians* and *Irish Music: A Fascinating Hobby*.[101]

A similar report on the falling fortunes of the uilleann pipes comes from "A Plain Piper," the pen name for a contributor to the *Kerryman*. This author, presumably male, implores readers to celebrate Ireland's traditional music as an object of national pride:

> The poverty-stricken piper became an object of contempt, and the contempt was naturally extended to his instrument, the cause of his indigence. It is only a few years since a friend of mine, a good fiddler, who expressed an intention of learning the pipes, was told by his relatives that if he did so disgrace himself he need never show his face at home again! Small wonder that the pipes ceased to be generally played just as the language ceased to be spoken and so many of the old customs to be observed! The race of "gentlemen pipers" had died out and no respectable person would touch the instrument.[102]

This tale corroborates O'Neill's similar interpretation of the pipes' decline in *Irish Minstrels and Musicians*.[103] If a male fiddler faced familial disgrace for wanting to learn the pipes in the late nineteenth century, a woman with the same desire must have risked opprobrium of an even greater magnitude, especially since the pipes lacked the connection with parlor music enjoyed by the fiddle / violin and the piano.

According to O'Neill's sources, however, several women did play the pipes in the nineteenth century, even if doing so in public was acceptable only for a woman faced with "dire necessity": "Tradition has preserved the name of Kitty Hanley, a Limerick widow, who on the death of her husband—a blind piper—buckled on his pipes and made a living playing on the streets."[104] And "from [Jimmy Barry, late nineteenth century] was learned the story of a woman known as 'Nance the Piper,' who flourished at Castlelyons and who had become a performer from dire necessity, on the death of her husband."[105]

O'Neill admits that blind Nance must have already played the pipes before her husband died, but in Kitty Hanley's case, a reader could assume that she strapped on the pipes without previous experience. This assumption is absurd—the pipes are difficult to learn to play: according to a popular saying often attributed to the twentieth-century piper Séamus Ennis, it takes seven years of learning, seven years of practicing, and seven years of playing to become a decent piper. We have no information to suggest that Kitty Hanley was a particularly good piper, but the fact that she was able to make a living at it suggests that she too was a proficient player.

These reports of nineteenth-century women musicians, however few, indicate that women were playing instrumental dance music, either privately or to avoid privation, before the institutions of cultural nationalism began to celebrate the sounds of the pipes, harp, and fiddle. Such cultural nationalism ultimately counteracted the stigma against the pipes and briefly allowed some young, probably middle-class, women access to national public performance opportunities on the uilleann pipes and the warpipes.[106] The fact that this level of access and encouragement was so short-lived makes it even more remarkable: only in the past two decades have women returned in significant—if still comparatively small—numbers to uilleann piping circles.

How, then, did the sensibilities of nationalist fervor enable upwardly mobile young women to play the pipes publicly in the early twentieth century? How did the rhetoric of Ireland-as-woman intersect with representations of women playing what had so recently been considered a lower-class, disreputable, and male instrument? O'Neill's sketches of Mollie Morrissey and May McCarthy demonstrate the rhetorical work necessary to portray women pipers as valuable semiprofessional participants in Irish public life rather than as unacceptable transgressors or as merely tolerable private amateurs. First, O'Neill and his sources emphasize these pipers' youth and femininity to render them harmless to the social and musical order. Second, descriptions of Morrissey and McCarthy resonate with poems and song texts that portray Ireland as a maiden—a stylistic device that naturalizes the idea that playing traditional music, even on the pipes, is an appropriate activity for young nationalist women. Finally, O'Neill and his sources avoid connecting musicianship with identity in their descriptions of Morrissey and McCarthy. This avoidance sidesteps class and potential gender role confusion and separates them from their male counterparts, for whom the label "piper" is an identifying feature and most likely a source of pride.

O'Neill's biographies of Morrissey and McCarthy leave no doubt that these two proficient pipers are women—young, graceful, and mild mannered. Unlike most of O'Neill's profiles of male musicians, which begin with reports of their musicianship, his accounts of Morrissey and McCarthy first situate each in relation to John Wayland, their teacher. In Morrissey's sketch, O'Neill also lauds the ease with which she memorizes new tunes—an important attribute, but hardly the cornerstone of traditional musicianship.[107] O'Neill quotes a 1905 article in the London-based *Ladies' Pictorial* at length:

> I give you an interesting portrait of Miss Mollie Morrissey of Cork, fideogist,[108] harpist, pianist, violinist, bagpiper and stepdancer, at the age of fourteen. I

venture to say that not many Irish colleens can boast of such a long list of accomplishments, but such are the attainments of this little girl, whose charming and unassuming manner has endeared her to all who know her. She is the youngest and most proficient female piper in Ireland, playing the famous Irish melodies with great expression, and is also a correct exponent of dance music. She appeared at the Cork International and Industrial Exhibitions with very pronounced success. The clever little artiste is decorated with many medals, won at competitions in piping and step-dancing, and at last year's Oireachtas she carried off first prize in female hornpipe dancing from all comers, her graceful carriage and movements combined with precision being much admired. Recently at Thurles Feis she won no less than three first prizes in step-dancing, and marched to the field in company with another young genius playing the now revived primitive Irish Warpipes. Miss Morrissey got a special invitation from the mayor of Carnarvon to attend a reception during Pan-Celtic week, which she could not accept on account of being indisposed at the time.[109]

Published eight years before *Irish Minstrels and Musicians,* this account emphasizes Morrissey's femininity and youth. Overall, O'Neill's sketch portrays Morrissey as a girl of fourteen, rather than as the adult woman she had become by 1913. In the *Ladies' Pictorial* article, her musical skills are "accomplishments" that would seem to lead to an advantageous match and a future playing in the parlors of middle- or upper-class homes. While the article calls her "the most proficient female piper in Ireland," it further feminizes her prowess by citing her expressive performance of airs even as it damns her renditions of faster—and arguably more challenging—dance music as merely "correct." At every turn, Morrissey's successes are diminished by phrases like "little girl" and "clever little artiste." The article's final reference to her "indisposition" reinforces an overall impression of delicacy that eclipses her prizes, precision, and proficiency and leaves the reader with a picture of an endearing young thing, a retiring, mild-mannered maiden whose medals and pretty face merely decorate the public practice of Irish cultural nationalism.

McCarthy's biography produces a similar tension between musicianship and its rhetorical erasure. McCarthy is also young—in her teens in 1910—and according to O'Neill, her "progress in piping and dancing is said to have been little short of marvelous."[110] Complimentary as that seems, "marvelous" suggests that McCarthy's progress is extraordinarily uncommon or even supernatural. Attribution of musical skill to otherworldly entities is common in stories told about

Irish traditional musicians—like the spéirbhean of aisling poetry, the fairies who bestow musical prowess are instruments of a magical nationalism that attributes exceptional qualities to the Irish.[111] Here, though, "marvelous" draws the reader's attention away from musicianship: McCarthy is not a musician, she is a marvel. O'Neill's next paragraph somewhat inexplicably links McCarthy with John Augustus O'Shea, a journalist and novelist stationed in France in the nineteenth century; identifies her as the daughter of Tipperary parents; and then returns our gaze to the young piper: "Their talented daughter, however, was born within earshot of the far-famed Bells of Shandon, and while neither big nor brawny this versatile Irish colleen can handle with ease a full-size instrument."[112]

O'Neill again focuses on the female body and its fully Irish origins rather than on the music that the body produces. McCarthy is small, no threat to anyone, and feminine—despite her ease with the pipes. Similarly, O'Neill's sketch of Morrissey avoids drawing attention to the physical control necessary to dance with "graceful carriage and movements combined with precision" in favor of her delicacy, small size, and youth.

If youth and femininity ensured that Morrissey and McCarthy presented no threat to the social and musical order, their participation in Gaelic League competitions establishes them as ardent nationalists and frames their musical performance as an expression of that nationalism. Cultural nationalist beliefs in the early twentieth century helped create an environment in which some parents allowed their daughters to learn the uilleann pipes, teachers agreed to teach them, and some newly formed pipers' clubs admitted women members.[113] McCarthy's performance career demonstrates the role of nationalist organizations in allowing her access to public stages in Ireland, England, and Wales. O'Neill mentions that McCarthy had been invited to play in a series of concerts in Wales in 1910, and then in Birmingham and Manchester around St. Patrick's Day, 1911.[114] Although O'Neill and the *Daily Sketch* article he quotes do not supply much detail about these concerts, McCarthy almost certainly performed for Irish diasporic audiences in Birmingham and Manchester, where a branch of the Gaelic League had been founded in 1905.[115] Her diary also lists nineteen concert dates in Cork, Kerry, and West Limerick in 1917.[116]

These concerts may have been part of an informal circuit of Gaelic League–supported events common in the early years of the twentieth century, a circuit on which the fiddler Bridget Kenny performed—as did the fiddler and dancer Teresa Halpin (Treasa Ní Ailpín) of Limerick, who appeared on the same bill as Kenny in Kilrush in 1903.[117] Rarely mentioned by traditional music historians, these concerts seem to have opened a musical public sphere for women performers akin to the political public sphere that Inghinidhe na hÉireann and Cumann na mBan created for women activists. Anecdotal evidence suggests that these two public spheres may also have overlapped: according to Mary Mitchell-Ingoldsby's history of the Cork Pipers' Club, May McCarthy was also a member of Cumann na mBan, whose 1917 constitution asserted that members "should participate in the public life of their locality, and assert their rights as citizens."[118] Since Cumann na mBan included cultural education among its goals, the organization may have made use of McCarthy's talents as a piper, although no available evidence supports that claim.

The fact that both Morrissey and McCarthy were participants in Gaelic League competitions and that McCarthy was a member of Cumann na mBan connects them to the nationalist movement in obvious ways. Moreover, if we assume that as maidens, they were destined to become bearers of children and tradition, we can imagine a suitably feminine future for Morrissey and McCarthy in keeping with the dictates of the Irish Ireland movement. O'Neill and his sources further cement the relationship between these musicians and the nationalist movement by echoing the words of songs and poems that personify Ireland as a young woman. Although the poetic use of adjectives like "fair," "sweet," and "graceful," as well as the Anglicized noun "colleen" predate the swell of nationalist broadside ballads and poems that began in the late eighteenth century, these words were familiar components of stock phrases like "fair Erin's isle," "sweetness of sweetness," and "sweet and mild" that referred to the Irish nation-as-woman.[119] Particularly striking is a stanza about Morrissey penned by her contemporary, the fiddle player Edward Cronin:

> Upon the height of steep Glenview
> That looks o'er Shandon's sweet-toned bells,
> A maid with eyes of heavenly blue—
> Fair Mollie of the music dwells.[120]

In four short formulaic lines, Cronin follows the form of most aisling poems, which begin by establishing the setting and usually describing the spéirbhean shortly thereafter, often beginning with her eyes.[121] Like Dark Rosaleen's "holy delicate white hands," Morrissey's eyes of "heavenly blue" align her with the angelic and saintly. "Fair Mollie of the music" invokes the famous poem and air "Seán O'Duibhir a' Ghleanna" ("John O'Dwyer of the Glen") and several similarly named works about the hardships of English occupation, thus supplying

FIGURE 1.1 Sir John Tenniel, "Two Forces," *Punch*, 29 October 1881. Used by permission of Punch Cartoon Library/Topfoto.

FIGURE 1.2 Raphael Tuck and Sons, "Erin Go Bragh Series" #177.

FIGURE 1.3 May McCarthy, in Francis O'Neill, *Irish Musicians and Musicians*, 333.

FIGURE 1.4 Mollie Morrissey, in Francis O'Neill, *Irish Musicians and Musicians*, 335

nationalist resonance to Cronin's otherwise superficial epithet. O'Neill's prose contains fewer artistic pretensions, but he also refers to McCarthy as a "colleen."[122]

Morrissey and McCarthy also visually match representations of the Irish nation as a young woman. Mangan's nineteenth-century verse gives us Erin's "waving raven tresses," Eiré's "golden tresses long and low," and "Maedhbh the young, of ringlets long."[123] In graphic representations from the late nineteenth and early twentieth centuries, Erin / Eiré / Hibernia often wears her hair down. Her overall appearance either shows her youth and need for Britannia's protection, as in an 1881 *Punch* cartoon by Sir John Tenniel, or invokes the imagined fresh-faced purity of the Irish nation, as in a scene on an early twentieth-century postcard, depicting Erin dancing to a patriotic song.

The photos of Morrissey and McCarthy included in *Irish Minstrels and Musicians* are consistent with images of Ireland-as-woman, and their flowing tresses show their youth and connect them with France's Marianne and America's Lady Liberty, iconic figures of national independence. McCarthy also sports her competition medals—a sartorial choice that binds her photographic image to the

Mother Ireland and the Queen of Irish Fiddlers **57**

work of the Gaelic League. Both portraits anticipate the obligatory curls worn by competitive women Irish step dancers today.

The enduring view that women are susceptible—and men immune—to the vagaries of fashion inflects O'Neill's descriptions of Morrissey and McCarthy. Unlike his accounts of male musicians, in which he uses nouns like "piper," "fiddler," "musician," and "composer," O'Neill's profiles of these two women pipers rely on words like "learner"; "artiste"; "performer"; and of course "daughter," "girl," and "colleen." In addition to emphasizing their sex and their relationships with teachers, parents, and audiences, these words relentlessly assert that for Morrissey and McCarthy, playing the pipes is something they do rather than an expression of who they are. Although the *Ladies' Pictorial* article that O'Neill quotes does refer to Morrissey as a "fideogist, harpist, pianist, violinist, bagpiper and stepdancer," it lists the pipes last among the instruments. Nowhere in his sketch of McCarthy does O'Neill refer to her as a piper or as a musician. This reluctance to call Morrissey and McCarthy pipers is remarkable, since O'Neill almost always refers to their male counterparts as pipers and frequently replaces male musicians' first names with "Piper," as with Piper Gaynor and Piper Jackson.[124] "Piper" thus defines the identity of these men and transcends their social class: Gaynor was a blind itinerant musician, but Jackson was a gentleman.

In a genre wherein "musician" still often becomes a male player's primary identity, O'Neill's word choice suggests that Morrissey and McCarthy used the music only as an accessory and that neither assumed the identity of a traditional musician. The distinction between doing and being offers clues to the scarcity of information about publicly active women musicians between 1922 and the 1970s. In reference to Morrissey and McCarthy, O'Neill and his sources term the playing of traditional music an "accomplishment" or an "attainment," a skill used to adorn the private parlor and entertain the family circle. If early twentieth-century male commentators constructed women's musicianship as a fashion and not a vocation, women's public performance became less threatening—both to male professional musicians and to the symbolic order that expected women to remain in the domestic sphere. By considering a woman's musicianship as peripheral to her identity, any expectation that she would continue playing through her adulthood was removed, thus enabling what the fiddler Bernadette McCarthy today calls "the disappearing act": the tendency for young women musicians to stop playing and vanish from the scene once they reach adulthood.[125] In this context, it is remarkable that McCarthy continued playing the pipes publicly as an adult and formed her own céilí band.[126]

Looking into the House Where the Music Is: Mary Kilcar and Lucy Farr

I close this chapter with a story about two women musicians absent from O'Neill's *Irish Minstrels and Musicians*: the flute player Mary Kilcar (b. c. 1890) and the fiddler Lucy Farr (née Kirwan, 1911–2003), who lived in County Galway in the 1910s and 1920s. Farr was barely two years old when O'Neill's book was published, so her exclusion is not surprising. However, although Kilcar was approximately twenty years her senior and by Farr's reckoning was a fine player, she remained unknown both locally and nationally. Previously, I examined the social conditions and symbolic connections that made public music performance possible for Kenny, Morrissey, and McCarthy. Now I ask what conditions relegated Kilcar's music making to the private realm, and what circumstances gave Farr the opportunity to narrate Kilcar's story from her position as a public musical figure reminiscing about her own childhood. Questions of access and (il)legibility are central to our understanding of the musical activity of all these women.

According to Farr, Kilcar never played the flute outside her own home in Lishenny, a small village near Ballinakill, in County Galway. We know that Kilcar was a spinster who lived with her sister, and we may assume that the women came from an economically secure family, since they seem to have lived by themselves—a residential situation that likely required some means. We must guess about Kilcar's early musical life, however. She may have learned to play the flute as a child or young adult, and like many girls of her generation, she most likely received some sort of formal music tuition: by the time she would have entered school, music had been part of the curricula of both the National Schools and convent schools for several decades.[127] East Galway also seems to have provided a supportive environment for music education for adults in the late nineteenth and early twentieth centuries. For example, violin classes for men and women were offered in the market town of Ballinasloe in 1905, and the organizers note that among the male students, all had "more or less a practical knowledge of the violin" before the classes began.[128] These classes seem to have focused on classical technique and repertoire, but the area was also known for its traditional music and remains famous for its traditional flute style. As in many other Irish communities in the late nineteenth century, opportunities for men and boys to learn and play wind instruments were plentiful, including local fife and drum corps and brass bands sponsored by area temperance societies.[129] However, Kilcar's sex limited her access to these avenues of public performance, and—unlike her contemporaries from Cork, Morrissey and McCarthy—she did not enjoy the support of a local pipers' or musicians' club that admitted women members.

It makes sense that Kilcar would have received musical instruction as a girl, and the category of "musical girl" at the beginning of the twentieth century was intelligible. But Kilcar inhabited another social category by the time Farr met her in the early 1930s: she was a spinster. As a single and aging woman in the socially conservative years of the Irish Free State, Kilcar would have been symbolically invisible: she was neither a mother nor a maiden in a society whose metaphors of nation defined the behavior and aspirations of real women. Although politically and rhetorically invisible, her position as spinster was legible within rural Irish society. The combination of her musicianship and her marital status, however, was not.

Why? After all, her younger friend Farr had few problems finding musical outlets. For Farr's family, music making may implicitly have been an expression of cultural nationalism, but it was explicitly a form of entertainment to which she had access as a child in a musical household—or, more specifically, as the daughter of a musical father. The way Farr reports a conversation with Kilcar emphasizes this access and Kilcar's awareness of it:

> And there was a lady in the next village, and her name was Mary Kilcar, and she would be—when I was twenty, she'd be about forty, and she played a flute, and—though she was never part of the scene in my young days—she never—women didn't come down into the houses where the men were. You'd hear Mary Kilcar playing the flute inside in her own house, but you'd never see her in any house where there was music. And so one day, I walked—I was walking around, and I knocked at the door.
> "Oh!" she said, "Lucy Kirwan! Come in!"
> "Well," I said, "I've come in because I'm playing the fiddle, and, um, we've all, we've all heard you playing outside, but you never come to our neighborhood dos."
> "Oh," she says, "They wouldn't have women—they wouldn't at all them dos."
> I said, "Well, we do, I do."
> "Ah, but you're living in the house where it *is*. I couldn't, I couldn't do *that*."[130]

"Living in the house where it *is*" ensures presence, but presence does not automatically produce legibility as a woman musician—yet Farr's fiddling seems not to have been particularly transgressive. Why not?

The answer lies in the pervasive ideals of the Irish Ireland movement of the late nineteenth and early twentieth centuries, which defined and reinforced the role of mothers as tradition bearers—a term usually invoked without acknowledging the gendered nature of "bearer." This connection between women, the home, and tradition has analogues elsewhere, particularly in those nations we now consider postcolonial. So while we might assume that progress and time march ever forward, and that Farr enjoyed more access to public music making than Kilcar simply because she was born later, that assumption overlooks a more significant point: Farr's status as a maidenly daughter of a musical father placed her, a future tradition bearer, on the receiving end of borne tradition. As a spinster, however, Kilcar was a transmissive dead end. Although she too may have once enjoyed legibility as the daughter of a musician, she does not fit into the category through which most women musicians of her generation are remembered: as mothers who passed tunes down to their sons.[131] Because she had no children, she became illegible as a tradition bearer, even though she did pass along her example and quite possibly her tunes to Farr. But woman-to-woman musical transmission—including the sharing of tunes between mothers and daughters—is rarely noted among Irish traditional musicians. In a tradition that values the lineage of tunes and players, especially within families or from master to apprentice, this omission is noteworthy. Another way of thinking about women as tradition bearers draws on Gayle Rubin's "The Traffic in Women": only women whose bodies held symbolic and actual exchange value—virgins and mothers—were part of the exchange of tunes.[132] For single women like Kilcar, bodies out of heterosexual reproductive circulation also meant tunes out of circulation.

We might interpret Kilcar's nonparticipation in community music making as shyness, but again, a comparison with Farr complicates this overly simplistic explanation. In her anecdote about Kilcar, Farr points out that women "didn't come down into the houses where the men were," and Kilcar's own story—albeit in Farr's words—reinforces this claim. Kilcar was not the only woman in Galway in the early twentieth century who never played music outside her own home: Farr says that her aunt Margaret, who eventually married, also played, but not in public "because there were no, no other women playing fiddles [in the scene], you see. There were *no* women fiddle players. My aunt Margaret, who played a bit—she never played out. Never went anyplace to play. She'd play indoors in the house. She's the one who used to dance a jig and sing and play the fiddle at the same time."[133]

Farr, whose access to the musical public sphere was much greater than her aunt Margaret's or than Kilcar's, also describes the discomfort of going out to sessions alone in London in the late 1960s:

> LUCY FARR: Well, I didn't used to go every Sunday morning, but I remember this one Sunday morning that I got all these looks—a *woman* walking in on her own, with a fiddle under her arm. And then all of a sudden I didn't feel too bad, 'cause I found Julia Clifford used to come in as well, but she had John—
>
> REG HALL: So was it—
>
> LUCY: I think that must be, I think that must be late, that must be around '68 or '9 or something.
>
> REG: Was it an all-man affair?
>
> LUCY: All old men.
>
> REG: Old men.
>
> LUCY: Yeah.[134]

To misquote William Butler Yeats's "Sailing to Byzantium," that was no country for single women. Kilcar and Farr's aunt Margaret could easily have disappeared entirely from the narrative of Irish traditional music, but like the narrator in Adriana Cavarero's "On the Outskirts of Milan," Farr gives both women the posthumous gift of their stories.[135] Her own position as a respected and publicly active traditional musician allowed her to give this gift, but her story reflects her own anxieties about legibility and access.

CONCLUSION

Single women like Kilcar were demographically distinguished and often economically disadvantaged compared with the maidens, wives, and mothers of popular nationalist imagery. Although the real women who fit these idealized categories were a minority in the early twentieth century, the categories nonetheless carried the rhetorical power of acceptability and approval, even when the women who fit them best did things that weren't quite acceptable or universally approved of, like playing instrumental dance music in public. As in the case of many of the women working actively toward Irish independence, alignment with the symbolic categories of mother and maiden enabled women playing music publicly to be seen as good nationalists working toward an Irish Ireland rather than as transgressive, even unwomanly, suffragettes. Their inclusion in *Irish*

Minstrels and Musicians ensures that they, unlike Kilcar, will be remembered, and O'Neill's prose dictates how they will be remembered.

The desire for recognition as human is related to the desire for recognition as a musician, and in traditional music circles, denial of one often leads to the denial of the other. An adaptation of a quotation from Judith Butler's *Undoing Gender* supplies a provoking set of questions to be asked of the multiple practices that constitute Irish traditional musicianship in the past and today. I acknowledge the life-or-death implications of Butler's original phrasing, but I suggest that music and identification as a musician may also help determine whether a life is livable. Here, I substitute "play(ing)" for "be(ing)" and "musician" for "person" or "human": "What, given the contemporary order of playing, can I play?." . . . [This question] concerns consequential decisions about what a musician is, and what social norms must be honored and expressed for 'musicianhood' to become allocated, how we do or do not recognize animate others as musicians depending on whether or not we recognize a certain norm manifested in and by the body of that other."[136]

Unlike Mollie Morrissey and May McCarthy, Mary Kilcar did not inhabit the body or the social position of the ideal Irish woman and thus did not honor and express the norms that would have allowed her entry into the music scene as a tradition bearer. For women traditional musicians in the early twentieth century, the nationalist movement and its symbols provided the "contemporary order of playing" that defined the norms of women's musical and social behavior that determined intelligibility or its opposite. As chapters below show, these questions remain relevant for women, queer musicians, and musicians of color in Ireland and its diaspora into the twenty-first century.

TWO

The Not-So-Strange Disappearance of Treasa Ní Ailpín (Teresa Halpin)

Class, Gender, and Musical Style in Early Twentieth-Century Ireland

INTRODUCTION

Winters in Limerick are bleak. With cold rain off the River Shannon and brief gray days, after the excitement of Christmas, the post-Lenten joys of summer seem distant. If you live in Limerick today, you might take refuge from the elements in front of your television or in a warm pub, listening to a trad session and warming your throat with a hot whiskey. Or you might be practicing your part for the Limerick Musical Society's upcoming production of *Fiddler on the Roof*, attending a fund-raising concert for the Irish Cancer Society, or performing—or watching your child perform—in a school recital. Soon, when spring comes and the gorse bushes bloom in the countryside surrounding the city, you might begin marking your calendar with music and theatre festivals happening in the county and farther afield. If you're interested in the Irish language, you might plan to trek down to Dingle, out to Connemara, or up to County Donegal to practice your *cúpla focal* ("couple of words") with native speakers in the *Gaeltachtaí* (Irish-speaking regions). And if you're an aficionado of traditional music, you might make the pilgrimage to Miltown Malbay, County Clare, for the Willie Clancy week or attend the competitions at the Fleadh Cheoil na hÉireann (Music Festival of Ireland, or the All-Ireland), whose location changes every two years.

For the fiddler and dancer Treasa Ní Ailpín (Teresa Halpin, 1894–1983), activities like these would have been recognizable.[1] Musical theatre, light opera, and charity events of all kinds were common in Limerick around 1910, as were variety shows, school recitals, and public dances. Touring musicians appeared periodically, including Limerick's own famous tenor Joseph O'Mara, and temperance societies sponsored brass band performances and guest lecturers. "Grand display[s] of animated pictures" and "performances" on the gramophone popularized new technologies and products.[2] And although pub sessions of Irish traditional music would not be common for several decades, house parties and dances were still part of local life. Public events, including the annual Oireachtas, presented language, music, and dance competitions and concerts to local, regional, and countrywide nationalist audiences.

Ní Ailpín was an active and sought-after participant in such celebrations of Irish cultural identity: by the time she was twenty years old, she had won several dance championships and had performed throughout Ireland and in England and the United States.[3] In a fiddle competition several years later, she would simultaneously win the praise of Bridget Kenny (the "Queen of Irish Fiddlers") and best another teenage fiddler, Michael Coleman—who later became the most influential Irish traditional musician of the twentieth century. In adulthood, she would publish the first bilingual Irish-English fiddle tutor (method book) and would spend most of her life teaching music and dance. Yet today, very few traditional musicians have ever heard of Ní Ailpín. Her status in the annals of Irish traditional music history is complicated by the common and heretofore unchallenged assumption that most "fiddlers" who performed in nationalist contexts in the early twentieth century were upper-class urban classical violinists, and indeed, today Ní Ailpín is presumed to have been one of these interlopers. Her disappearance from the history of Irish traditional music points to powerful but unacknowledged connections among gender, class, national identity, and "authentic" performance practice. These connections are based on nationalist ideals of Irish traditional music as masculine, organic, and untaught, in opposition to the feminized refinements of "foreign" classical music education.[4]

In this chapter, I first trace the gendered and classed associations that inform today's common assumption that nearly all fiddlers who participated in the high-profile music competitions of the early twentieth century were classical violinists. Then, by analyzing archival sound recordings, newspaper clippings, and written accounts of Ní Ailpín's playing between around 1907 and 1929, I challenge the claim that she was "merely" a classical player. The connection between women musicians and Western art music styles has meant both that many of the women musicians active in the early twentieth century have disappeared from the narrative of traditional music history and that the potentially significant influence of classical violinists on Irish traditional musicians of both sexes during that era has gone unexamined. By drawing attention to the inextricability of gender and class in determinations of genre and style, I question the notion that traditional music was a stable category in Ireland in the early decades of the twentieth century. Because attributions of traditionality have been so closely associated with citizenship in the Irish nation, these naturalized connections among masculinity, class, and traditional music have complicated the full recognition of women musicians.

Most important, Ní Ailpín's story—and its omission from the dominant historical narrative of Irish traditional music—complicates understandings of the relationship between folk authenticity and ethnic nationalism that continue to determine which stories we tell, which musical styles we hear as authentic, and how past and present aesthetics shape the experiences and remembrance of musicians. By linking gender, class, ethnicity, and musical style, Irish traditional music discourse in the twentieth century created a paradoxical situation in which actual or perceived style effectively erased the Irishness of performers like Ní Ailpín while also creating the conditions for nonethnically Irish musicians to sound Irish. This slippage is central to the book's overall argument that Irish traditional music has the potential to free itself from the fetters of ethnic nationalism.

CLASS, GENDER, AND ART MUSIC IN EARLY TWENTIETH-CENTURY IRELAND

To understand the public activity of women performers of traditional music in the early twentieth century and their subsequent disappearance from traditional music history, we must investigate the presence of women classical musicians at the same time—a presence that has led to the assumption today that all publicly active women fiddle players of that era were classically trained. We must also consider the relationships between traditional and art music in nationalist circles, especially between the founding of the Gaelic League in 1893 and the founding of the Free State in 1922. Such an investigation challenges the separation between genres that endures in academic scholarship and in traditional music discourse, if not always in performance.[5] With the exception of some work on the harper Turlough Carolan (c. 1670–1738), the dominant historical narrative of Irish traditional music has largely ignored art music except as a contaminant whose techniques and methods of transmission threaten to dilute or destroy the "pure drop."[6] From the perspective of art music composition, the musicologist Harry White has argued that the cultural isolationism of the Irish nationalist movement in the early twentieth century prevented the development of a significant art music tradition in Ireland.[7] Thus, the power dynamics between art and traditional music in Ireland were highly contestable in the early 1900s and remain so today: while art music has historically enjoyed institutional power and class prestige, traditional music has increasingly been empowered as an instrument of ethnic nationalism.

Where, then, were women musicians in this fin de siècle clash between foreign European high culture and homegrown Irish artistic forms? They were everywhere and nowhere: despite their visibility on local, regional, and national stages, large numbers of early twentieth-century women musicians disappeared into a space between art and tradition—the field of amateur classical music. In the following section, I demonstrate that the ubiquity of women amateur classical musicians established a feminized, foreign, and bourgeois background against which the emerging Irish nation could sound out its struggles for identity and independence. Moreover, the marginalization of instrumental traditional music in nationalist institutions in the early twentieth century exacerbated ongoing tensions between traditional and classical music. This combination of circumstances has supported today's common but mistaken assumption that most of the women who played fiddle publicly in the early 1900s were classical rather than traditional musicians.

Piano Girls and Clever Young Artistes: Irish Women Amateur Musicians

As in England and the United States, in Ireland music education for girls and young women was common in the nineteenth century, and proficiency on an instrument—especially the piano—was a desirable accomplishment for a genteel young woman.[8] Music education had been part of the National Schools curriculum since the 1850s, and while middle-class families tended to approve of the methods, repertoires, and ethos of British music education, the majority of the Irish population found the subject matter irrelevant at best.[9] At worst, some nationalists feared it would destroy traditional music in its attempt to cultivate appreciation for European high art. In response to nationalist critiques, schools incorporated some Irish melodies, but teaching methods and aims remained the same. By 1888, the Irish Intermediate Education Board had ruled that "music shall cease to be a subject of examination for Boys" in state-supported schools.[10] In denominational schools, many of which were associated with foreign religious orders, the goals and often the repertoires of music education for girls and boys differed. For girls at convent schools, vocal and instrumental art music tuition was designed to inspire religious feeling and elevate taste, while for boys at Christian Brothers' schools, songs from Sir Thomas Moore's *Irish Melodies* and hymns were often selected to develop nationalist and moral sensibilities.[11]

The differences in goals and expectations of formal music education for girls and boys are clear in the gendered disparity in musical participation of all kinds in the early 1900s. In 1911, the *Limerick Echo* published a list of examination results of the Incorporated Society of Musicians, a London-based organization founded in 1882 that administered musicianship tests to students in Britain and Ireland.[12] Of the fifty-two students who passed the 1911 examinations, forty-nine were girls: forty-three pianists and six violinists.[13] Such statistics are not unique to Limerick, and if the figure of the "piano girl" was already disappearing from English and American parlors by 1911, it was still part of everyday entertainment in Ireland, where unmarried women provided nearly all the piano accompaniments at local events. Indeed, although male musicians generally enjoyed more prestigious gigs, the contributions of women instrumentalists to local Irish musical life in the early 1900s were plentiful and encompassed a range of genres. In Limerick's 1911 musical calendar, "Clever young Irish Violinist" Nora O'Hea graced the stage with the famous tenor Joseph O'Mara; Miss Kathleen Hennessy provided piano accompaniment at the annual Rathkeale Gaelic League concert; and the champion warpipes player Miss Maggie McDonnell lent her talents to an event put on by the Temperance Society Boat Club, as did the fiddler and dancer Treasa Ní Ailpín.[14] In the period 1915–25, women likewise dominated the piano and strings competitions and the Irish fiddle contest at the Feis Ceoil, a primarily art music-centered festival established in 1897. At the *feis* as in everyday life, brass, woodwinds, and the uilleann pipes remained the province of men, as did public traditional music performance in general.[15]

If middle-class women and girls represented the majority of art music performers in their home communities, much of the repertoire associated with amateur musicians of both sexes reinforced the notion that this music was foreign, trivial, or both, damned by nationalists for its foreign provenance and by would-be music critics for its lack of "seriousness." The works of William S. Gilbert and Arthur Sullivan were an obvious target for both criticisms, in spite of their popularity—or perhaps because of it.[16] Members of the Gaelic League frequently complained about such foreign imports: a particularly vituperative commentator who wrote under the name of Clan-na-Gael fumed to the *Kerryman* in 1913, "We want no songs from Dixie Land or the gutter productions of London back lanes or elsewhere."[17] Very little of the instrumental music played in concerts during this time is identified in newspaper reports, but articles often noted the songs performed: Verdi arias were popular items, and sentimental Irish songs likewise found plenty of singers and listeners. The test pieces listed in the syllabus for the 1926 Feis Ceoil, however, contradict the notion that women never played serious art music and suggest that some of these female amateurs were very adept technicians: participants in the senior violin competition were required to play the Chaconne in G Minor for Violin and Continuo attributed to Tommaso Antonio Vitali, and competitors for the Eileen Cup for Advanced Violin Playing performed Beethoven's Romance in G, op. 40; an arrangement of a Handel passacaglia by the Irish composer Hamilton Harty; and Franz Ries's Perpetuum Mobile, op. 34.[18] We may deduce that by the 1920s, women soloists were not discouraged from playing music written by serious male composers, however romantic and non-Irish that repertoire often was.[19]

But Is It Traditional? Irish Repertoire at the Feis Ceoil and the Oireachtas

Instrumental traditional music, however, found no institutional home of its own in either the language-focused Oireachtas or in the Feis Ceoil, two festivals first held in 1897. At the Oireachtas, the premier event of the Gaelic League's annual calendar, Irish-language competitions dominated the syllabus. Music and dance were an indispensable part of the festival's grand concerts, and instrumental competitions were generally popular, but the promotion of dance music remained peripheral to the organization's goals. The Feis Ceoil, in contrast, was organized and evaluated by classical musicians, and the organizers' interest in traditional music was largely antiquarian, with monetary prizes offered for "the discovery and vocal or instrumental performance of ancient Irish melodies hitherto unpublished."[20] This impulse to preserve repertoire resulted in the recording and transcription of tunes played by a number of feis participants, as well as the publication of a collection of tunes in 1914. Unfortunately, the fragility of wax cylinders and the convention of reusing them for subsequent recordings has resulted in the loss of most of these performances.[21] Despite this contribution to traditional music, one 1914 commentator expressed her consternation at the feis's preference for "the foreign, so-called 'classical' element in music"—a sentiment shared by other traditional musicians and fans.[22] Others, including the pianist and Oireachtas judge Carl Hardebeck, noted that the formality of concerts and competitions was ill suited to the communal ethos of traditional music.[23] By the 1920s, the feis had become primarily a venue for art music performance competitions. Although it still held contests for pipes, fiddle, Irish harp, and tune arrangements as late as 1926, not one musician "from the tradition" held a leadership position in the organization.[24]

These early twentieth-century arguments against the Oireachtas and the Feis Ceoil were sound, but the related and enduring claim that classical players consistently won traditional music competitions is not supported by archival evidence. Through an analysis of feis results in the period 1897–1935, Barry O'Neill has demonstrated that the judges' decisions in the pipes competitions were defensible from a present-day traditional music perspective.[25] By "hearing" the published results of the Feis Ceoil in 1915–25 in connection with available recordings, we can extrapolate that the feis judges also recognized and rewarded traditional fiddle playing: Bridget Kenny's daughters Christina Sheridan and Josephine Whelan, members of the Siamsa Gaedheall Ceilidh Band, consistently placed in the top three at the feis fiddle competition in 1915–25.[26] Commercial recordings demonstrate that both women were undeniably traditional players. Today, however, most feis and Oireachtas fiddle champions from the early 1900s are assumed to have been eminently forgettable classical violinists. Why does this assumption persist?

Class, Gender, and Traditional Music: A Set of Logical Fallacies in Action

The answer lies in the connections among women, the middle class, and art music. Although middle- and upper-class musicians have played, collected, or appreciated traditional music over the past two centuries, it remains ideologically rooted in rural peasant practice. Art music patronage and performance, in contrast, were associated with the Anglo-Irish elite—a class whose often nationalist political sensibilities did not generally extend to a deep understanding of the concerns of the classes beneath it and whose cultural, familial, and political connections with England were suspect until proved otherwise.[27] The stated purposes of the Feis Ceoil—to promote Irish music and music in Ireland—framed the pursuit of art music by Irish people as a nationalist activity, but the blanket term "music in Ireland" did not automatically erase these class associations from art music from outside Ireland.[28]

Looking back at the Oireachtas and especially at the Feis Ceoil, the assumption that most of the middle-class participants were not traditional players makes some sense because we know that published arrangements of Irish tunes for piano and voice introduced the repertoire to many members of the middle and upper classes. This assumption, however, relies on the inaccurate and romanticized generalization that musicians who played in a traditional style were almost always small farmers, buskers, or traveling music masters.[29] Equally dangerous are assumptions that no members of the working classes received tuition in art music. Nevertheless, these stereotypes continue to inform our understanding of the history of traditional music and its players. Taken together with and reinforced by the ubiquity of women amateur classical musicians in the early twentieth century, these assumptions lead to the retroactive conclusion that publicly active women strings players must have been classical violinists. The logic, however fallacious, works something like this:

(a) If all traditional musicians were lower class, then no middle- or upper-class musicians played traditional music.
(b) If a woman was middle or upper class, then she did not play traditional music.
(c) Lower-class women were mentioned in newspapers only because of their misfortunes or criminal activity. Therefore, if a woman was portrayed in newspapers without reference to crime or misfortune, she was middle or upper class.[30]
(d) If a woman played music at a respectable public event, she was middle or upper class.

Conclusion: if a woman played music in public, she was not a traditional musician.

Even though this logic seems ridiculous when stated sequentially because each premise is clearly based on a biased sample, every one of these statements is true often enough for the complete argument to go unquestioned. Bridget Kenny, the renowned "Queen of Irish Fiddlers" who "played for a precarious pittance along the highways and byways of Dublin,"³¹ becomes the exception who proves the rule, and having found one appropriately classed lady fiddler, the collective traditional music memory may relegate the remaining early twentieth-century Oireachtas and Feis Ceoil fiddlers to the ranks of middle-class women who were amateur classical violinists. Such is the background to my investigation of Treasa Ní Ailpín, whose biography, musical style, and erasure all require that we examine these assumptions about class, gender, and musical style to ask what makes a musician "traditional."

THE "RISING STEP" AND UPWARD MOBILITY, OR TREASA NÍ AILPÍN AS CHILD STAR[32]

But that principle of existence which assigns to the life of man its periods of youth, maturity, and decay, has its analogy in the fate of villages, as in that of empires. Assyria fell, and so did Garryowen! Rome had its decline, and Garryowen was not immortal! . . . The still notorious suburb is little better than a heap of rubbish, where a number of smoked and mouldering walls, standing out from the masses of stone and mortar, indicate the position of a once populous row of dwelling-houses. A few roofs yet remain unshaken, under which some impoverished families endeavour to work out a wretched subsistence, by maintaining a species of huxter trade, by cobbling old shoes, and manufacturing ropes.[33]

Treasa Ní Ailpín—or Teresa Halpin, as she was most often called in newspaper accounts of her exploits in the 1900s and 1910s—was born on 3 June 1894 in Garryowen, a neighborhood of Limerick whose fame for boisterous and destructive lawlessness had been immortalized in song as early as the mid-1800s.[34] The 1911 census reports that most of its houses at the turn of the twentieth century had only two, three, or four rooms. The Halpins were fortunate to live in a four-room dwelling, which housed Seósamh (Joseph, a carpenter who was then forty years old) and his wife of twenty years, Mary Ellen (then thirty-nine), as well as their eight surviving children (Treasa was the second oldest).[35] Of the entire family, Mary Ellen is the only member marked monolingual in the census—the rest of the family is reported bilingual in Irish and English. This attention to the Irish language may be read as a political statement, and Joseph and Treasa were both active in Gaelic League events and meetings as early as 1899.[36]

Treasa's first public appearances were as a dancer. In 1901, she won first prize in the double jig and reel dance competitions at the Oireachtas, and in 1903, she and her father received special billing as "The Champion Amateur Dancers of Ireland" at a concert presented by the Limerick Pipers' Club in Kilkee, County Clare, where they shared the stage with the fiddler Bridget Kenny.[37] In 1904, Treasa—who was not yet ten—and Joseph appeared at the St. Patrick's Day Festival concert in London,[38] and in 1911, they represented Limerick in a battle of steps in Nenagh, County Tipperary: "Great Challenge Contest in Irish Dancing. Limerick V. Nenagh. Joe Halpin and Miss Teresa Halpin, Champion Dancers of Ireland, will represent Limerick; Paddy Brett, International Champion Dancer, and Miss May Hayes, Gold and Silver Medalist, will represent Nenagh. To be followed by a CONCERT, in which several highly-talented Ladies and Gentlemen will take part, including Songs and Selections by All-Ireland Prize-winners, &c."[39] Treasa would continue dancing after her father's death in the early 1910s and would begin teaching dance to children at the Coláiste na Rinne in 1923.[40]

This family tradition of dance gives us insights into the social position of the Halpins. Along with its antiquarian obsession with finding ancient and purely Irish tunes and songs, the Irish Ireland movement went to great efforts to promote and codify the forms of dances its leaders identified as native. Very often, though, members of the movement dismissed the dance styles they found in working-class Ireland with labels such as "buck-jumping" and likened them to English clogging and African American–inflected dance styles popular on the vaudeville stage.[41] As the dance historian Helen Brennan argues, "many of the Gaelic League codifiers were unaware of the existence of a vigorous, energetic and largely adult-male style of vernacular step dancing. . . . The strength and vigour of this genre of dance with its unacceptably urban and working-class associations was classified as un-Irish."[42] According to Brennan, Joe Halpin was an exponent of this style, and his dancing may have been the target of anonymous jibes in at least one newspaper.[43] We can only assume that he won his Oireachtas medals before the Irish Ireland movement had solidified its views on the relative Irishness of dance styles, and evidence shows that he remained a popular performer at events in and near Limerick until his death.

Along with the family's Garryowen address, such reports of Halpin's dance style help establish the family's working-class roots—a social position that would surely have been apparent to audiences in the early 1900s but that is less obvious today. The family's upward mobility, including its attention to schooling, further complicates class identification in retrospect: Treasa received a first-rate education, and even her four-year-old sister is marked as literate in the 1911 census.

The Not-So-Strange Disappearance 73

Treasa attended the Laurel Hill School, a prestigious convent school established by the Paris-based Faithful Companions of Jesus in 1846 that also educated the author Kate O'Brien (1897–1974).[44] O'Brien's fictionalized account of her time at the convent, *The Land of Spices*, addresses class distinctions at the school in the early twentieth century and unflatteringly portrays the nationalist mistrust of schools run by European orders.[45] Although O'Brien, a boarder, and Treasa, a day student, almost certainly attended Laurel Hill at the same time, they may not have known each other: an 1863 advertisement noted that although "a day school is also attached to this establishment [its] apartments [are] entirely separated from those occupied by the boarders, with whom they never have any communication."[46] Laurel Hill maintained separate schools for boarders and day students until at least 1909, and in the 1911 census, only boarders and members of the order are counted as convent residents. Such separation may have reinforced long-standing class distinctions.[47]

Treasa as a Traditional Musician: 1907–13

In addition to providing clues about her family's social mobility, we know that Treasa's education at Laurel Hill exposed her to art and sacred music and that she had piano and music theory lessons there.[48] Based on this information and the convent's European connections, we might conclude that Treasa also had violin lessons at Laurel Hill, but several sources suggest otherwise.[49] The school may also have been sympathetic to her interest in traditional music, if we take Laurel Hill's growing commitment to Irish-language education to indicate wider support for other performances of cultural nationalism. But according to a biography of Treasa's husband, Seán Ó Cuirrín, she learned fiddle first from her father and then from a traveling musician named Clancy—possibly Martin Clancy, whom Francis O'Neill identifies as a "fiddler of great repute."[50] Several additional details support the assumption that the Clancy in question is Martin: in 1911, he lived in Newmarket-on-Fergus, about seventeen miles from Limerick, and was therefore the closest Clancy we know of who taught fiddle. Furthermore, Martin may have moved to Limerick after the 1911 census.[51] We also know from concert reports that Treasa sometimes traveled across the Shannon for musical events.[52] If Treasa was Martin Clancy's pupil, her pedigree is impeccably rooted in rural musical practice, just as the existing wax cylinder recording of her playing supports the conclusion that she was a traditional player.

Here, I quote O'Neill at length to fill in the details about Clancy and to perform the kind of unhurried anecdote telling that often accompanies traditional musicians' origin narratives. If Martin was her teacher, Treasa would surely have had her own stories about him, but in the absence of such stories, I will substitute O'Neill's:

> A fiddler of great repute named Martin Clancy has been brought to notice by our friend Patrick Powell of Tulla, County Clare. For years Clancy has been patronized by Hon. William Halpin of Newmarket-on-Fergus, an ardent revivalist, on account of his exceptional talents. Mr. Halpin's nephew, Frank O'Coffey, now connected with the *Irish American* of New York City, speaks very highly of Clancy's musical versatility. Now about seventy-one years of age, he was born at or near Kilrush. Most famous as a fiddler, he has quite a few pupils, but he also plays the flute, Union pipes, and perhaps one or two other instruments. He is generally regarded in Clare and Limerick as without an equal, especially as an exponent of the traditional style. His rendering of "The Fox Chase," "*Taim im Chodhladh*," "*Eamonn an Chniuc*," [sic] and other ancient pieces, has gained him much local renown. "Rocking the Cradle," in which he mimics the crying of the baby, is another of his masterpieces. Unfortunately the jovial Martin has his little eccentricities, like most famous musicians, the most pronounced being his free use of the fiddle to enforce domestic discipline while in his Bacchanalian moods. Though but little of the original instrument remains, as a result of frequent repairs, the temperamental Martin's veneration for it is unfaltering. He talks to it as if it had been endowed with life, and sleeps with it snugly reposing under his pillow.[53]

This biographical sketch first establishes Clancy's excellent musical reputation and identifies him as a likely source of the ancient repertoire for which Treasa was lauded. It also suggests the vestigial survival of a system of patronage. No other information links this William Halpin with our Limerick Halpins, and Joseph was born in Clonmel, County Tipperary. If discovered, however, any family relationship would provide another link between Martin and Treasa, as well as perhaps giving clues about how the Halpins funded Treasa's education at Laurel Hill.[54] The anecdote about Clancy's drunken excesses adds nothing to our story of Treasa, but is worth noting because it fits comfortably within a recognizable genre of tales of unmarried alcoholic male musicians and their anthropomorphized fiddles: Pádraig O'Keeffe called his fiddle his "wife," and it is not outlandish to imagine that Clancy likewise gendered his fiddle female.[55] And the fiddles of both men outlasted (and perhaps became) the women in their lives: Pádraig's sweetheart immigrated to America as a young woman, and by 1911, Clancy was a widower.

Treasa Ní Ailpín as the Tradition: The Feis Ceoil Collection of Irish Airs Hitherto Unpublished

What determines traditionality? Is it the predestination of biological pedigree, a traceable line of begats that situate one as the heir to generations of musical participation, if not always to the prowess of those who have come before? Or is it a more biographical genealogy that gives one a place in the master-student relationship? Is it possible to become "traditional" only if one is caught and catechized young enough? Or is grace possible through a series of good works and idiomatic playing, a sort of educated conversion? And the fall—is one taste of the apple sufficient to get one cast out of the garden? So far, I have established that Treasa Ní Ailpín's lineage and training ground her firmly in the tradition. We also know that she was a popular entertainer around Limerick and a successful competitor and performer at national Gaelic League events in the early 1900s. But what sort of player was she? Like Martin Clancy and scores of other traditional fiddlers active in the first decade of the twentieth century, Ní Ailpín receives a sketch in O'Neill's *Irish Minstrels and Musicians*. Unlike his profiles of the pipers May McCarthy and Mollie Morrissey, though, its brevity and lack of detail suggest that O'Neill had not met her. His entry emphasizes her repertoire and, perhaps more important, the quality of her versions of tunes: "A very clever violinist by all accounts is Miss Halpin, daughter of the late Joseph Halpin of the city of Limerick, a celebrated dancer in his day. Although yet in her teens, she possesses an extensive repertory of old tunes in very good settings. Her name appears among the list of prize winners for unpublished airs at the Dublin Feis Ceoil in 1907."[56]

This point is significant for several reasons. First, her knowledge of this repertoire suggests an understanding of and proximity to at least one traditional style—perhaps that of her teacher, Martin Clancy. Such exposure to the tradition would have distinguished her from those who learned from sheet music. Second, the possession of old tunes was and continues to be a valuable attribute for a traditional musician and is one marker of traditionality. Finally, Ní Ailpín's repertoire allowed her to participate in the nationalist game of unearthing antique Irish artifacts—a unique position for a teenager (she would have been thirteen in 1907). And because she possessed a number of special tunes, she became one of the very few traditional musicians to be recorded on wax cylinder, and one of only two women instrumentalists included in the 1914 *Feis Ceoil Collection of Irish Airs Hitherto Unpublished*. Her inclusion in this collection demonstrates the respect in which her repertoire was held in 1914, and the rarity of this repertoire meant that she was included in the recording session that produced our best information about her playing as a teenager.

A Few Words About Nomenclature: "Fiddle" versus "Violin"

In O'Neill's sketch, as in newspaper accounts, Ní Ailpín's instrument is most often referred to as a violin, not a fiddle, but we cannot depend on this usage to indicate musical style in the early twentieth century. For example, the classic 1959 *All-Ireland Champions: Violin* album bore the now-questionable noun until the 2001 reissue changed the name to *An Historic Recording of Irish Traditional Music from County Clare and East Galway*.[57] The prevalence of the term "violin" requires that we be attentive to the stereotypes that suggest that a violin in a woman's hands would not produce traditional music. Newspaper columnists and other writers may also have chosen to call young women of any class "violinists" to avoid any suggestion of impropriety evoked by the term "fiddle."

Reading Ní Ailpín: *The* Feis Ceoil Collection of Irish Airs Hitherto Unpublished *in Print*

What can we learn about Ní Ailpín's playing from printed sources? O'Neill mentions her prize for unpublished airs at the Feis Ceoil, and that competition provides our first clues about her repertoire and style. The printed collection, like other compilations of tunes published in the late nineteenth and early twentieth centuries, ostensibly aims to preserve repertoire believed to be in danger of disappearing, although one might sometimes wonder if the impulse was more that of the bounty hunter than of the diligent archivist.[58] In accordance with the works of O'Neill and other collectors, the *Feis Ceoil Collection* only includes single-voice melodies and makes no attempt to indicate ornamentation or double-stops on the fiddle or droned accompaniment on the pipes. Following convention, the collection only provides skeletons of tunes. It does not offer extensive suggestions on how the tunes should be played, save for occasional tempo markings.[59] By checking some of the tunes supplied by pipers against surviving recordings, Breandán Breathnach has identified numerous errors and liberties in some of the transcriptions, as well as some overlap with other collections.⁶⁰ Unfortunately, most of the wax cylinders have been lost or destroyed, so we cannot compare Ní Ailpín's contributions to the book with their source recordings. Although the collection is not always a reliable source for tunes, it provides insights into the repertoire considered rare in 1914 and gives us some idea about the personnel of the early twentieth-century nationalist music scene.

By today's standards, competitions for unpublished airs in the early 1900s were disorganized affairs. The Feis Ceoil contests were open to singers as well as instrumentalists, and entrants could send in manuscripts or arrive with a list of titles from which the judges selected several they wished to hear. Robert Young, one of three judges at the first feis in 1897, described the process by which tunes were collected: "At length, when the happy moment came that, as far as the memories of Bunting, Petrie, Joyce, or Holden served, the judges thought a hitherto unwritten air was being played, the phonograph was brought into position, and a durable record taken on one of its tiny waxen cylinders, duly preceded by the name of the player and of the tune."⁶¹

According to Breathnach, Bridget Kenny participated in the contest the following year and "came furnished with a list of thirty-three titles." The judges asked her to play seven of these tunes, and four were recorded.⁶² Ní Ailpín appears among the prizewinners in the 1907 and 1909 competitions: in 1907, she and the blind fiddler Michael Daffy tied for third place, and in 1909, she and Kathleen O'Callaghan (instrument unknown) were noted, although we no longer know whether they tied or whether Ní Ailpín placed second and O'Callaghan third. In both years, the first prize was withheld—a common practice when the adjudicators did not deem that any performance warranted that honor. Indeed, few first prizes were awarded in 1907–14, and I wonder whether the judges were reluctant to give first place in ancient airs to fiddlers as young as Ní Ailpín and Daffy, who were both in their teens in 1907.⁶³

Ní Ailpín's contributions—"The Death of Staker Wallace" (an air) and "The Tinker's Wife" (a reel)—were probably recorded in 1907.⁶⁴ They are preceded only by an air and a hornpipe by Kenny and an air from her husband, John, a piper who also played fiddle. Other contributors include the noted pipers Denis Delaney, John Cash, Dan Markey, and Stephen Ruane, but the only other women mentioned in the collection were lilters identified as Mrs. Elizabeth McCall and the late Miss Ellen Newport and an unnamed "old woman in the town of Sligo" who performed the song "Molly, My Own Love." Kenny's pride of place in the collection is understandable: of all the musicians included, she seems to have been the most widely known participant in the competitions and concerts put on by the Gaelic League up to that time. Indeed, the order of the book may reflect the performers' level of participation in nationalist endeavors, in which case both Kenny and Ní Ailpín would rank highly.

Hearing Ní Ailpín: "The Ennistymon Jig" on Wax Cylinder

The eighty-five tunes included in the Feis Ceoil collection were the result of over a decade of work, and the compilers delayed the volume's release several times because tunes slated for inclusion had been printed elsewhere, including in Frank Roche's acclaimed 1911 collection. Thus, not every tune recorded at the Feis Ceoil made it into the book: omitted were Kenny's performances of "The High Road to Galway" and "The Boys of Wexford," as well as Ní Ailpín's rendition of a jig she called "The Ennistymon Jig," today better known as a version of "Boys of the Town." Despite the poor sound quality of the recording, "The Ennistymon Jig" provides evidence that Ní Ailpín's playing was indeed "traditional" as we understand the term today. Probably recorded in 1907, the hiss and crackle of the wax cylinder overpower the timbral nuances of her playing. Because volume was of utmost importance in making a clean recording, Ní Ailpín may also have sacrificed some finer points to direct a usable sound into the horn of the Edison phonograph.[65] Nonetheless, her playing is audibly in time and rhythm, with a slight but not excessive emphasis on the beat. Her uncontrived articulation of each note suggests that she does not "drive" the bow in the way characteristic of classical violinists but instead lets its momentum propel the melody forward. She does not use vibrato, and her tone is clean as far as is audible through the surface noise of the recording.

Two qualities of this performance may have been contingent upon the circumstances of recording. First, Ní Ailpín plays the tune only one time through, and unlike the common version of the tune today, she plays it singly—AB, rather than AABB. Given the time constraints of the recording medium and possibly of the recording situation, I do not think we should assume that she always played the jig that way. Also, and more important for my discussion later, she does not vary the tune, and her ornamentation is sparse. Again, we must remember that these wax cylinders were being recorded as a source for transcribing tunes believed to be in danger of disappearing, not to showcase style or to preserve performance. Decorating the basic melody with dense ornamentation and extensive variation would have been hubristic and counterproductive, and therefore these recordings must not be compared with later 78 rpm albums intended for entertainment and repeated listening.

"Hearing" Ní Ailpín through Accounts of the 1913 Oireachtas

That was Ní Ailpín's playing at age thirteen, in a performance that any Irish traditional musician today would recognize and applaud for its lack of affectation. The judges' remarks at the 1913 Oireachtas in Galway, as printed in the *Connaught Tribune*, suggest that Ní Ailpín's playing six years later retained these qualities and provide information about some of her rivals:

> Eoghain Ó Maoileoin gave a fair rendering. Mine Ní Domhnaill, Dublin, performed in excellent style. She was a competitor at the 1910 Oireachtas. Treasa Ní Ailpín, Limerick, was given Carl Hardebeck's opinion as to the necessity for regularity in playing the violin at the accustomed tone. This young competitor also gave a faultless selection. The next competitor was Miss C. Carrigan, Glenamaddy, who gave a selection from Moore's melodies, and, by request, contributed some traditional pieces, with commendable execution. Mr. Luke Kelly, Aughrim, Co. Wicklow, who was a winner in the dancing and bagpipes competitions, played with beautiful harmony in fast and slow times. The most youthful competitor was Seaghan Ó Bruadair, Bohermore, Galway. He played in easy and graceful style, and his selection was one of the best performances of the competition.
>
> The following were the awards:—Teresa Halpin, Limerick, 1; M. O'Donnell, Ballsbridge, Dublin, 2; Luke Kelly, Wicklow, 3.
>
> Carl Hardebeck, in announcing the decision said it was very difficult always when good playing was heard as on that day, to decide [the winners of] a competition. They had to take into account the tone, traditionality and the slow air, and the time of the dance music. The first prize winner's playing was excellent. The tone of the playing of the second prize winner was also excellent, but the air she played was not traditional or played in that style. Luke Kelly, as far as traditional playing was concerned, was better than Miss O'Donnell, notably his slow air. His tune [*sic*], however, was rather weak and delicate.[66]

Perhaps the most striking feature of the adjudicators' comments is the recurrent distinction between what was traditional and what was not: pieces from Sir Thomas Moore's *Irish Melodies* were not traditional enough, nor was Miss O'Donnell's air or the style in which she played it.

Despite this frustrating (but not unusual) lack of detail in Hardebeck's account of the competitors' playing, his comments indicate that for these two judges (Hardebeck and Kenny, whose comments were not published), tone was more important than either the traditionality of repertoire or phrasing in placing Mine O'Donnell over Luke Kelly. Rather than leaping to the conclusion that the judges were swayed by O'Donnell's possibly classical technique, I instead suggest that political considerations may have led the judges to determine that a strong and consistent tone demonstrated more of the qualities the nationalist movement wanted to promote than did traditionality of phrasing or repertoire. Put another way, perhaps the adjudicators responded more favorably to ways of controlling the bow—and therefore one's body—that produce a strong, clear tone. In an independence movement that valued temperance and sought to prove Ireland's fitness for self-rule, this kind of bodily control would have provided a subtle yet powerful counterargument to stereotypes of the Irish as uncontrollable simian colonial subjects who brawled, drank, wept, and danced with abandon.[67] Furthermore, it would have provided an unofficial analogue to the standardization of dance forms that was also emerging in the 1910s and 1920s through An Coimisiún le Rincí Gaelacha (the Irish Dancing Commission). These methods of tone production were also more legible within an art music context, and therefore more closely connected with ideas of social and moral uplift indexed by art music—an aspect of stylistic choice that we also hear in Ní Ailpín's use of vibrato in her 1929 recording of "An Buachaill Caol Dubh."[68] And on a different register, perhaps we should not be surprised that the judges rewarded tone, since Kenny's playing demonstrated her own mastery of the bow and preference for a brilliant, forceful sound—a characteristic she passed along to at least two of her daughters, Christina Sheridan and Josephine Whelan, who swept the prizes at the Feis Ceoil in 1915–25. Today, this kind of tone remains highly regarded.

Perhaps this judging was based on Hardebeck's classical training: before he moved to Belfast and joined the Irish nationalist movement, he worked as an organist and pianist in London.[69] But Kenny, "Queen of Irish Fiddlers," was the second judge, and her presence tempers the possibility that Hardebeck's classical training clouded his judgment. Thus, Ní Ailpín received Kenny's stamp of approval in 1913, along with the winner's purse of £3—a queenly sum in those days. Another participant in this event is worth pointing out: Michael Coleman, whose recordings would later make him one of the most revered Irish traditional musicians of all time, also competed in this fiddle contest. Although he had competed in local *feiseanna* in his native Sligo with some success and had tied for third place in the fiddle contests there in 1909 and 1910, Coleman did not place at the 1913 Oireachtas.[70]

NÍ AILPÍN AS A TRADITIONAL MUSICIAN: THE 1920S

If Ní Ailpín had put down the fiddle forever at the Galway Oireachtas in 1913, any claims that she was a classical interloper in the traditional fold would be unsupportable. Newspaper reports; O'Neill's published biographical sketch; her family background; and most important, recorded evidence of her musical style all confirm her place in the tradition. But she did not stop playing in 1913, and the nature of her surviving recordings shifts the question somewhat: if Ní Ailpín had been merely overlooked as a fiddle player for the reasons I have outlined, then my work would end at noting those reasons and inserting her back into the historical narrative of traditional music. But the reality is infinitely richer: she recorded two 78 rpm albums in 1929 and published a bilingual Irish-English violin tutor in 1923. All three items provide ammunition for the argument that she was not truly "traditional." We must therefore ask an additional set of questions. First, for what purpose were these materials created? What musical elements steer us toward hearing or reading them as not traditional, and is this judgment sound? Can we assume that what we mean by the term "traditional" today is comparable to the way listeners in the 1920s categorized what they heard? And most important, why should we care if Ní Ailpín was "traditional "or not?

In 1923, Ní Ailpín published a violin manual with the assistance of the Irish author Seán Ó Cuirrín, whom she would marry on June 23, 1923.[71] On the cover page of the book, titled *Teagosc-Leabhar na Bheidhlíne* (Instructional book for the violin), Ní Ailpín is listed as "professor of music" and Ó Cuirrín as "professor of Gaelic." Although these titles may simply have indicated that the musical contributions were Ní Ailpín's and that Ó Cuirrín had written the text, "professor" may also have referred to the jobs each held at the Scoil a Leanbh (Children's school) at Coláiste na Rinne (College of Ring), an Irish-language boarding school in the Ring Gaeltacht of County Waterford. Founded in 1905, the school continues to hold summer classes in Irish language, music, and dance. Ní Ailpín had been a student there in 1917 and would teach music and dance at the school from 1923 until 1970.[72]

The book offers instruction on the proper use of the bow and placement of the fingers, as well as practice material and an "enjoyable selection of lullabies, laments, and happy tunes of the Gael."[73] Of seventy-eight tunes included, all are

Irish airs and dance tunes, but the book also features adaptations of exercises typical of classical violin method books, including material for practicing scales, intervals, arpeggios, and bowing.[74] Unlike other violin method books, however, *Teagosc-Leabhar* also includes lengthy instructions for playing Irish dance music and exercises specifically designed for honing a student's skills at playing jigs, reels, and hornpipes. Although traditional musicians today would balk at some of Ní Ailpín's notational choices—for example, she chooses to notate reels and some jigs in a dotted rhythm, attempts to write out melodic ornamentation, and does not discourage readers from using vibrato in traditional tunes—the logic behind these choices seems to come from one well versed in traditional style. Her remarks on reels echo those of many other traditional musicians: "Freedom and flexibility of wrist should be thoroughly acquired before attempting to play Reels, as it is the bowing that gives the characteristic ring and spirit to the music."[75] She also discusses the use of semitones in airs—a topic given much less space in more recent publications.

Ní Ailpín's book is unique and deserves more attention than I am able to give it here. Clearly aimed at a nationalist audience, it uses words like "*suantraidhe*," "*goltraidhe*," and "*geantraidhe*" ("lullaby," "lament," and "happy music") to invoke Edward Bunting's late eighteenth-century collection of harp tunes, further connecting this book with renowned traditional sources. Moreover, *Teagosc-Leabhar* was part of a growing body of textbooks in Irish published after independence.[76] But most important, this violin tutor represents a distinct reframing of the endeavor of learning music in Ireland. Although its audience was most likely the same middle-class demographic group to whom arrangements of traditional tunes were marketed, *Teagosc-Leabhar* assumes that its students are picking up the instrument to learn traditional music rather than to gain skills for classical performance. Even if learning through printed notation is not the traditional way, the student of *Teagosc-Leabhar* is no longer fully implicated in the colonialist project of European art music pedagogy and performance. Although this repurposing of classical technique to Irish nationalist ends did not endure, it must be counted among attempts to support the idea of an Irish art-traditional hybrid music rather than as the mere appropriation of traditional material by clueless dilettantes.

The text is not specifically addressed to children, and perhaps the book's ideal user was an urban adult beginner caught up in the excitement of newfound Irish cultural identity—much like the intended audience for Matt Cranitch's celebrated *Irish Fiddle Book*, which also begins with a lesson in basic staff notation.[77] The 1926 Feis Ceoil syllabus identifies another audience for Ní Ailpín's work and may indicate the presence of a second book, or possibly a revision of *Teagosc-Leabhar* with the addition of several tunes: competitors in the feis's fiddle contests are directed to her *Violin School* as a source for test tunes.[78] For the 1926 feis, entrants for the senior and under-sixteen fiddle competitions were required to play specific tunes from this book.[79] These tunes had been printed elsewhere and so were not unique to Ní Ailpín's book, but they were presumably selected for inclusion for their pedagogical value and Irishness. Under the list of selections for the under-sixteen competition, the program provides helpful information for participants: "All these tunes are contained in the *Violin School* by Teresa Halpin. . . . Traditional playing *only* will be accepted. Competitors *must* play the tunes named as above."[80] Once again, the feis presents traditional material in decidedly nontraditional circumstances: unlike in classical violin competitions, which often prescribe the repertoire for competitors, the only customary direction for tune choice in traditional music settings is for specific rhythms (reels, jigs, and so on) for dancing. In contrast, pipers chose their own material for competitions, possibly because the feis organizers presumed that they would invariably choose Irish tunes. From this information, we may infer that the book was not marketed to established traditional musicians and that some anxiety about nontraditional repertoire existed in relation to the feis fiddle competition. We cannot, however, assume that its author was therefore primarily a classical musician.

A TALE OF TWO 78 RPM RECORDS

These facts and conjectures can tell us only about Ní Ailpín's political sensibilities, ideas of appropriate repertoire for beginners, and audience—not about her playing. But two 78 rpm sides can tell us how she sounded on one day in 1929, when representatives of London-based Parlophone Records came to record in Dublin. This record—one of the thirty-eight recorded on that trip and issued in the E3000 series—features Ní Ailpín playing the slow air "An Buachaill Caol Dubh" ("The Dark Slender Boy") on one side, and the Halpin Trio's rendition of "Over the Moor to Maggie" on the other. The members of the trio are not identified, but presumably Treasa was one of them, since one of the fiddlers' sound matches hers on "An Buachaill Caol Dubh." These two sides and another surviving 1929 78 rpm recording of a more polished version of "Over the Moor to Maggie" under the title "Rogha an Fhile" ("The Poet's Choice") present a mystery and a challenge: why do the musicians play them the way they do, and might the answer to this first question change the way we hear these tunes today?

"Over the Moor to Maggie"

Today, "Over the Moor to Maggie" is a common three-part reel in G major. It bears no particular associations with any region, style, or musician but has a long history of recording, beginning with a performance by the accordion player John Kimmel in 1919.[81] Like other reels, "Over the Moor to Maggie" is customarily played at a speed of between approximately 100 and 120 beats per minute. Most players subtly emphasize the beat and give the offbeat a slight accent. Fiddlers achieve this emphasis using a combination of bowing patterns (slurred and single notes), bow pressure, and left-hand ornamentation. Although musicians use varying amounts of swing, the tastes of traditional playing today disdain excessive accenting of reels, and one would not play or notate a reel with a dotted rhythm. The phrase below (Figure 2.1) illustrates how a traditional fiddler might play this part of the tune.

The Halpin Trio's performance of "Over the Moor to Maggie" is a surprise to the listener who expects to hear the reel by that name: rhythmically, this tune is not identifiably a reel, and although it begins with the A part of "Maggie," another reel, "The Morning Star," is spliced in. Although the melodies of both tunes are more or less the usual versions, the rhythm is distinctly and intentionally dotted. At about eighty beats per minute, it is much slower than a standard reel and sounds more like a hornpipe, a tune type usually played with a more dotted rhythm. The players decorate longer notes and important notes within phrases with a moderate vibrato that is slightly slower and wider than the fast, narrow vibrato considered acceptable today in slow air playing (but not usually found in reels, jigs, and other dance tunes). The whole tune sounds rather refined—"sedate," even, as one reviewer remarked when the "Rogha an Fhíle"

FIGURE 2.1 "Over the Moor to Maggie" [A part (with bowing) music transcription].

version of the tune was rereleased on a 2001 compilation.[82] Taken in isolation, this performance raises several questions. Was this how Ní Ailpín always played dance tunes? Did she play every reel as though it were a hornpipe, and was vibrato a defining characteristic of her adult style? The question of vibrato is impossible to answer from the evidence available, but the Halpin Trio's relatively unpolished performance on the Parlophone 78 rpm leaves several clues that suggest a provisional answer about her dance tune playing.

Form is our first clue that we should not assume that this recording of "Over the Moor to Maggie" merely represents unidiomatic reel playing. Irish dance tunes have a regular form based on eight-measure phrases, often repeated as AABB, where A + A = sixteen measures, and B + B = sixteen measures. The whole tune is then repeated as many times as the players desire or the dancers require. The length of the form sometimes varies, and a body of "single" reels (AB) exists, as well as a number of tunes with more than one part—like "Maggie," which is usually played AABBCC.[83] But the total number of measures in any standard reel (or other kind of dance tune) will always be a multiple of eight. The Halpin Trio's version of "Maggie," however, begins with a four-measure introduction based on the A part. This lead-in is our first hint that what follows is not a casual rendition of the tune. During a first hearing, we might assume that this is an arrangement created specifically for the recording, a reel turned into a piece to be played on the gramophone in someone's tidy parlor, where wild peasant reels are not wanted. Unfortunately, the surviving copy of the Parlophone 78 rpm recording does not contain the Halpin Trio's full performance: it ends abruptly at the end of the second time through the C part.

The recording of "Rogha an Fhile" also presents a mystery: according to the identifying information included in Reg Hall's notes to the 2001 reissue, this disc too was a product of a Parlophone recording session in Dublin on 12 July 1929.[84] It seems unlikely that two Parlophone recording sessions would have been held in Dublin the same year, so presumably "Rogha an Fhile" is another take from the same session. But is it the same recording as "Over the Moor to Maggie"? Other than changing the name of the tune, the Halpin Trio's performance here is remarkably similar to its rendition on the Parlophone 78 rpm: although the playing sounds cleaner and more closely in unison on the later recording, the tempo and ornamentation are nearly the same. Missing on "Rogha," however, are an unintentional plucking of the E string in the first full measure of the C part and a slight increase in tempo in the C and D parts.

Whatever its provenance, this recording confirms the form—a nearly pal-

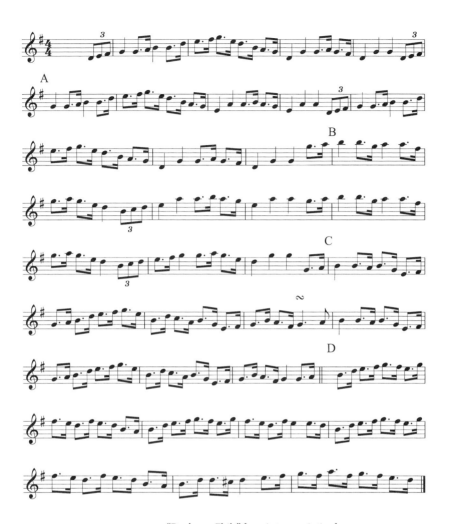

FIGURE 2.2 "Rogha an Fhile" [music transcription].

indromic sequence of parts after the introduction: ABCDCBABCDCBA(B). The final B part (shown in parentheses) may be unintentional: toward the end of the recording, at least two of the players seem temporarily confused about where the tune goes next. In the penultimate B, one of the fiddlers nearly goes back into the C part instead of into the A, and the piano player continues into the final B part after the fiddlers have stopped at the end of the A part. They rejoin the pianist and end with a flourish, emphasizing the V-I cadence in a way that suggests that one or both fiddlers want to make absolutely sure the tune ends there.

The discrepancy between what seems to be the intended form and the actual performance suggests that the musicians were not using written music as a guide.

But what about this self-conscious form and its four-measure introduction? Here, the name of the tune and its subtitle, "New Irish Traditional Dance," help solve the mystery. The name "Rogha an Fhile" had not been associated with either "Over the Moor to Maggie" or "The Morning Star" before this recording, but according to a biography of Ní Ailpín's husband, it was the name of a couples' dance that the two composed.[85] Hearing this as a piece specifically designed and played for dancing puts it into a very different category than if we assume that "Maggie" and "Rogha" are intended primarily for listening.[86] First, the short introduction makes sense: such introductions are common practice at dances, where they allow dancers time to count in before they begin dancing. Moreover, another enduringly popular céilí dance, "The Three Tunes," is built on a similarly contrived arrangement wherein one of the tunes, "Haste to the Wedding," is played at the beginning and ending of the dance. Perhaps the Halpin Trio or the recording companies Parlophone or HMV may have hoped to market one or both of the albums to dancers.[87] Indeed, the music on these recordings might not have been most important to Ní Ailpín—instead, she might have hoped that the albums would help the new dance catch on. But unlike other céilí dances composed in the first half of the twentieth century, "Rogha an Fhile" is relatively unknown today. Ní Ailpín's role as a composer of céilí dances requires a brief explanation of the intersecting worlds of Irish step, set, and céilí dance, however.

Irish Dance Genres

Mention Irish dance, and most people imagine young girls with impossibly curly hair wearing dresses covered in Celtic knotwork. Today, the world of competitive Irish step dance goes about its own business without much attention to or from traditional musicians. Set dancing—the dance form based on the popular quadrilles of the nineteenth century that were banned by the cultural nationalist movement in the early 1900s—has enjoyed a revival in the past several decades, and this scene typically wants little to do with the artifice and regulation of competitive step dancing. By now, set dancing has its own claims to tradition as the "authentic" activity of the people, unsullied by the "purity" imposed on the terpsichorean arts by the authoritarian Irish Dancing Commission in and after the 1910s. Between these two kinds of Irish dance—step and set—lies céilí dance.

Céilí dancing encompasses a limited repertoire of group dances reputed to be entirely Irish, beginning with a handful of dances considered "ancient" by the nationalist movement in the late nineteenth and early twentieth centuries. However, the movement needed more than a few dances if it hoped to lure the Irish populace away from the compelling and numerous sets (quadrilles) that had taken rural Ireland by storm in the nineteenth century. To that end, fervent nationalists revived old dances, and some may even have composed new dances—although this whisper of recent authorship is controversial. Today, a set dance event might include one or two céilí dances, especially if children are present. Because they share footwork and the institutional oversight of the Irish Dancing Commission with step dancing, however, céilí dances are more often aligned with step dance schools and with the more restrictive elements of the nationalist movement. Set dancing, on the other hand, is more closely associated with the so-called revival of Irish traditional music in the middle of the twentieth century. Both set dance and traditional music are implicitly and explicitly portrayed as organic, grassroots activities independent of institutional power and built on ideals of inclusion, even if they are not always organized around inclusive practices. These divisions among Irish dance genres and between music and dance have had an enormous influence on the practice, discourse, and historiography of the traditional arts. However, such later separations between music and dance must not influence the ways we look back on the creative output of early twentieth-century musicians like Ní Ailpín who were also active dancers.

Ní Ailpín and "Rogha an Fhile" Revisited

The form and rhythm of "Maggie" or "Rogha" strongly suggest that Ní Ailpín intended these recordings for dancing. In the notes to the third volume of his 1927 tune collection, Roche provides additional confirmation of Ní Ailpín's penchant for creating new dances. He refers to her by her married name, Bean Sheáin Ó Cuirrín [sic] (Mrs. Sean Curran), in connection with an unnamed dance, quite possibly "Rogha an Fhile":

> A praiseworthy effort was made some years ago by Bean Sheáin Ó Cuirrín of Limerick in arranging a new dance for couples on Irish lines suitable for the ballroom, but it has not, so far, appeared beyond a rather limited circle. It is to be regretted that this, and others of a similar nature had not been provided earlier, and popularised, as they would have removed the anomaly complained of as well as helping as a protection against those corrupt foreign influences

that have been creeping in, and spreading so widely amongst us, for the past decade, or more.[88]

The description of the dance matches the brief account of it in the Irish-language biography of Ó Cuirrín, and it also establishes that Ní Ailpín's motivations for creating the new dance were political as well as artistic. Roche's further lament about "corrupt foreign influences . . . creeping in" also reminds us that by the late 1920s, the nationalist Catholic establishment's fear of so-called jazz dancing was intense.

No evidence proves that Ní Ailpín herself subscribed fully to the crusade against foreign music and dance, but she clearly channeled her creative energies into composing and performing Irish material. Research done by the highly respected dance historian Joe O'Donovan suggests that she contributed two now-ubiquitous céilí dances to the Gaelic League's roster of "approved" dances:

> The Gaelic League then busied itself with finding enough "truly Irish" dances with which to replace the sets. The hot potato is whether they restored old Irish dances to popularity, or made up new ones. Joe O'Donovan, a dance teacher at UCC [University College Cork], taking his lead from Francis Roche's 1957 volume, *Irish Dances, Marches and Airs*, says Bean Sheáin Ó Cuirrín, secretary of the Gaelic League in Limerick, composed such staples as *The Walls of Limerick* and *The Siege Of Ennis*. Tom Marry, who was elected chairman of the Steering Committee for céilí-dancing's Centenary Year at Sunday's meeting, has never heard of the woman.[89]

In the world of Irish dance, O'Donovan's statement that Ní Ailpín wrote these two dances is earth-shattering: merely attributing them to a modern author is an incendiary move because it removes the patina of timeless Irishness from the core repertoire of céilí dance. Indeed, some would find identifying a recent composer—not to mention a woman composer—for "The Walls of Limerick" and "The Siege of Ennis" nearly heretical. Tom Marry, chairman of Cairde Rince Céilí na hÉireann (Friends of Céilí Dancing of Ireland) dismisses this claim with the weak argument that because he has never heard of Bean Uí Chuirrín, she cannot possibly have composed these two important dances.

Marry's response leads me to two important points about tracing the life and performance of someone like Ní Ailpín—a woman and a native speaker of Irish who used the Irish version of her name in times and places where the English version would have been much easier (albeit less patriotic). First, Marry's surprise makes sense, given the distant and sometimes uneasy relationship between traditional music and dance and Irish-language activism today: with the exception of musicians from or living in Gaeltachtaí, most traditional musicians and dancers are not proficient Irish speakers.[90] With such attitudes toward Irish in place even among traditional musicians, Marry's lack of familiarity with Bean Sheáin Uí Chuirrín is not surprising because she seems to have been more active in Irish-language environments as she got older. It is more puzzling that he wouldn't recognize her from her work with the Gaelic League, but her involvement in the organization may have ended before Marry was born. It's also unclear whether Ní Ailpín and Uí Chuirrín remained in Limerick or whether they moved to Waterford after their marriage—a move that might have effected a clear split between the Limerick Teresa Halpin / Treasa Ní Ailpín and the Waterford Bean Sheáin Uí Chuirrín. That split, whether geographically reinforced or not, has meant that very few written sources have made the connection between the two.[91] Today, Bean Sheáin Uí Chuirrín is a name even less familiar than Teresa Halpin / Treasa Ní Ailpín.

Issues of name recognition would not have been a problem for a man, since Irish and English versions of surnames are usually fairly easily deciphered and do not change at marriage. With the caveat that the Gaelic League and Irish Dancing Commission may not have found it politically expedient to advertise the recent composition of "The Walls of Limerick" and "The Siege of Ennis," the idea of a woman as a creative force in Irish céilí or set dance is nearly unheard of. To the Gaelic League establishment, the recent creation of dances undercuts their claim to pure Irishness, while to the generally anti–Gaelic League set dance community, céilí dances themselves are less exciting, damned by some as "thinly disguised quadrilles cobbled together and passed off as authentic."[92] For both sides of the argument, the idea of composition is inherently problematic, and a composer of new dances must either be invisible or a mere collector: as Seán Donnelly writes, "Surely, these people collected these dances, rather than composing them; certainly, Nan Quinn is also spoken of as the source of 'The Sweets of May,' not as the composer."[93] Thus, Marry's lack of familiarity with Bean Uí Chuirrín becomes a metonym for not knowing women as creative forces in dance, especially before the mid-twentieth century. Men were still considered the producers of new dances in the early twentieth century, while women as a group were merely the dancing consumers of new figures and steps. Sometimes they were excluded altogether: male traveling dancing masters were still making their rounds in the west of Ireland around 1900, and some did not allow girls to take their classes.[94] Nevertheless, traditional musicians, set dancers, and scholars have long romanticized the figure of the dancing master. With the standardization of step dance through national competitions and the formation of the Irish Dancing Commission in 1930, male adjudicators and musicians increasingly regulated the bodily movements of dancing women and girls. And as of 2018, although women dancers outnumber men in competitive step dance, a significant portion of the leadership of the Irish Dancing Commission was male.[95]

"Over the Moor to Maggie" Revisited

I believe that the incomplete "Over the Moor to Maggie" recording is more than just a rehearsal for "Rogha an Fhile." As in the Halpin Trio's performance of "Rogha," the roughness in "Maggie" tells us something about the fiddlers who played it into the microphone in 1929. Remember that the side named "Over the Moor to Maggie" actually contains melodic material from another tune, "The Morning Star" (see parts C and D in "Rogha an Fhile"). Like "Maggie," the reel version of "The Morning Star" is built mostly on eighth notes. While the Halpin Trio plays a stripped-down version of "Maggie" that suits the dotted rhythm they give it, they retain long passages of eighth notes from the reel version of "The Morning Star." Why they keep all these eighth notes remains a mystery, but perhaps the dance "Rogha an Fhile" incorporated movements that didn't match the bouncy rhythms of a reel transformed into a semihornpipe.

What happens in performance, though, is that the two fiddlers are not quite able to hold the moderate tempo of "Maggie" after the change into "The Morning Star," and they speed up slightly in measures 3–4 and 7–8 of the C part (the A of the original reel) and at the end of measure 6 and the beginning of measure 7 in the D part (the B of the original). As the players speed up, they also subtly but noticeably smooth out the rhythm and establish a swing that is closer to what we today would consider traditional reel playing. In the "Rogha" recording, they have this section better under control, but the unevenness of the earlier recording suggests that one or both of the fiddle players more often played the tune faster, as a reel.

In both recordings, the individual sections are unusually consistent between iterations, and the sparse ornamentation recurs in the same places each time the parts are repeated. These characteristics differ from the customary practice of traditional music performance, in which musicians are assumed to vary a phrase each time it occurs. And although some musicians use less ornamentation than others, it is now also considered an important part of performance practice. Here, however, the fiddlers play only one roll on the penultimate G of the fourth measure of the C part, and they add what some fiddlers today would call a short roll on the second B in the next measure.[96] One fiddler also breaks the unison sound in the fifth measure of the D part to add a small and very idiomatic variation, a quick C that turns the first two notes into a BCD triplet. Otherwise, the only gestures toward ornamentation are the inclusion of several double-stops and some vibrato. This consistent and conservative use of ornamentation represents an aesthetic and perhaps a practical choice: if the point of these recordings was to popularize a new dance, rhythm and clarity of phrasing would have been more important than the virtuosic use of ornamentation. Therefore, as with the wax cylinder of the "Ennistymon Jig," we have no record of Ní Ailpín playing traditional dance tunes for their (or her) own sake—only recordings in the service of preserving an old tune or popularizing a new dance. In such recording contexts, she had no opportunity to demonstrate the kind of virtuosic ornamentation and inventive variation for which Coleman, her 1913 rival, was already famous.

Listening to the B Side: "An Buachaill Caol Dubh"

Ní Ailpín's solo performance of the well-known air "An Buachaill Caol Dubh" appears on the other side of the 1929 Parlophone 78 rpm from "Over the Moor to Maggie." Most slow airs are instrumental versions of songs in either Irish or English, and in playing slow airs, traditional musicians strive for phrasing that matches the song's lyrics. Rather than using dance music's rhythm-contingent ornaments, a musician will often attempt to mimic the placement, melodic content, and affect of a singer's ornamentation. Ní Ailpín does both: her phrasing is faultless, and with the exception of two awkward roll-like decorations in the first part of the air, her melodic ornamentation is entirely idiomatic and traditional.

So—to use an old turn of phrase—where is the pill in all this jam? If she gets the all-important phrasing and the ornaments right, then where's the problem? Is there a problem at all? Yes and no. In her performance of the air, Ní Ailpín uses vibrato liberally, and some of her long notes sound sickly sweet to ears accustomed to hearing fiddlers today attempting to approximate the nasal timbre of sean-nós singers. We don't know why she chose to use vibrato—perhaps she hoped to reach audiences who valued a more classical sound, or maybe she was consciously participating in a fad for vibrato or simply adopting a technique that she thought sounded good. Contributing to the classical feeling established by her relatively wide vibrato, she also audibly slides to a higher hand position a couple of times to reach higher notes on the E string—something traditional fiddlers don't officially do. And herein lies the real problem, or problems: this performance exposes a historiographic blind spot embedded in the contrast between discourse and practice.

Simply put, our current definition of "traditional music" prevents us from accepting the widespread influence of art and popular music. We selectively accept certain aspects of this influence, including group performance and tracks that are three and a half minutes long. However, audible sentimentality and the extensive use of vibrato have been deemed distasteful for long enough that most traditional singers and instrumental musicians today studiously avoid them. Upon encountering such vitriol as this 1978 passage from Tomás Ó Canainn's now-classic *Traditional Music in Ireland*, most traditional musicians would shy away from the use of vibrato: "Any general use of vibrato, particularly in dance music, is completely out of place in Irish traditional music and its use is a pretty sure indication that the performer is not a traditional musician."[97] Ó Canainn then lists the requisite exception of using vibrato sparingly as an ornament—a use very much in keeping with that of baroque performance practice. The fiddler and scholar Matt Cranitch makes this connection:

> Certainly I would consider vibrato merely as an element of technique rather than a fundamental part of slow-air playing. When I play slow airs some notes may not have any vibrato at all—others a little, depending on what I want to do at the time. It's not unlike early Baroque fiddle playing, where vibrato was only used to emphasise or heighten some notes. It's a pity that vibrato is taught nowadays as a basic and continuous element of violin playing, rather than for occasional emphasis.[98]

Therefore, by Ó Canainn's widely accepted definition, Ní Ailpín was probably not a traditional musician. Vibrato is the forbidden fruit that retroactively casts her from the garden of the tradition. Upon hearing her performance of "An Buachaill Caol Dubh," a musician steeped in the aesthetics and practices of the past half-century might dismiss her as not traditional with hardly a second thought.

Why is vibrato so reviled? In a discussion of sean-nós singing, Ó Canainn likens musical restraint and an essential "naturalness" to the "Irish ethos": "The voice-quality of the traditional singer is quite unlike that of the so-called 'trained' singer. He does not use vibrato nor does he employ dynamic effects. The song is allowed to speak for itself, with a minimum of artificial intrusion or histrionics on the part of the performer. One might see an analogy here with other artistic expressions of the Irish ethos."[99] One might also see florid melismatic ornamentation as artifice. But the typical traditional musician does not, even though similar characteristics in other contexts betray a lifetime of formal training in art music. Melodic ornamentation has come to stand for all that is native and natural, and vibrato for all that is foreign and artificial.

This polarization has had profound effects on art and traditional music in Ireland. Harry White has approached this split from the perspective of art music, which he believes has suffered from the use of "the native repertory" as an instrument for establishing Irish national identity.[100] However, traditional musicians have tended to view this division as a necessary means of maintaining stylistic integrity in the face of potential incursions from a genre whose prestige and presumed technical superiority threaten to overwhelm all it encounters. From this point of view, a musician who uses vibrato extensively does not just make a certain sound but threatens to destabilize the polarity between art and traditional music, thereby endangering the integrity of traditional music as a whole.[101] In this context, Cranitch's analogy with baroque music makes political as well as musical sense: for traditional musicians seeking greater recognition in the academy in the past fifty years, likening Irish traditional music to baroque music has provided a way in without requiring surrender to the art music practices and repertoires that traditional music has defined itself against for at least the past century.

Metaphorically and demographically, gender distinctions are implicit in this polarization. In Ireland, the overwhelming presence of women amateurs in local art music performance in the early twentieth century reinforced familiar connections between effeminate men and art music. Of the techniques considered classical, vibrato has long indexed femininity and sentimentality, and the polarization between art and traditional music in the twentieth century has reinforced the notion that vibrato is for women.[102] But quite a few male musicians in the history of Irish traditional music recording have played slow airs with just as much vibrato as Ní Ailpín used in 1929, and while she is forgotten, their status in the tradition is uncontested. What happens when Paddy Reynolds (1920–2005), Andy McGann (1928–2004), Eugene O'Donnell (1932–2019), and other male musicians born in the 1920s and 1930s use vibrato in playing slow airs?

Here, the disappearance of a woman musician—itself obviously a problem— also exposes an avenue of historical inquiry that has been blocked by the polarity between art and traditional music: the influence of recorded classical music on traditional music in Ireland in the first half of the twentieth century. During this era, 78 rpm records of virtuoso violinists were just as available in Ireland as the celebrated recordings of the fiddler Michael Coleman—and Coleman met and played with Fritz Kreisler, a violinist particularly known for his vibrato.[103] Pointing out this as-yet-unstudied aspect of traditional music practice may help us understand why Ní Ailpín chose to play "An Buachaill Caol Dubh" with extensive vibrato without fearing that it would ruin her traditional reputation. Furthermore, it may also help contextualize the playing of Reynolds and other male musicians in what I believe was a more widespread appreciation of vibrato than we have assumed. Such an assumption has led to the undervaluation of most of these musicians' air playing in relation to their performances of dance tunes, and in contrast with the respect given to other performances of slow airs that better fit later tastes.[104]

CONCLUSION: WHY DOES IT MATTER IF TREASA NÍ AILPÍN WAS "TRADITIONAL"?

Why does it matter whether Ní Ailpín is accepted into the mainstream history of traditional music? First, recognizing her as a traditional musician requires that we revisit histories that have assumed that all publicly active musicians in the nationalist movement were classical, and therefore not worth remembering. In making this determination, today's traditional music establishment risks repeating history: willfully forgetting Ní Ailpín and other such musicians of the past because they do not fit today's ideals of Irish traditional style repeats the Gaelic League's attempts to eradicate set dancing to protect and promote "pure" Irish dance. Set dancing survived, but will the names and music of early twentieth-century musicians fare as well? Moreover, the story of Ní Ailpín forces us to consider whom we include in the tradition, and how and why. At the beginning of this chapter, I asked what it takes to be "traditional," and how determinations of "authenticity" shape the experiences of musicians and influence whether and how they appear in historical memory. Is "traditionality" a birthright or a learned behavior? Nature or nurture? As long as the bodies of would-be traditional musicians are or appear to be ethnically Irish, these questions and their answers remain negotiable. But as the population of traditional musicians in Ireland and elsewhere becomes more ethnically diverse, these questions become increasingly urgent.

Ní Ailpín's story focuses on the slippages between definitions of "authenticity" based on Irish ethnicity and those based on musical style—slippages that expose the constructed nature of "authenticity" and bring the idea of an essential "Irish" identity into question. By exploring her early life and music, I hope to have demonstrated how connections among gender, class, and reception led to her erasure from Irish traditional music history. In contrast, the next chapter discusses the life and music of a woman musician who is very much remembered and revered in Irish traditional music: the Sliabh Luachra fiddler Julia Clifford. Her story offers an unparalleled opportunity to consider the benefits and constraints of biography and to begin to explore the topic of trad subjectivity.

THREE
Biography, Musical Life, and Gender
Julia Clifford as a Woman Traditional Musician

INTRODUCTION

In 1998, I first heard the music of Sliabh Luachra, the region whose center lies at the point where Counties Cork, Kerry, and Limerick come together at the headwaters of the River Blackwater. Even though many Irish traditional musicians consider the Sliabh Luachra style and repertoire simple, even simplistic, I was drawn to the music's at once lively and wistful melodies, its rolling rhythms, and the easy sociability of its players. In short order, its ghosts also captured my imagination: Pádraig O'Keeffe, the rakish trickster; Denis Murphy, the gentle giant; and especially Julia Clifford, who in a famous photograph stands bespectacled, holding her peculiar Stroh fiddle and laughing at someone's off-camera quip.[1]

Clifford is the protagonist of comparatively few of the stories that constitute the colloquial history of Irish traditional music, and her narrative often seems contingent on the fame of her teacher, O'Keeffe, and her brother Denis Murphy. Yet when asked directly, musicians will sometimes say that Clifford was the best fiddler of the three. You wouldn't know it from the stories, though.

Few women in Clifford's generation played traditional music in public. Between the founding of the Irish Free State in 1922 and the 1980s, women instrumentalists were rarely seen playing in public and even more rarely recorded—a

FIGURE 3.1 Julia Clifford with her Stroh fiddle. Used by permission of the *Irish Examiner*.

scarcity that obscures the existence of women who played in private settings. Above, I described the conditions that enabled women instrumentalists to perform traditional music in public during the early twentieth-century fight for independence, and I argued that their prominence as women musicians was contingent on centuries-old idealizations of the nation as mother or maiden. Through an account of the fiddler Treasa Ní Ailpín (Teresa Halpin) in chapter 2, I then investigated the roles of the masculinization of traditional music and its attendant connections with art music, effeminacy, and foreignness in today's assumption that early twentieth-century women fiddlers were classically trained violinists with no authentic connection with traditional music.

But while biographical details have necessarily informed my arguments, my focus has been on women musicians as a category rather than on the life stories of individuals. Following Adriana Cavarero, I have focused on the *what* rather than the *who*—on the social positions (including identifications as woman, spinster, wife, and mother) that too often stand in for the *who* (the uniqueness of every person that is only discernible by an outside observer). Cavarero illustrates this concept of the *who* by citing the Danish novelist Karen Blixen's tale of a man who unconsciously traces the figure of a bird with his footsteps. In the moment, Blixen's character knows only that he runs frantically from house to pond to fix a leak in a dike, and it is not until the next morning that he sees from his window the outline of a stork in the mud. To Cavarero, the *what* of "woman" is imposed by the masculine symbolic order, but seeing *who* she is requires a sympathetic narrator to discern what patterns her particular relationships traced.[2] Thus, my discussion so far has been framed as a set of arguments about the conditions that have enabled or prevented women musicians as a group from gaining public recognition as traditional musicians. I have therefore not presented a collection of stories that tells us what sorts of people Bridget Kenny, May McCarthy, Mollie Morrissey, Mary Kilcar, Lucy Farr, and Treasa Ní Ailpín were.

The tradition has not forgotten Clifford's name or her music, but the ways she is remembered invariably erase her gender or emphasize it: those who never knew Clifford view her only as a *what*—a woman musician—because stories that demonstrate *who* she was are not in wide circulation. In contrast, the people who did know *who* she was are reluctant to intentionally reduce her to the *what* of "woman." Such reluctance to contemplate Clifford as a woman reinforces the common assumption (usually made by men) that no "gender trouble" exists in the Irish traditional music scene, while viewing women musicians solely as women presumes that their sex is more meaningful than their music.[3] This chapter begins with a discussion of the dangers of emphasizing gender in biography: I argue that in writing the musical lives of members of a group marked by difference, we must guard against reducing biographical subjects to their social identities, because doing so denies individual subjectivity even as it bestows recognition. But if reducing a protagonist to her sex is a danger in writing a woman musician's life, so too is the tendency to erase gender in asserting her equal worth. This tendency also applies to other kinds of minoritized identity, such as sexuality, race / ethnicity, and ability. Within the Irish traditional music scene, this tendency is reinforced by the idealized notion of the session as a meritocracy in which musicians of equal skill play together without regard to differences of gender, sexuality, race / ethnicity, or class. I therefore use Cavarero's formulation of *what* and *who* to investigate the unique situation of one Irish woman instrumentalist in the mid-twentieth century as a way of uncovering the simultaneous emphasis and erasure of gender. By telling Clifford's story, I offer a narrative that is part biography and part analysis. This narrative challenges the erasure and emphasis of gender and sexuality even as it consciously questions our understanding of what constitutes *what* and *who* in lived life and in biography.

BETWEEN THE GREAT MAN AND EVERYMAN, WHERE ARE THE WOMEN? SEARCHING FOR THE INDIVIDUAL IN THE EXEMPLARY

The central challenge in focusing on individuals in an ethnography is that individuals by definition are not simply ordinary, and neither are they entirely exceptional—if indeed either of those categories is meaningful in life as we live it. For example, the seemingly ordinary musician becomes somewhat extraordinary by their position in a published text, and the exceptional musician still fits within a network of societal and musical relationships and shares this network with hypothetically ordinary musicians. In this way, Clifford was simultaneously ordinary and exceptional. Like many women of her generation, she migrated to England to work in the 1930s, where she married and had two children. Like many of her fellow emigrants, she tended to socialize in Irish enclaves in London and made several attempts to return to Ireland. But unlike most of her peers in Ireland and its diaspora, she played publicly in multiple performance contexts and released several commercial recordings during her lifetime, although she never recorded a solo album. And although she learned her music from male musicians, Clifford may be unique in being—in death as in life—a woman who was a much more famous musician than her accordion-playing husband John or her son Billy, a flute player (both tremendous musicians in their own rights).

The project of using biography to question received notions of women instrumentalists' musical participation requires that we look more closely at two different branches of biography, which seem at first to work toward opposite ends. The first and most common brand of biography retains its original and enduring connection with "great man" narratives, which recount the escapades of figures deemed to be extraordinary. The second, championed in the late 1970s by scholars in the social sciences, calls for biographical attention to "the common man," as a way to examine the workings of groups and cultures.[4] The rhetorical contrast between these two approaches is striking on several levels, particularly in the relative positions of biographer and biographical subject. As Daniel Aaron writes: "Great biographies like Froude's *Thomas Carlyle* are rare, because such happy conjunctions of writer and subject are rare; great figures more often than not are the victims of their biographers' ineptitudes and biases. Froude undertook the life of Carlyle as a sacred obligation. . . . [He] revered his master."[5] And according to Stanley Brandes: "Usually, to be designated ethnographic, an autobiography is recorded and edited by a social anthropologist, or by some other professional with interests closely allied to social-cultural anthropology.... [The informant] is generally illiterate or semi-literate, and, in any case, is far from being an introspective, intellectual person who would be likely to be self-motivated to produce an autobiography. The protagonist of ethnographic autobiographies is almost always a commoner, an ordinary member of his or her society, whose individual achievements are not noteworthy in and of themselves."[6]

In typical great man biography of the sort that Aaron lauds, the biographer kneels at the feet of his "master," while in Brandes's "ethnographic . . . autobiography," the biographer—by definition a professional academic—presents the world of his illiterate, low-status informant. Outdated as they are, these quotations nonetheless point toward two different and enduring conceptions of the role of biography. The first places the biographer in the position of acolyte and underscores the singular greatness of the biographical subject, while the second depends on situating the informant as an exemplar, someone whose very ordinariness seemingly bestows the authority to speak for a larger group.

Here, I could easily argue that the first approach obscures the power of the biographer and that the second denies the informant subjectivity. Instead, I want to highlight the distinction between the biographical protagonist as an individual and a member of a group to examine the way power circulates in both of these approaches to biography. Implicit in my examination of these power dynamics is a variation of my opening question, which resonates with Cavarero's distinction between *who* and *what*: what are the politics behind situating one's biographical protagonist either as an exception or as an exemplar, especially when that protagonist somehow differs from the constructed norms of their social context?

From a feminist perspective, both approaches are problematic: between Aaron's great man and Brandes's Everyman, what happens to women? Gender, sexuality, class, and race-based challenges to biography's great man narratives open the genre to new protagonists, but these new protagonists remain marked by the difference that previously relegated them to the fringes and shadows of Western biography. Whether biographies aim to add members of these groups to the roster of extraordinary personages (like Gayle Wald's work on Sister Rosetta Tharpe) or intend to use the lives of exemplary figures to shed light on the experiences of a group of people (as in Susan Cheever's 1994 *A Woman's Life: The Story of an Ordinary American and Her Extraordinary Generation*), each biographical protagonist's association with a marked group runs the risk of denying her the individuality that still identifies the subjects of "great man" biography as important.[7] Here, it's useful to consider Peggy McIntosh's point, paraphrased in Richard Dyer's *White*, that "a white person is taught to believe that all that she or he does, good and ill, all that we achieve, is to be accounted for in terms of our individuality."[8] I would argue that even now, four decades after Aaron and Brandes published the passages I quoted above, the reception of biographies of women and other historically othered people still hinges on a politics of identity that implicitly emphasizes group membership rather than individuality and thereby renders these biographical protagonists less powerful and less important than their unmarked counterparts.

Thus, unmarked individuality is a position of power. I now turn to Julia Clifford and the Irish traditional music scene, which has an ambivalent relationship with stylistic individuality. Despite this ambivalence toward innovation and some kinds of individual creativity, the community tends to celebrate the idiosyncratic personalities of skilled and revered musicians. In this scene, being heard as a truly traditional musician means that one has deep and audible connections with repertoires and musicians who have come before, even if one's own playing is significantly different from that of other players. As long as one's playing is suitably traditional, quirks of personality are tolerated and even embraced, and they eventually contribute to one's enduring legend. Many well-known male Irish traditional musicians fit into this category, including Pádraig O'Keeffe, whose playing was brilliant and whose influence was immense, but his position in the pantheon of musicians of note is also dependent on his role in stories as a trickster and rebel. Thus, Pádraig and his music are especially memorable because of his idiosyncratic individuality, and this individuality in turn is possible because he otherwise belongs to the unmarked category of the Irish, rural, and male traditional musician.[9]

What about Julia Clifford, then? Along with her teacher, Pádraig, and her brother Denis Murphy, she was a quintessentially Sliabh Luachra fiddle player. But she is remembered in a very different way from the way Pádraig is remembered. If the many stories about Pádraig reinforce his individuality, his Pádraigness, the few stories about Julia in wide circulation situate her as a woman or as Pádraig's student, Denis's sister, or John Clifford's wife, but almost never as Julia. I do not mean to suggest that her sex was irrelevant but instead intend to point out that a typical biography of Julia as a woman fiddle player would implicitly or explicitly foreground her position as exemplary of a small group of women musicians rather than as a musician extraordinary in her individuality. Although such an approach might be politically expedient in the project of writing women back into traditional music history, and although seeing her as a woman might be particularly attractive to other women musicians, telling the story of Julia as woman further separates her from the ways that musicians like Pádraig are remembered. A biography written from this perspective would suggest that we are primarily interested in Julia and her counterparts because they belong to a group whose members are often missing from historical narratives—that we are interested in them only as *whats,* never as *whos.*

The Pleasures of a Good Session: A Selection of Vignettes

Most Irish traditional musicians live for a good session. Musicians go home from a good session happy, energized, fulfilled, with tunes ringing in their ears for hours or days—and great sessions become legendary, the fodder for reminiscences for musicians who were there and wistful thoughts from those who were not. Such memories live in fragments—sensory traces that resist articulation and find expression in a shorthand of tunes, names, and places. In remembering the magic of a fleeting moment, these tunes, names, and places can become magical themselves.

What makes a good session?

Perhaps it is an evening of music shared among old friends, where the tunes are sparse but beautiful and the conversation plentiful.

tralee, co. kerry, autumn 1999
"what's that one?" "'the linen cap,' in o'neill's."

Or perhaps all the musicians are energetic, rabid, gasping for a tune—and the jigs and reels come tumbling out in twos and threes, taken up as eagerly as the pints of stout on the table and consumed just as fast.

sunday session at ri ra, washington dc, 2003
the guitar drives the tune inexorably forward.

Maybe the session is epic, a festival session that sees musicians arrive and depart in shifts while the music continues, gradually changing hues as afternoon becomes evening becomes night becomes sunrise.

hotel bar, castleisland, co. kerry, autumn 2001
we played every polka we knew, and then some.

It might be in a city pub, hours strictly regulated by the publican and the Gardaí (police): "Come on, lads. Please. It's time!" One musician is clearly senior, and the rest of us defer to him while pretending assiduously not to lest he feel self-conscious. But by now we all know and love his favorite tunes and suggest them at appropriate intervals.

nancy blake's pub, limerick, autumn 2003
"how about the brosna slides?"

A good session—like those I describe above—can take on many forms. Often, there's a clear hierarchy—some musicians are more senior or more adept or have more tunes, and others might be only learning or might not know tunes that belong to a specialized regional repertoire. Melody players call the shots, accompanists follow, and singers take their turn. But when the session is going well, the hierarchy seems to evaporate, at least among the melody players at the session's core. At those moments, there's no clear power differential: we each follow the tune in close heterophonic conversation with our comrades. We play an ornament here, a variation there—or perhaps nearly in unison, and then one of us leaps down an octave to "play the bass," as it's called in Sliabh Luachra. I anticipate where the flute player will take a breath, the flute player guesses when I'll dig in with the bow for extra emphasis, and with the exchange of a glance, the box (accordion) player and I drone on D together for a beat or two. To invoke the terms of Suzanne Cusick's famous manifesto, in this kind of session, nobody's on top all the time.[10]

I wax rhapsodic advisedly, though. Although the players at the heart of the session may go home with the feeling of having had profound, even transcendent experiences through the communal enjoyment of playing tunes, a player on the fringes of the same session might depart feeling excluded for reasons musical or otherwise. Maybe the peripheral musician is new to town or musically or socially inept, or perhaps they are not part of the in crowd. These dynamics are often present in sessions, and sex, appearance, age, race, and national identification often influence the reception and experience of players in a session.[11] This disjuncture between the ideal of the session as a site of democratized musical participation and the reality of musical and social hierarchies and exclusions can be a shock to some newcomers to the music, and this reality sometimes affects even seasoned players. But even with that caveat firmly in mind, I still assert that most players of Irish traditional music are always pursuing musical experiences in which they can forget the exigencies of everyday life and, for a few short hours, create an "escaped" and intimate musical relationship with other players and the music through shared repertoire and style.[12]

I am not sure to what extent the social experience of session playing gives male musicians a break from the gendered and classed expectations of quotidian life, or whether a good session is more often a nonverbal extension of the pleasure of casual conversation and good-natured "slagging" (poking fun) in the pub associated with groups of men—a pastime during which social roles can be policed as much as they are negotiated. Most likely, it's a combination of the two, balanced differently depending on time, place, and personnel. As I discuss further in chapter 4, musicians' relationships with "the music itself" may produce pleasurable feelings of relinquishing control and letting the tunes take over—a sense of freedom that may be experienced as queer or may be akin to the abdication of conscious control associated with religion or perhaps with addiction.

These meditations on sexuality and Irish traditional music can help us think through the problems inherent in researching and writing a biography of a prominent yet marginalized woman musician like Julia Clifford. First, the idealization of the session as a space where social equality is achieved through musical performance helps explain why white male heterosexual musicians usually seem baffled by the idea that gender, sexuality, and / or race / ethnicity might affect one's participation in the music. Moreover, the implicit assumption that "musician" is an identity that supersedes other identity categories derives in part from the power attributed to "the music itself"—but because Irish music performance has historically been the province of men and the sonic expression of masculinized Irish nationality, the unmarked term "musician" is invariably gendered male. Thus, the privileging of "musician" as an identity has profound implications for writing the lives of musicians of both sexes, and the temptation to confuse the *what* of "musician" with the *what* of "woman" presents particular problems for producing biographies of women musicians.

Julia Clifford as a Musician

If I have succumbed to an identification with my biographical protagonist that affects how I hear her story, it is primarily in this way: even though I have fought diligently to avoid objectifying Clifford as a woman, I have blithely allowed myself to research and write her life as though she were limited to another subject position—that of musician.[13] According to Cavarero, "musician" can just as surely be a *what* as can "woman" in "the pervasiveness of a symbolic order where the androgynous subject is what defines *what* they are: mothers, wives, care-givers, bodies to be enjoyed."[14] That symbolic order defines how Clifford is a traditional musician and how I am one—and suddenly "woman traditional musician" becomes a *what*, not a *who*.

Is resistance futile? Is this a tale about the education of a girl into the ways of being a woman traditional musician? Or does *who* Clifford was emerge from the stories that construct her identity as a traditional musician instead of as a woman? Or in carving out a path by which to become a traditional musician and negotiating the symbolic order of the intensely Catholic Irish Free State to gain the freedom to play tunes in public, did Julia create a *who* from modes of resistance that were later appropriated by the symbolic order—modes once revolutionary that now define *what* rather than showing *who*, and now so established as to seem timeless?

But most of us who embrace identification as the *what* of "traditional musician" today have not heard Clifford's stories, of her either as a woman or as a traditional musician. By combining her reminiscences with those of other musicians, I offer this story of her as a woman traditional musician, along with the understanding that it is not her only story. The two narratives of this chapter—one more theoretical, which serves as a frame story to the second, the tale of Julia's musical life—stand in relation to each other and to the sounds of her music.

THE MUSICAL LIFE OF JULIA CLIFFORD

Over the past several decades, the *Journal of Cumann Luachra*, which focuses on the Sliabh Luachra region, has included profiles of local musicians. Each titled "My Life and Music," these short autobiographies follow a pattern: first, the musician—almost always a man[15]—describes his or her family background and how he or she came to the music. These musicians pay special attention to music teachers, and anecdotes about Pádraig O'Keeffe, the local fiddle master, are de rigueur, whether he taught them or not. The musician then explains his or her transition into adulthood in both musical and personal terms but focuses on gigs, festivals, and musical comrades rather than on family life or day jobs. And at the end of several printed pages, each musician concludes with a pithy statement about being a musician or about the tradition. I include several of these statements to illustrate the common trope of music and its tradition as a gift, lifelong calling, and beloved master:

I hope the Lord will give me the health to continue my music for many years to come. It is my wish that music will be kept in the traditional style, as I learned it. (Sonny Riordan, fiddle)[16]

Music has been good to me and I have been lucky enough to play in England and the United States. I thank the Lord for whatever talent he has given me and the health to continue playing and sharing my music with many people. (Maurice O'Keeffe, fiddle)[17]

I hope [my children] will continue the tradition handed down to me by my father. Music has given us all many years of happiness and what can be better than a good session. I have never seen anyone playing music with a sad face, and in today's world especially it is nice to see people with a cheery look. (Jimmy Doyle, accordion)[18]

I don't know whether I am good or bad, but everybody seems to think that I am good at it. Anyway, I'll keep on playing until I drop. (Paddy Cronin, fiddle)[19]

Life has changed a lot since my young days, but as I mentioned previously, it gives me great pleasure to see so many of our young people playing Irish music and dancing sets. Long may it continue and with God's holy help, I will do my part for our great tradition, while I'm able. (Mike Duggan, fiddle)[20]

The enduring notion that a serious traditional musician lives for the tunes is well known outside the covers of the *Journal of Cumann Luachra*. I will not investigate the implications of this claim here, but I note that the tension between devotion to music and family or career obligations is familiar in traditional music's history, and many of the genre's most famous musicians have remained bachelors or chosen occupations that have allowed them ample time for musical pursuits.[21] The problems for women musicians, who can less easily escape family responsibilities and who have historically faced barriers to working outside the home, are obvious.[22]

The ideal Irish traditional musician, then, views his love for the music as innate, passionate, and enduring and as part of an unbroken tradition that connects him with past, present, and future musicians. He plays for the love of the tunes, and his musical activities are always somehow in service of the tradition. Such devotion to a genre characterized by camaraderie and convivial settings is no sacrifice—but it is a brand of devotion that women have historically been discouraged from pursuing. The 1937 Irish constitution reinforced the ideal of women's devotion to family, home, and the Church, and most women musicians were not known outside their families for being, as the saying goes, "mad for the tunes": they were presumed to be loyal to familial duty rather than musical pleasure. Male Sliabh Luachra musicians, however, often remember their mothers as singing and lilting tunes incessantly, learning tunes from the radio, and keeping instruments close at hand for playing when the mood struck.[23] But these women seem rarely to have played in public, even in neighbors' houses: Clifford's son Billy, who spent most of his childhood during the 1950s with his maternal grandparents in Lisheen, near Gneeveguilla, County Kerry, does not remember women musicians playing out in the community, and does not remember his aunts—Bridgie, Mary, and Hannie—playing in public. Understandably, Billy is less familiar with the activities of his aunts Mary and Hannie after they immigrated to New York, and Mary in fact ran an all-female band called "The Maids of Erin" for a time.[24] But women's public musical activity in Ireland in the mid-twentieth century seems to have been rare—or at least, we have been encouraged to think so.

Clifford, however, does seem to have lived for the tunes in public as well as in family settings, and the closing words in her *Journal of Cumann Luachra* autobiography are very similar to those of her male counterparts: "The love of music has never left me and, just like my beloved brother Denis, I intend to play until the moment the Master says: 'Julia, your next tune will be in Heaven.'"[25]

This passion for the music led Julia to pursue the music at home, as well as to risk punishment at home and social censure for following the tunes to traveling shows, house dances, and dance halls. Like many traditional musicians, Julia remembers being warned not to break older siblings' instruments, and she writes, "Even when I was very small I was mad to play."[26] She credits her brother Thady with teaching her her first tune, a jig she calls "The Ducks in the Oats," and remembers music in the house in the evenings when she was a young girl:

> In the evening when any bit o' work—doing turf or hay or something—was finished, they'd [her father, Thady, and Denis] get in the kitchen and start playing music—and the three of them'd be sitting there playing away . . . and they'd play for about a couple of hours and they'd leave the fiddles lovely in tune . . . and get up and go away out. . . . O'course I didn't use to go. And the very minute they'd go I'd go for the fiddle.[27]

Eventually, though, Julia—the youngest child in the family—was allowed time to play the fiddle.[28]

Although Julia credits her mother with "[keeping] us under control" and

Julia's son Billy remembers his grandmother as the disciplinarian in the family, Julia nonetheless managed to escape some parental restrictions at a time when the clergy were particularly outspoken about the need to regulate the activity of young women. No evidence exists to suggest that Julia was sneaking out of the house to engage in illicit liaisons, but it's worth noting that during the 1920s and 1930s, Church and state were in a panic about the rise in illegitimate births, which averaged about 1,700 per year in the 1920s.[29] And in their famous study of life in County Clare, the anthropologists Conrad Arensberg and Solon Kimball reported that in rural areas, both premarital sex and birth out of wedlock were a disgrace for a woman and her family.[30] Therefore, sneaking out of the house was no small matter for a teenage girl. Perhaps, though, in an era when priests condemned dancing, especially jazz dancing, as morally ruinous, Julia's interest in traditional music was read as pure and nationalistic—perhaps she even benefited from the image of the "clever little artiste"[31] popularized by Treasa Ní Ailpín, May McCarthy, and Mollie Morrissey a generation earlier. But once her interest in traditional music was firmly established, Julia's parents could probably be confident that Julia was well chaperoned by her brother Denis or other siblings—and we should remember that her older sisters also played music, even if not in public.

In any case, sneaking out of the house to play tunes was not something every teenage daughter did in the 1920s, and the best-known story about Julia is about one of her clandestine excursions:

> I must have been around the age of fifteen when I took part in a competition for the first time. It was organised in Knocknagree by a traveling showman, known as Gordy, but I had to be persuaded to take part as my parents did not know I was in Knocknagree. Anyway, I entered and, much to my surprise, won first prize of 10 shillings, a mighty sum in those days. Gordy advised me to learn how to read music and I went to Pádraig Keeffe, who showed me how.[32]

This version of the story, which Julia contributed to the *Journal of Cumann Luachra* in 1987, is remarkably subdued compared with another version of the tale in circulation, and with Julia's retelling of it in an interview conducted by Reg Hall in 1990. Although the 1987 version introduces the idea that Julia mightn't have been allowed to go to Knocknagree to the show and suggests that she went alone—surely not something a parent of a fifteen-year-old daughter would encourage—this telling portrays the young Julia as modest and humble. She "had to be persuaded" and was surprised that she won—although a few sentences later, the bold, tune-obsessed Julia returns: "The win in Knocknagree gave me a lot of confidence and nothing in the world would keep me at home after that, if there was a dance or amusement in the district."[33]

Like the other autobiographical sketches in this series, Julia's published version of the story pays homage to Pádraig O'Keeffe, who became her teacher soon after the Knocknagree contest. So too does the version of the tale that appears in the liner notes to *The Rushy Mountain: Classic Music from Sliabh Luachra 1952–1977*:

> Julia tells a story of how as a child she crept out of the house one night while her parents were asleep to enter a local music competition which she won. Over the following three weeks she stole out of the house on the night of each successive heat until eventually she won the final. When her parents discovered what she had been up to, they were so delighted by her success that they engaged Pádraig O'Keeffe to give their children proper music lessons on a regular basis.[34]

Two details of this story are particularly striking. First, it suggests that she might not have been allowed to participate in the contest had she asked her parents for permission, with the easily reached interpretation that because she was a girl they might have prohibited her from entering the contest. Second, by invoking O'Keeffe, this story becomes a way to explain how Julia becomes his student rather than an account of a resourceful young musician who resorts to disobedience to get what she wants.

A third version of the story comes from a 1990 recording of an interview in her home in Thetford, Norfolk. In addition to her interviewer Reg Hall, the Cork accordion player John Coakley and the Galway fiddler Lucy Farr were also present, and among friends, Julia tells the story this way:

> My father started me off learnin' me how to play, but I wasn't very good. I was getting better, and there was a concert run by a traveling man by the name of Gordy, and he put up this big competition—talent competition, and I went in for it. Denis went in for it as well, and . . . schoolteachers and everything went in for it! I think 'twas five pounds, or ten pounds—I'm not sure, but 'twas a lot of money anyway. . . . And I won it! And the man that gave me the prize said, "You should get a music teacher." So I told my father, and they brought in Pádraig O'Keeffe. So Pádraig taught me. But he never taught me to read music. He was too lazy![35]

Here, after a brief nod toward humility—"I wasn't very good"—Julia emphasizes her victory, and in this version of the story, the prestige of the contest and the size of the winner's purse increase significantly. She prevails in a pool that included her brother Denis—who today is probably slightly better known than Julia—and a host of adults, including schoolteachers. And while it is possible the prize money could have been as much as £5, the fiddler Maurice O'Keeffe recalls that in 1930, a fiddle could be bought for 25 shillings (£1.25), and an introductory lesson from his teacher, Johnny Linehan, cost 10 shillings. Pádraig O'Keeffe is remembered to have charged six pence per tune taught.[36] Moreover, this rendition of the story offers the only unequivocal critique of Pádraig O'Keeffe's fiddle teaching that I've encountered—and in doing so, it goes very much against the usual reverence accorded this legendary musician. We do know, however, that Julia respected other aspects of his musicianship, including the repertoire she learned from him, and she and Denis joined him to record the material that would eventually be released as *Kerry Fiddles*.[37]

The element of secrecy is entirely absent from this last version of the fiddle contest story, and with it disappears the implication that being a girl had anything at all to do with her path toward musical proficiency. Indeed, no evidence suggests that Julia's parents treated her interest in music any differently than they did their sons'—an equality that was by no means present in every family in the 1920s. The elder Murphys understood the appeal of dances and musical gatherings, as Julia describes: "Mary, my sister, had a house dance and, of course, I had to be there. My father and mother were not supposed to know. However, at about 10 o'clock, when the dance was in full swing, didn't I see the donkey's two ears outside the window. My father and mother had pulled up outside: like me, they could never say no to a dance."[38]

Again, Julia circumvents what seems to have been fairly relaxed parental control to follow the music, and although she never refers to her siblings as chaperones, family members seem to have been present at most of the events she attended. She and her brother Denis often played for house dances and were later in demand at local dance halls: "Denis and I used to play at an amount of house dances and we were often out two or three nights in succession until clear day in the morning. But, this didn't knock a shake out of us. We'd play away all night for polka-sets. . . . When the dance halls got popular, we were kept very busy."[39] Julia continued playing for dances through most of her adulthood, but no anecdotes about her exploits at these dances are commonly told.

This silence contrasts with a number of such tales about Denis and especially about O'Keeffe. And because these stories constitute the popular history of Irish traditional music, they determine how—and if—musicians are remembered as people beyond their immediate circles. Historically, the exploits of women musicians, who may not be able or welcome to participate in homosocial male environments and activities, have either gone unremarked or remained untold out of delicacy and a desire to maintain a lady's respectability. Therefore, stories about Julia are vital if she is to be remembered as Julia Clifford, not just as a woman musician or the disembodied source of the splendid fiddle playing we hear on her recordings.

Telling Tales across the Irish Sea: Clifford's Well-Traveled Fiddle

By the time Clifford came of age in the 1930s, the effects of the economic war with England and worldwide depression had profoundly affected the Irish economy.[40] Despite independence and the establishment of the Irish Free State in 1922, emigration remained a fact of life for Irish men and women. In the period 1926–36, Ireland's population declined as its people left to seek work, and women emigrants outnumbered their male counterparts: an estimated 46,000 women left Ireland, compared with 30,000 men.[41] In "My Life and Music," Clifford writes, "My youthful days were very happy and carefree. I practised hard and I learned my music well. . . . But sooner or later, I had to go earn a living."[42] In 1933, at the age of eighteen, she left for Falkirk, Scotland (near Glasgow), to join an aunt who found her a position where she could train to be a nurse.[43] Clifford soon returned home to Kerry, though, in large part because she missed the music: "I was trained to be a nurse, and I didn't like it, and I met no musicians there. . . . And I got so lonesome that I packed it up and came home for Christmas. . . . So I went home anyway, and played away at home with Denis."[44] Later in life, she continued to tell the story of leaving Falkirk because it offered no opportunities for playing Irish traditional music.

The Cork fiddle player Connie O'Connell remembers hearing her talk about her brief sojourn in Scotland:

> But she told me she had the fiddle under the bed, in this [bed]sit in Glasgow, and she said, "Connie," she said, "there was dust down on top of it—'twas never taken out of that spot." . . . She nearly fecking died there, like. Well, I think . . . after making up her mind that she wasn't going to live in Glasgow for the rest of her life, she really delved into music big time then, and she played it, and all her friends and all her company—and anything that she touched after that, there had to be music involved in it somewhere, in her whole life.[45]

After a little while at home, Clifford went to London in 1935 and found work as a maid in various hotels in the Bloomsbury-Euston area.[46] This time, she seems to have enjoyed relative freedom, and she arranged her life around playing music in the dance halls in Tottenham Court Road and later in Cricklewood.

At home in Ireland, however, priests were railing against the dangers of urban depravity for young women emigrants in the cities of Ireland's erstwhile colonizer. The historian Louise Ryan describes the threat to Irish nationalist patriarchy that women's emigration represented and cites live-in domestic service positions as one means of containing women in safe spaces. Press commentators in Ireland in the 1930s encouraged women emigrants to seek such jobs rather than work as hotel chambermaids, shop girls, or in factories.[47] However, Clifford chose the relative freedom of hotel work and seems to have relished the ability to travel between Ireland and England frequently—a pattern she maintained throughout her life. She describes her early years in London in an interview quoted in Alan Ward's extensive notes to the Cliffords' Topic recordings: "When I came to London I came to nobody, I came to a job. I answered an advert in the paper and came to a job. I used to go [back home] very often. I'd get a fit, a notion. I'd save up, I'd get the ship and I'd stick over for three months then I'd get fed up with home and I'd come back again!"[48]

Hotel work, too, seems to have offered Clifford more opportunities to play the fiddle than nursing did Lucy Farr, who also came to England in the 1930s. The hotel schedule was more adaptable to nights spent in dance halls, and time and space for playing the fiddle were easier to find in hotels than in hospitals. Farr describes some of the obstacles that prevented her from playing fiddle when she was working at a hospital in Hither Green, London, in the late 1930s: "I did tentatively try to pick it up and play a few tunes, but you were always interrupting someone—you were interrupting the night staff if you played in the daytime, in the mornings, and you were interrupting the day staff, 'cause, you see, your room was there, and the next one is there, and the next one is there, and you couldn't do it. And nobody else had an instrument, so you couldn't do it."[49]

Moreover, Farr worked the night shift and had few evenings off to go to the dance halls as a dancer, much less to make the connections necessary to join a band. For Clifford, hotels—as well as public transport—offered opportunities for a resourceful young fiddler to practice her music, as she relates in this anecdote: "I used to play on the top of buses coming home from the dances, and I'd hear a new tune some place, you know, and I was really so keen, and in case I forgot the tune—we used to go into the hotel at night—I'd go into the coal cupboard and get the fiddle and play the tune inside the coal cupboard."[50] Such are the actions of one "stone mad for music," as the saying goes—ladylike behavior be damned!

Marriage, World War, and a Return to London's Dance Halls

Unlike many Irish traditional musicians, Julia Clifford left behind a significant amount of autobiographical material in the form of interviews, liner notes, and the "My Life and Music" article. But as in any telling of a life, even one's own, her accounts are fragmented and often leave her motivations for actions unspoken and unexamined. So written and recorded accounts do not leave a clear picture of her move to Bristol in 1940 or her marriage to John Clifford in 1941. Julia worked for a doctor in Bristol, and she and John began seeing each other more frequently there.[51] He was a neighbor from home whom she also knew from the London scene, and one of Julia's tellings of the story suggests that they were both in Bristol purely by coincidence—while a later version suggests that they intentionally moved to Bristol at the same time.[52] John worked for a manufacturer of war materials in Bristol, which was most likely better-paying work than the hotel porter position that Julia had helped him get in London.[53]

Why did Julia marry then, and why did she marry John? None of her accounts of her life in Lisheen or London make much mention of John, although he was certainly a familiar face from home and was by all accounts a brilliant button accordion player. But if we are to take Julia's reminiscences of her childhood and teen years as representative of her life then, she lived for the tunes, and especially for playing music with her brother Denis. And unlike some women of her generation, including Farr, courting does not enter Julia's narration at all. Music, however, does, and even if Julia and John's meeting in Bristol was by accident rather than by design, it makes sense that they would have seen more of each other in a smaller place, with fewer musicians, dance halls, and social gatherings.

So far, I have portrayed Julia as a woman driven by her love for traditional music—a tracing of who she was that matches the memories her fellow musicians have of her. While I acknowledge the certainty that other stories exist, I believe this particular way of tracing her life best enables us to understand her choices. She and John were both emigrant musicians with a shared repertoire little known outside Sliabh Luachra at that time and a large number of friends and acquaintances in common. If, in accordance with the era's social mores and economic exigencies, Julia had to or wanted to get married, marrying another traditional musician was the best way to ensure that she could keep playing.

Furthermore, playing for dances was financially rewarding: Julia remembers that in the 1940s, each musician was paid £3 for a night's playing.[54] Two musicians in the household meant double the income from music, and because John was an accordion player and Julia a fiddler, they were often the core personnel in the bands they played in as a couple, although both also continued to play with bands separately after they were married. Later in Ireland, they formed the Star of Munster Céilí Band with their son Billy and with members of the Moloney family of Templeglantine, County Limerick.[55] And in the days before portable tape recorders were widely available, the memories of two musicians were better than those of one for remembering new tunes picked up at dances or in sessions.[56]

John may also have been something of a musical proxy for Julia's brother Denis. Back in Ireland, John and Denis had been friends and close musical companions in their teenage years, and Ward identifies their partnership as Denis's "earliest really formative period," during which the two played together and learned new tunes from gramophone records of Michael Coleman and other fiddlers.[57] In the same publication, John tells two stories of his adventures with Denis in the late 1930s—one about John's first radio broadcast and another about cycling from Lisheen to Cork and back in one day for another broadcast—a total distance of about a hundred miles! John was the first of the three to pass the required audition for playing on the radio, but Denis soon joined him, as did Julia during visits home from England.[58] These radio performances extended all three musicians' fame beyond Sliabh Luachra, and when Julia was asked how the managers of the dance hall known as "over Burton's" came to hire her and John, she matter-of-factly answered, "Oh, we had a name made for ourself in Ireland before we came over, you see . . . playing for the radio, one thing and another."[59]

John and Julia were fixtures in London's dance hall scene for decades and played in traditional as well as "mixed" bands—which performed both traditional tunes and music for popular dances like the quickstep and backed singers. Such bands usually featured a range of instruments, from fiddle / violin and accordion to saxophone, trumpet, piano, and drums, and musicians needed to be versatile in repertoire and musicianship. John, who had wowed Irish radio listeners with his button accordion playing, arrived in London to find his instrument unsuitable for much dance hall playing because most button accordions cannot play in the full range of keys in use in the dance hall bands.[60] Soon after he arrived in London, he bought a piano accordion to adapt to the needs of dance hall performance.[61] Julia, however, was well able to play in whatever key the music required—a skill that set her apart from other traditional fiddlers—including, perhaps, even her brother Denis, who once said, "There are things which Julia does on the fiddle which I could never do!"[62] Indeed, Julia was known in the London scene for this ability, as Farr remembers from their first meeting in the Brewery Tap bar in London:

> So we went up on spec, and there you were, and somebody went up the same night to sing a song. . . . And this bloke . . . said, 'Listen to this, now,' and I thought, 'Well, I wonder why'—and he said, 'The only person I know who can—whatever key this man sings in, whoever goes up there to sing, whatever key he sings in, Julia Clifford can get it!' And you know what? You proved it to me.[63]

However, in the interview Julia replies that she does not remember this occasion, which probably occurred sometime in the 1960s—for her, accompanying singers was so routine as to be unremarkable, and while meeting another woman traditional musician may have been an event, Farr did not have her fiddle with her that day.

During World War II, the dance halls remained in operation, and after they returned to London from Bristol, Julia and John played several nights a week. Julia remembers running home during air raids to check on their two children, Billy and John. In the following exchange, the Cork button accordion player John Coakley, another immigrant to London, has just asked Julia about attendance at the dances she and John played:

> JULIA: Oh, big crowds there, all right, dancing and everything 'til 4 o'clock in the morning. . . . And—this is during the war and all, and the bombs were dropping, and the hall would shake back and forth, and we were on the stage, and we still kept playing.
> JOHN COAKLEY: They kept the whole thing going during the war?
> JULIA: They kept the whole thing going during the war.
> REG HALL: Goodness.
> JULIA: And I used to have the kids at home, and somebody looking after them, and when the siren would go, I used to run from the stage down the road, home. And I used to have to lie down in the road from the shrapnel before I got indoors, in case a bomb would drop on the house before I [got into it].
> REG: Goodness!
> JULIA: Oh, 'twas very nerve-wracking.[64]

Eventually, Julia and John took the children to live with John's parents in Ireland for the duration of the war, and Billy spent much of his childhood after the war with his mother's family in Lisheen. In these years, Julia and John went back to Ireland often—they were allowed to travel freely as long as they had jobs and a residence to return to in London.[65]

A LIFE IN MUSIC: JULIA CLIFFORD AFTER THE WAR

Clifford's autobiographical reminiscences about the years after the war seem less colorful and more rote—although we have more photographic, audio, and even video evidence of her playing available from that period, supplemented by the memories of musicians who knew her in Ireland and England after the 1950s. Therefore, the next section will put Clifford's playing and image in dialogue with the facts of her life and the memories of musicians who knew her. Here, I do not attempt an exhaustive history of her life but instead offer an intentionally loosely woven set of images, sounds, and discussions to represent decades of musical, emotional, and quotidian life held together by the melodies and social practices of traditional music—decades when the *what* of traditional musician stands in for the *who* of Julia Clifford.

Therefore, I resume with Julia's own words, again from "My Life and Music." Other than a paragraph in which she marvels at her older sister Bridgie's good health and the concluding paragraph I quoted above, these three paragraphs represent the only column space Julia devoted to the last four decades of her life. In them, she focuses on the music and chooses not to mention her many relocations between England and Ireland during those decades, episodes of ill health, John's death, and other personal events in her later life. Because she chooses to focus on the music and in respect of her family's wishes, I will therefore present vignettes of Julia's life after World War II primarily through attention to her music.

According to Julia:

> We [she and John] never lost touch with Lisheen and made frequent visits. We decided to return more or less permanently in 1953 and went to live in Newcastle West, Co. Limerick. We formed our own band, "The Star of Munster," and it was rated as one of the best in Ireland, playing regularly in Limerick, Kerry, Clare and Galway and on Radio Éireann. However, things were bad economically in the 1950s and it was not easy to make a living so we returned to London in 1958.
>
> We played away in London and, with the decline of the old dancehalls, began to concentrate on Irish pubs, which were popular haunts for lovers of traditional music in the 1960s. Musicians like Martin Byrnes, Bobby Casey and

FIGURE 3.2 "Danny Ab's Slide" [basic melody].

Willie Clancy were in their element while our son, Billy, on the concert flute, joined John and I [sic] to form The Star of Munster Trio.

We made several records and I'm playing today as well as ever, thanks be to God. Most of my time is spent in Norfolk, England, and I'm teaching some English youngsters how to play the real Irish music.[66]

Slides, in 12/8, are peculiar to Sliabh Luachra, and with its recurring scalar motifs and quarter-eighth / quarter-eighth rhythmic pattern, "Danny Ab's Slide" is a good example. A different recording of this tune appears on *Kerry Fiddles*, and the liner notes to the 1993 CD reissue provide some information about the tune: "Julia remembers how she and Denis induced 'Danny Ab' of Tureen Cahill near Lisheen to teach them the two slides on track 6 in exchange for cups of tea!"[67] Here, Julia and Denis play together, and characteristic of the Sliabh Luachra style and their duo playing, one of them plays the melody an octave lower than the other. Julia probably takes the lower part: she was particularly known for her skill at "bassing," as it's called in Sliabh Luachra, and legend has it that Pádraig O'Keeffe encouraged (or instructed) her to do so. Julia and Denis play slides so similarly as to confound attempts to distinguish them, but her tendency to use more slurs provides additional corroboration that she plays the lower part on both tunes. Julia may take the lower octave because she may have been more adept at transposing than her fellow musicians: by 1952, she would have had nearly two decades of experience playing in hybrid traditional-popular bands, which required musicians to be comfortable playing in more keys and registers than are customarily used in Irish traditional music. In addition to showing off her skills, the lower part may also have appealed to Julia because it allowed her to distinguish her musical voice from those of her brother and her teacher. Moreover, because many tunes in the Irish repertoire do not lend themselves to doubling, she also had ample opportunity to enjoy the pleasures of tight unison as she played in the same register as Denis or other fiddlers in other tunes.

The Star above the Garter (1969) remains one of the most important albums of Irish traditional music, and it was the first LP devoted to Sliabh Luachra style and repertoire. The original liner notes to the album's 1992 CD reissue are prefaced by a brief and superlative paragraph that asserts its impact on the tradition: "Masters of Irish Traditional Music [the reissuing series] presents classic recordings by artists whose performances have literally defined the music. This album . . . is the finest representation of music from County Kerry ever produced. Denis and Julia were giant figures in Irish music . . . [their music] stands as some of the most powerful and eloquent Irish music ever made."[68]

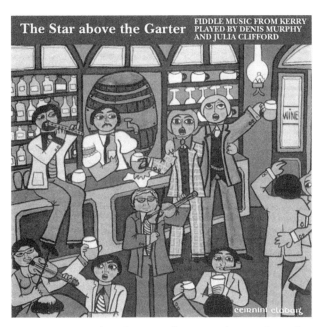

FIGURE 3.3 *Star above the Garter* album cover [artist unknown]. Appears by the kind permission of Claddagh Records Ltd.

In a 1990 interview with Reg Hall, Julia remembers that she and Denis recorded all the tracks for the album in one day, and that they put down more material than would fit on the LP. According to her, the listening public would eventually hear that material in another way: the Chieftains learned the tunes and, as Julia says, they "played it [the music] everywhere they went—but fair play to them—they used to say where they came from. . . . They always say, 'This is Kerry music from Denis Murphy.'"[69] This record is the main reason Julia Clifford's name endures outside her immediate circles of friends, family, and fellow musicians in Kerry and London. Musicians from Texas to Tokyo to Toomevara cherish the recording and play tunes named after Julia and Denis, including "Julia Clifford's Polka" and "Denis Murphy's Slide." If Julia and Denis are household names among aficionados of Irish traditional music, John Clifford is not, and the liner notes do not mention him. Nor is he pictured in the album cover's cartoon caricature, which shows Julia seated in the bottom left corner, Denis standing in the center, and Billy sitting on the bar playing flute. But if Julia and Denis earned fame and respect from this album, very little of either seems to have rubbed off on John, and according to one musician who knew them in London, John became increasingly jealous of Julia's success.

Julia, of course, is the only woman in the cartoon.

The 1960s and 1970s were eventful: in 1964, Julia won an All-Ireland title, and she and Denis released *The Star above the Garter* in 1969. She moved back to Ireland in 1968—first to Lisheen and then to Tipperary Town to be near her son Billy and his wife, Catherine, in the early 1970s.[70] John remained in England. In 1973, he collapsed with severe bronchitis, and Julia returned to England to take care of him. Denis died unexpectedly in 1974.[71]

One track from this era, on Julia and John's 1976 release *The Humours of Lisheen* haunts me: "Freddy Kimmel's / The Home Brew," two hornpipes. The first tune is unique, and no one has yet managed to figure out where Julia and John got it. The title suggests a misnamed attribution to John Kimmel, the famous American accordion player of the early twentieth century, but this connection has not been proved. The second tune is better known by its alternate titles, "Delahunty's" and "The Wicklow Hornpipe." Here, I will concentrate on "The Home Brew" to point out a few of the subtleties that distinguish Julia's playing. Although this transcription of her playing during the first time through each part of the tune is useful for following along with the recording, I make no attempt to represent the ornaments or variations in each part of the tune.

2:21 in the recording

FIGURE 3.4 "The Home Brew" [music transcription].

And of course, transcribing Irish tunes as a way of describing performance is an exercise in folly, however handy "the dots" are for learning or remembering basic melodies.

After a brief two-note pickup, Julia and John start "The Home Brew" together, both strong and audible on the A—although as in "Freddy Kimmel's," John's accordion is low in the mix, and distinct phrases of his playing emerge only occasionally. The piano—presumably played by Reg Hall—is even more in the background, perhaps as a reaction against so many 78 rpm recordings on which the piano is distractingly loud. Here, though, the piano is consistently sparse and plays mostly on the off beats. Julia's fiddle comes out loud and clear—so much so that it seems no attempt was made to balance the fiddle and the accordion. With John's presumably poor health and diminished playing capacity by 1976, this choice is logical.

Julia's playing in this tune is quintessentially her own, and quintessentially Sliabh Luachra. In the A part, she ornaments the quarter note C in the second full measure with a typically subtle ornament—she begins by briefly leaning on the previous note, a B, and then moving to the C only to flick her ring finger up to interrupt it with a D. The whole thing happens so quickly that a listener might not notice it consciously, and a scribe would have a difficult time parsing the note durations. This ornament is generally unnamed in Irish traditional music pedagogy, in which the common names of some ornaments—cuts, rolls, triplets or trebles, and crans—assert their existence, codify their forms, and prescribe their use.[72] In the Sliabh Luachra style, however, ornaments do not always fit neatly into this lexicon. This ornament has the overall effect of making it seem as though Julia has made a shallow, slight slide into the C, and even if we don't think about what's happening, we notice that note just enough: she's not forcing us into it but makes it appealing enough to stick in our ears. Julia was a great one for making certain notes ring out with a combination of unassuming ornaments and slight increases of bow pressure—something she did without conscious effort, or so think some of the musicians who knew her. In contrast, Denis's ornamentation was much more by the book and obvious, from his wide slides into notes to his rhythmic rolls.

The intonation of this C (shown in the transcription by a triangle pointing downward)—and of several others in this tune—is also interesting, and it stands apart from other slight out-of-tunenesses in this recording. Like many other fiddlers of older generations, Julia is a great exponent of what I call "C-supernatural": slightly closer to C-natural than to C-sharp, it sounds wrong to ears unused to the playing of older Irish musicians and highlights the tension between modality and tonality that arguably characterizes Irish traditional music as a whole.[73] This "C-supernatural" is intentional, and Julia is well able to position that finger in the proper place for C-sharp, as she demonstrates in the C-sharp in the triplet in the sixth measure. Did she think about this finger placement intentionally? Probably not—she grew up around players like O'Keeffe and would have heard its use from so young an age that she probably picked it up without too much thought. Was she aware of it? Most traditional musicians today like to think of the older generations as innocent, playing the way they learned without regard for trends and judgments from outside, and I'm sure that's true to some extent. But Julia would have encountered many musicians in her lifetime, and perhaps by 1976 she was aware of the choice. Today, "C-supernatural" indexes just the kind of traditionality associated with Julia, Denis, and other fiddlers of their generation and before it.

Julia's restraint in this hornpipe is characteristic: her variations and ornaments are never obtrusive, and instead of dressing the tune within an inch of its life, she brings out the beauties of the melody and the lift of the rhythm. Sometimes her versions of tunes deviate significantly from standard settings, as in the B part of

FIGURE 3.5 B part of "The Home Brew" [common setting].

"The Home Brew": play this variation in a session, and people who know this recording will know where you got it. No one I have talked to knows whether the Cliffords got this variation from someone else or made it up themselves, and the most plausible speculation I've heard is that it is a way of fitting the B part on a one-row melodeon with a limited range—so perhaps John learned it on a more limited instrument in his youth and continued playing it that way after he switched to the piano accordion. The variation also suits Julia's style, I believe, because it gives her a chance to lean on the high G to transform the usual version to a plaintive call to which the second section of the B part responds. This variation gives Julia ample opportunity to bring out certain notes of the melody—here, the high Gs and the A, and then the low G.

Now that I have performed the sort of genealogical exegesis we Irish traditional music aficionados live for, and a certain kind of musical analysis, let me tell you why this recording gets under my skin, beginning with this mysterious variation in the B part. If we believe that John brought the variation to the musical partnership—or, put another way, if we think that he imposed his version on Julia—we may hear the performance as an audible manifestation of Julia's lack of musical agency in the relationship. There's quiet evidence for that. But perhaps Julia came up with it, so we might reach the opposite conclusion: that she wore the musical pants in the family. There's evidence for that conclusion, too. Or maybe this variation says nothing of the sort. Maybe, like the vast majority of musical negotiations, the Cliffords easily reached a consensus: it's nice, so we'll do it this way—or, I like my version better, but I don't mind playing it your way.

I hear biography in these notes, although I can only guess what tales they tell. This B part represents everything I love about Julia's playing, and in it, I hear everything I know—or think I know—about her life.

John survived another five years after this recording was released. After his death in 1981, Julia spent the last years of her life in Thetford, Norfolk, near her son John, and was sought after at sessions and folk clubs near Cambridge. She recorded an album, *Ceol as Sliabh Luachra* (Music from Sliabh Luachra), with her son Billy in 1982 and was a featured guest at the 1994 Éigse na Laoi festival at University College Cork.[74] She died in 1997, at age eighty-three, in Norfolk.[75]

PERFORMING "(WOMAN) MUSICIAN" IN IRISH TRADITIONAL MUSIC

Julia Clifford occupies a simultaneously ordinary and extraordinary place in the annals of Irish traditional music history. Told one way, her life seems stereotypical: a country girl emigrates to find work, marries an acquaintance from home, bears two children, and maintains her connections with members of a family that defines itself by its Irish origins. How, then, did she become an internationally known fiddle player and the most famous woman traditional musician of her generation? I suspect that if we could ask her, she'd reply in her delightfully matter-of-fact Kerry way, "Ah, sure, I just did." Upon reflection, she might add that the gigs and recordings that led to her recognition as a superb traditional musician were possible in part because she moved to London but traveled home often. Moreover, she and her peers benefited from increasing interest in so-called folk music in Britain, which peaked in the 1960s and 1970s.[76] She would probably also credit her brother Denis, her teacher Pádraig O'Keeffe, her husband John, and her son Billy for their musical camaraderie. At times, the presence of Denis or John may also have helped ease Julia's entry into musical situations, including the dances where she and her brother played in Kerry as teenagers and certain pubs in London in the 1960s, as Farr suggests: "Well, I didn't used to go [to the Brighton pub in Camden Town] every Sunday morning, but I remember this one Sunday morning that I got all these looks—a *woman* walking in on her own, with a fiddle under her arm. And then all of a sudden I didn't feel too bad, 'cause I found Julia Clifford used to come in as well, but she had John."[77]

Farr then clarifies that the Brighton crowd was almost entirely "old men," but that other pubs were less intimidating for women by the late 1960s. However, Julia had become an integral member of the dance hall scene thirty years before, so it is unclear whether she would have felt the need of male company to enter a pub where music was played. Indeed, in her own statements, Julia often seems barely conscious of her sex—and ironically, this seeming disregard might have enabled her to participate more fully in the musical life of her era than other women did. By contrast, Farr is a keen observer of gendered differences in traditional music practice and sounds at times painfully aware of her own status—an awareness in which appropriately feminine behavior mirrors the exactitudes of upward class mobility. Julia doesn't seem particularly concerned with class status, nor was she willing to sacrifice musical fun for appearance's sake. Here again, gender and class considerations confound easy interpretation: for example, was her publicly indulged taste for beer and whiskey a reflection of lower social status, resistance to proper femininity, both, or neither?[78] Likewise, Julia's obsession with music could easily have been seen as her abnegation of proper gender and class roles, but in a family as mad for the tunes as hers was, her priorities were understandable, as her son Billy's laugh asserts: "God—I think anything else, anything other than music was a chore for my mother, really. . . . I'd nearly go so far as to say that even to make the breakfast, like [chuckles]. . . . It had to be music, and that was it, like, d'you know."[79] Billy's statement echoes an anecdote told about Denis Murphy in which his wife claimed she could tell what kind of tune he had in his head by the way he drove the car: for him as for Julia, music infused every aspect of daily life.[80]

But Julia did not completely ignore her position as a woman in a male-dominated music scene, as is clear from this exchange in an interview that Reg Hall conducted in 1990:

> REG HALL: So what was it like, sort of being the only woman in the pub playing the music? Was that difficult, or easy?
> JULIA CLIFFORD: It wasn't difficult, no.
> LUCY FARR: You were really the first of the women players, weren't you?
> JULIA: I was the only one![81]

Here, Julia insists that she was the only woman musician in the London pub session scene in the 1950s and early 1960s—and in the same breath, she implies that her sex didn't make playing in sessions difficult. This contradictory awareness and dismissal of difference resonates with the self-presentation of some women composers, including Kaija Saariaho, who has said that although she has to "face [her] womanhood every day" in negotiating her place in Finland's male-dominated contemporary music scene, she nonetheless does not consider gender an issue in her composition.[82] Cristina Scabbia, the lead singer of the Italian heavy metal band Lacuna Coil, has expressed similar thoughts about being one of the very few woman in the genre—that she is a musician first and relates to her peers from that subject position, rather than as a woman.[83] From the available evidence, for Julia, "musician" also seems to have prevailed over "woman"—at least, in the way she appeared to the musicians who knew her.

MEN, MUSIC, AND TRADITION

The idea that one might be a musician first and a gendered subject second may seem to take gender out of the equation, and to many male musicians, it does—an appealing notion that places music above quotidian negotiations of labor in the home and workplace. The session, with its theoretically inclusive ethos, might seem to maintain the patterns of homosocial interaction even with women present: as long as no one mentions gender in a traditional music context, male musicians can imagine that sexism is not a problem. For those who wish to think so, the session thus becomes a sexless space, a homosocial *musician* environment where individuals can choose to identify themselves as musicians first and as gendered beings second. This well-intentioned erasure of gender constitutes a different dismissal of gender than that of male musicians who simply ignore the women in a session. In her critique of patriarchy in Irish traditional music, the Australian ethnomusicologist Helen O'Shea describes the latter through the very real effects of polarized gender positions within sessions. While such an analysis is long overdue, O'Shea misses nuances of power and positionality by presuming separate and singular understandings of masculinity and femininity. Such an opposition allows little room for recognizing resistance or negotiation.

Thus, when O'Shea encounters this quotation from the great whistle player Mary Bergin, she focuses on the speech act that she interprets as transforming Bergin into an "honorary male," rather on the event that Bergin suggests inspired the comment:

> [Subtle variation within the tune structure] is how musicians really appreciate each other. Often in the middle of playing a tune with someone they change a few notes, and that really gives the tune a lift. I feel like going, "wow!" It's brilliant! Even one note can make such a difference. People have shouted at me a couple of times, "Good man, Mary!" (laughs). I would have done something and not even have known it. That's the nice thing about all that, it's the magic of it.[84]

"Good man, yourself," is a common phrase that is occasionally modified to "Good woman, yourself," and occurs in musical and nonmusical contexts. As O'Shea rightly suggests, the incongruity of "Good man, Mary" illuminates the erroneous presumption that the best traditional musicians are inevitably men. But by ignoring Bergin's discussion of the music, O'Shea misses a series of related points that tells us more about the connections among gender, sexuality, and musicianship in Ireland. If Bergin has indeed been made an "honorary male," this status is multifaceted and full of internal contradictions beyond the simple differences between the sexes. First, what has been conferred, masculinity? No, musicianship—but the two are so close that they become nearly synonymous. How has Bergin won this status? Through her playing—specifically, through details Bergin doesn't notice herself producing. And here we discover another important though perhaps not surprising fact: although she is a virtuoso on the tin whistle, Bergin does not win approval as a traditional musician through flashy playing or extensive variations of the kind that made Michael Coleman's reputation in the 1920s. She gains respect through subtle stylistic choices and a fairly conservative approach to variation—and in doing so, she joins the ranks of male traditional musicians known for their loving protection of the tradition.

So to be declared a traditional musician in the same utterance that names one a "good man" makes sense: the conservative aspects of Irish traditional music are gendered male. But like some male musicians in Western art music and jazz, traditional musicians like Michael Coleman, Paddy Keenan, and Matt Molloy are also recognized for a paradigm-shifting virtuosity that is clearly gendered male. In a genre historically dominated by male musicians, men occupy the positions of both traditionalist and innovator. Moreover, ongoing associations between traditional music and virile nationalism counterbalance the competing notion of innovation (and virtuosity) as linked with modernization. So instead of setting up a binary between feminine, domestic, Irish, backward-looking tradition and masculine, political, foreign, and forward-looking modernity, male Irish musicians almost always occupy both sides of the binary. Furthermore, male musicians enjoy the freedom to travel between both polarities. For most women musicians, however, being recognized for traditional playing requires a much more conservative approach: it is much more difficult for a woman musician to retain her status as "traditional" if she adopts repertoire or stylistic practices associated with the innovative side of this false binary.[85]

A SORT OF A "NEUTRAL GENDER": ALMOST (BUT NOT QUITE) ONE OF THE BOYS

If "good man, Mary," does not exactly confer masculinity but instead performs the public recognition of a woman's playing as valuable to the traditional music scene, what extramusical qualities help a woman achieve this recognition? In the context of the session, this particular form of praise usually indicates camaraderie and social acceptance as well as admiration of musical skill. For example, male or female strangers in a session are less likely to be praised by name, although their contributions may elicit responses like "Lovely!" or possibly "Good man, yourself," or "Good woman, yourself." But the personalized incongruity of "Good man, Mary," is contingent on Bergin's social place in that session and the scene—a social place that is established by more than musicianship.

Here, I explore how Julia Clifford resisted stereotypes of idealized Irish womanhood even as she performed femininity in other ways. This mostly nonmusical negotiation of gender stereotypes, I argue, helped her participate fully in the social practice of traditional music at a time when few women played outside their own homes. In chapter 1, I discussed the ways that publicly successful women musicians in the early 1900s were visually and rhetorically connected with the idealized female figures of Erin and Mother Ireland. With the adoption of the constitution of 1937, which asserted the special position of the Catholic Church in Ireland, these tropes of virgin and mother did not disappear. Instead, they retained seemingly inescapable social power: such personifications helped define and reinforce expectations for women's behavior and provided additional rationale for Church-led efforts to remove noncompliant women from society through institutions like the Magdalen laundries.[86] Stereotypes based on these three archetypal figures—mother, maiden, and whore—have complicated the integration of women into the publicly social practice of Irish traditional music.[87]

Needless to say, few women completely fit these stereotypes, but they defined ideal and transgressive behavior for women for most of the twentieth century. How did Clifford manage to fit in—if not as "one of the guys," then at least as someone around whom "you wouldn't be too worried to have an awful lot of manners," as O'Connell described her? For Irish men, typically brought up to be devoted to their mothers, the presence of a middle-aged woman in the session—as Clifford was by the time pub sessions became popular—would most likely have had an effect on sociability, no matter how good a musician she was.

But Clifford was not a stereotypical Irish mother, just as she seems not to have been a demure maiden in her youth: she chose work in a hotel over domestic service or nursing and was bold enough to have found and made opportunities to play the fiddle in public. And although she did marry and have children, she did not follow her mother's lead and become fervently religious in later life.[88] In fact, Clifford seems not to have had much use for organized religion, according to this anecdote from O'Connell. The events of this story took place in 1994, when Clifford had been invited to play at a festival in Cork and brought her older sister Bridgie with her for the weekend: "But Julia was up on the Sunday morning, anyway, and she was sitting below inside in the sitting room, and she was practicing her tunes for the concert. And Bridgie was around the house . . . and she came in to Julia, and she said, 'Julia, will you put that fiddle away—we'll be late for Mass!' And Julia stopped playing. . . . 'Bridgie,' she said, 'Do you know, Bridgie, that I *hate* Mass?'"[89] Such humorous irreverence would have made her an entertaining presence in a session, where the chats between sets of tunes can be as important as "the music itself." And combined with her liking for a pint, Clifford's lack of self-conscious piety would have established her as the sort of woman unlikely to stand in the way of convivial chatter.

O'Connell also affirms that Clifford was conversationally adept, and rather than performing femininity through quiet shyness, she was quick to talk with anyone about any number of subjects:

> She'd have a lot of talk—she was a great woman to talk—she was not a kind of a person . . . that you'd sit down and that there'd be an awful lot of silence. There'd be never any silence, like. She kept talking about something—she'd be talking about a dog, or she'd be talking about something that went wrong that morning, or, you know, that she probably couldn't light the fire, or—there was something going on always, and, like, it mightn't be music, it might be a car that broke down.

Later, he remembers, "She was happy to go outside the door and smoke a fag with anyone, like, and chat away to 'em."[90] From O'Connell's stories, Clifford seems to have been no delicate flower. Perhaps her conversation would have shocked the men more than she would have been shocked by anything they said.[91] Likewise, the Kerry fiddle player Donal O'Connor remembers her as "a very easygoing person—she never worried too much about anything." He also notes her sense of humor, but unlike O'Connell, O'Connor recalls that in the sessions he attended, "she would never be a person that would start telling stories in the bar"—a striking difference that we might attribute to differences in personnel on the occasions that the two men met her, or perhaps to her age: O'Connor probably met Clifford about two decades before O'Connell did, when she might have been more concerned with how she appeared to others.[92] Although Clifford seems to have had some shy moments, she most likely developed her sense of humor, affability, and social ease early in life and around men, including her brother Denis—who is said to have had a similar personality.

By avoiding stereotyping as a delicate, religious woman around whom a man might have to watch his manners and his language, Clifford put her male musical comrades more at ease than other women might have done. O'Connell concludes that her personality and skill transformed her into "a neutral gender," and that a musician's sex is irrelevant:

> She was a very forthcoming woman, you know, and she was not a terrible ladylike woman in the sense that you wouldn't be too worried to have an awful lot of manners around her—you know that sort of thing? So that made her more of a neutral gender, like—it didn't make any difference whether she had pants, or a cap, or a hat.... That's what I think, anyway.... Her circle of friends and her social outings and everything was centered around music—they were all associated with music, and they didn't give a damn what she was—if she had two heads—as long as what she was able to do, she was able to do it![93]

But a "neutral gender" and the irrelevance of sex are not the same thing, although O'Connell and many others conflate the two. Here, I believe O'Connell's perception of Clifford as a "neutral gender" indicates that because she did not fit into the stereotypes of mother, maiden, or whore, Clifford did not read as a conventionally feminine woman to him, although he is quick to add that she was "a lovely-looking lady." The fiddler Bernadette McCarthy, who knew Clifford in London in the 1960s, said that she maintained a personal style that seemed "ladylike" but perhaps not overly feminine: "She was kind of ladylike in her own way, as well. She always wore a white mackintosh coat, like a rain mac, and she'd have her hair all nice, and smoke Woodbines or rollups or something like that, you know."[94] It is also worth noting that Clifford was well into middle age when O'Connell and McCarthy first met her and was therefore less likely to be sexualized, compared with a younger woman.[95]

Unfortunately, no one who knew Clifford as a young woman in Kerry is around today to describe her presence at musical events before the 1940s, so tracing long-term shifts in her public persona is difficult. However, we can contemplate subtle differences in her demeanor in Ireland and in England between roughly 1950 and 1975, which suggests that she may have presented herself as more verbally outgoing in London, even if she was eager to play wherever she was. Although more information is necessary to support this notion, the following accounts identify a significant difference in Clifford's musical presence in Ireland and in London.

In the first, O'Connor was remembering sessions in Ireland in the 1950s, when Pádraig O'Keeffe was still alive. I had asked him, "Was she the kind of person who—the second a tune starts, she's mad for the tunes?" He answered: "Oh yes, she was. She was really steeped in the music, and she was very, very interested, and when she got her own group—the group that understood, that had an understanding between them—Denis and herself, and Pádraig—or that sort of a group, she was better, because they had the arrangements, they had the tunes, they were very, very close."⁹⁶

In the second, McCarthy was remembering Clifford's performances in London in the 1960s. When I asked, "Was she at all reticent about playing in front of people, or did she just get up there and—" McCarthy replied:

> She'd just get up. . . . The compère [emcee] would say, "Now we'll have a tune from Julia Clifford," and "Oh, yes, of course" [she'd say] in that Kerry accent, and up she'd get, and she'd play away. . . . Lucy Farr was more kind of like, "Oh, sure, I can't play at all"—that kind of approach. But she was only dying to get up there at the same time, whereas Julia—you wouldn't have to ask twice, and she just came across—she just got up, and she played away, and she'd have them all laughing.⁹⁷

In the third, O'Connell was remembering sessions with Clifford in Ireland, probably in the 1970s: "'Twas absolutely great to play with her—really great. And again, very relaxing, and there was no pressure on anyone, you know. . . . She wasn't going to go on a big show and play all solos all night—never ever did that. She never did it—under fierce pressure she'd probably start a tune. Everybody else started 'em, like.⁹⁸

All three quotations portray a Clifford dedicated to the music, but the two accounts of her at sessions in Ireland suggest that she might have been less comfortable playing alone or with strangers and reticent about starting tunes, while McCarthy's memory of Clifford at London folk clubs asserts the opposite—that Clifford was eager to play solos and was utterly unaffected by nerves. This difference suggests some amount of code switching between London and Kerry, perhaps intensified by the company she kept—which in Ireland would have included family members and neighbors she'd known since childhood. This reading of Clifford's code switching suggests that she was somehow less comfortable playing in Ireland, and one interpretation seems obvious—urban, progressive London offered greater opportunities and freedoms to women than did rural, socially conservative Ireland. While Clifford may have felt more free in some areas of her life, I am not sure that these differences between London and Kerry affected her music making to a large extent within the enclaves of recent Irish immigrants who formed the core of the traditional music scene.

Another interpretation of Clifford's geographically specific musical demeanor makes more sense within the larger context of her life and offers a new perspective on her recordings. Simply put, playing music in Ireland may have meant ensemble playing to her: from childhood, she and Denis had played together and with O'Keeffe. Moreover, sitting among players well versed in the Sliabh Luachra style and repertoire (a group that includes both O'Connor and O'Connell), Clifford may have found solo playing unappealing compared with the fun of matching the sound of other fiddles, leaping down to play a tune in a lower octave, and playing polkas and slides with others who played them with the right lift.

By contrast, Clifford's musical life in London included membership in dance bands, solo folk club performances, and group playing in pub sessions, as well as the recordings she made there in the 1960s and 1970s. And because most of her fellow musicians in England were not steeped in the Sliabh Luachra style, Clifford became associated with core repertoire that would have gone unmarked at home: for example, Farr and musicians who knew Clifford in Cambridge in the 1980s and early 1990s remember the quintessential Sliabh Luachra reel "The Banks of the Ilen" in connection with her. Associating tunes with specific musicians is a mark of esteem, and among the musicians Clifford encountered in England, she became an unofficial ambassador of Sliabh Luachra, including to musicians who had emigrated from elsewhere in Ireland.

She also seems to have enjoyed a significant amount of musical agency, especially in the making of the Topic recordings in the 1970s. Indeed, although the second of the two 1976 recordings, *The Humours of Lisheen*, bears John's name as well as hers, its musical content represents what we can see as an emerging solo career for Julia: John appears on only seven of the twenty tracks, and Julia's solo playing is strong, confident, beautiful.[99] The solo material on *The Star of Munster Trio* and *The Humours of Lisheen* proves Julia's prowess, but unlike other albums in this Topic series, these two records were never reissued on CD and have not yet been officially digitized.[100] Her later album with her son Billy, *Ceol as Sliabh Luachra*, is equally hard to find. Therefore, *Kerry Fiddles* and *The Star above the Garter* remain the most available of Julia's recorded output, and these albums have shaped the way today's musicians think of her: as an ensemble player known for her slow airs, not as the fine solo player of dance music she also was. Her playing of slow airs is unparalleled, and as an implicitly more femininized subset of the traditional repertoire, these airs may have brought her extra respect as a woman musician and a solo player at a time when women dance musicians were seldom recorded and seldom seen playing in public.

If *who* Clifford was drove her to pursue fiddle playing at the highest levels, *what* she was demonstrated that women could indeed join the ranks of Irish traditional music's greats. While this point should be self-evident, women in Irish traditional music still struggle for equal recognition and equal treatment in musical contexts as well as in society more generally in Ireland, the United States, and elsewhere. Queer musicians and musicians of color face similar challenges, as the next two chapters discuss—and like Clifford, they are enticed by the delights of "the music itself."

The next two chapters shift to the ethnographic present of the 2010s, although my interlocutors and arguments are sensible only through the recognition that the past and future are vital participants in the phenomenological present of Irish traditional music, and that "the music itself" often plays the role of participant rather than remaining solely the medium of performance. Although parts of previous chapters have brought the Irish diasporas of the United States and Britain into earshot, the following two chapters listen to trad specifically as a transnational genre. In using the thoughts of musicians from outside Ireland to support my argument for a postnationalist understanding of Irish traditional music, I seek to subvert conventional framings of insider and outsider, because this dichotomy describes neither the lived experiences of musicians nor the production of meaning within the genre. Instead, chapter 4 explores the pleasures of playing trad alongside experiences of (hetero)sexist and / or racist harassment to demonstrate that the embodied joys of "the music itself" are theoretically available to anyone, even though identity-based discrimination presents particular challenges for women, queer, and nonwhite musicians.

FOUR

Subjectivity, Flow, and "the Music Itself"

> Apollo, the god of light, of reason, of proportion, harmony, number—
> Apollo blinds those who press too close in worship.
> Don't look straight at the sun. Go into a dark bar for a bit and have
> a beer with Dionysios, every now and then.
> *Ursula K. Le Guin,* The Left Hand of Darkness

> It's the only music that brings people to their senses.
> *Joe Cooley, interview with Cathal O'Shannon*

The summer before I entered graduate school, I was standing at the bar at a festival chatting with a well-known Irish musician and scholar. As we sipped our beers, I expressed my excitement about moving to New York and (as one does in the scene) tried to remain appropriately cynical about the prospect of studying the music in a formal setting. This musician admonished me to stay away from what he called "sociology" and urged me to do the kind of work that "really matters," which I presumed meant that I should study either the great musicians of the tradition or to dig into "the music itself" and study regional repertoires and ways of playing, ornamentation, bowing, and so on.[1] I fidgeted nervously and probably nodded in a noncommittal fashion—I was entering a PhD program as an ethnomusicologist, after all, and I knew that attention to cultural context would be central to my training.

We would not have to work hard to imagine a version of this conversation between a senior scholar of Western art music and a student—a conversation that could have happened at any point during the twentieth century and likely still happens in some quarters. As in Western art music scholarship (especially before the 1990s), citing "the music itself" in Irish traditional music is often shorthand for asking readers or listeners to pay attention to text or sound rather than to the social, economic, or historical circumstances that situate a performance.[2] However useful studies of musical sound can be, invoking "the music itself" in this way is not neutral, especially when used to control discourse and shape the production of knowledge. The Irish musicologist Harry White makes a similar critique and writes that "in its empirical assent to antiquarian models of collection and recension, [Irish traditional music has] eclipsed the prospect of historical interpretation and sociological discourse."[3] And as scholars like Christopher Small, Ruth Solie, Suzanne Cusick, Judith Tick, and others have amply demonstrated in the context of Western art music, foregrounding the discussion about social context removes the illusion that "the music itself" as text is "objective"—and therefore more worthwhile than "subjective" accounts of lived experience.[4]

What I propose to do in this chapter is reclaim the phrase "the music itself" by exploring some of its more phenomenological aspects—a project that benefits Irish traditional musicians of all kinds in its focus on the embodied, sensory aspects of playing trad. That I do so in talking about the experiences of women, queer, and nonwhite musicians is testament to the importance of paying attention to the experiences of those of us who have historically been othered. I also recognize the irony of building my argument through literatures that have long been dominated by white men. This chapter seeks to queer these literatures by mobilizing them to explore nonnormative musicians in a genre customarily undervalued by musicology, ignored by philosophy and psychology, and only provisionally claimed by ethnomusicology. Instead of focusing on either text or context, I intend to demonstrate that Irish traditional music provides ideal ground for resisting the binary thinking that separates mind and text (and, implicitly, musicology) from body, performance, and context (and, implicitly, ethnomusicology). After explicating the relationship of Irish traditional music to magical nationalism as a precedent for understanding "the music itself" as agential, I then describe musicians' encounters with "the music itself" through the embodied experience of what I am calling "trad flow" as an affective state. In relating the negative experiences of some of my interlocutors, I enumerate some of the circumstances that can prevent nonnormative musicians from entering flow states. I then posit that recognizing "the music itself" as an agent gives us new insights about humanism as it relates to women, musicians of color, and queer practitioners in trad.

MAGICAL NATIONALISM AND "THE MUSIC ITSELF"

Symbol, object of adoration, interlocutor, soul—when Irish traditional musicians and scholars speak of "the music itself," we invoke one or more of these things. Especially when it refers to instrumental music, "the music itself" is simultaneously singular and unbounded, and with its ostensibly distinct stylistic boundaries, vague sense of spirituality, and seemingly limitless signifying power, trad continues to play a role in magical nationalism.[5] Like magical realism, magical nationalism incorporates marvelous or supernatural aspects and actors into everyday expressions of national identity. For example, the literary scholar Jonathan Allison discusses William Butler Yeats's matter-of-fact treatment of the supernatural in his nationalist poetry as anti-imperialist because in privileging the marvelous and the magical within his accounts of everyday life, Yeats (and, by extension, the Irish) resists the hegemonic power of "Anglo-Saxon administrative rationality."[6] By casting Irishness as proximal to the supernatural, poets, politicians, the tourist industry, and ordinary Irish people claim an exceptionalism in relation to the imperial, ostensibly rational powers of both Britain and the United States.

In the first few chapters of this book, I recounted the histories of women musicians active in the early twentieth-century nationalist movement. There, I argued that one of the reasons these women have been forgotten is because traditional musicians and the institutions that support trad have sought to distance the genre from militant nationalism while reinforcing a vision of national belonging rooted in an idealized past. Like aisling poetry with its supernatural spéirbhean who told welcome stories of Ireland's liberation in the eighteenth century and the Gaelic revival's retellings of legends of like those of Cú Chulainn and Fionn mac Cumhaill in the early twentieth century, trad has its own relationship with the magical. Commentators deem musicians like the piper May McCarthy (profiled in chapter 1) "marvels," and stories of fairies who give musicians tunes or magical abilities are widespread. For example, the origin story of the jig "The Gold Ring" begins, "A long, long time ago—if I were there then, I wouldn't be there now; if I were there then and now, I would have a new story or an old story, or I might have no story at all—the birds could talk, giants roamed the land, and fairy music filled the air."[7]

The past of talking birds, giants, and fairy music seamlessly joins the more recent past of house parties and crossroad dances, hearth-baked bread, and *poitín* (Anglicized as "poteen," an illicit distilled beverage). The homespun delights of an

Irish Ireland become exceptional because this blend of human and supernatural is treated as unexceptional: meeting a fairy on the road is something that might reasonably happen to anyone at any time.[8] This form of Irish exceptionalism is extraordinarily alluring, as the steady flow of tourists to Ireland demonstrates.

Trad is an effective instrument of magical nationalism because it indexes both the valorized domestic sphere and the national supernatural of trickster heroes and fairy forts. In this context, "the music itself" has the potential to be signifier, object, and actor—an audible representation of Irish nationalism, a beloved, and a coconspirator. For the Clare fiddle player Martin Hayes, trad has a language, speaks, and knows itself in relation to other musics: "I learned the language of 'the music itself' and how it could expand, and that rolled into how it could relate to other music forms and how other music forms could connect with it and if there were places where they could contribute to each other."[9]

Similarly, other musicians and commentators (including several of my interlocutors) identify the spirit of the genre in the spaces where humans and sounds shape each other. The US-based journalist Bill Margeson connects Paddy O'Brien's appreciation for the "nicest tune" with the "soul of Irish music," and in using "wizard" to describe O'Brien, he mingles the supernatural, spiritual, and musical. In this formulation, a certain set of repertoire choices and performance practices become the music itself, the center and soul of Irishness as performed through trad:

> The music. Button box wizard Paddy O'Brien gets it. Really gets it. "What I like in a musician now," states Paddy, "is the one who plays the nicest tune, even more than the technical musicianship." In that one sentence the legendary Offaly-born button box player encapsulates a life spent in the center and soul of Irish music. And that center is the music itself. Not the current fashion. Not the current "hot" group. Not "the buzz." The music. Period. Full stop.[10]

This aggressive paragraph depends on the reader understanding "the nicest tune" as "old," and thus something imagined as simpler, despite ample available recordings that demonstrate that some musicians of the past, like Bridget Kenny and Michael Coleman, were quite "technical" players. I point out this confluence to show that trad inhabits a discursive space that is both homely and otherworldly. This quality is what makes "the music itself" such a powerful signifier—even if its use as a signifier of secular Irish nationalism tends to strip away its agency.

Rather than downplaying trad's supernatural or spiritual associations (which can also elicit feelings of embarrassment because they do not match Ireland's more modern persona since the economic boom of the 1990s), I take up the invitation offered by magical nationalism to ask whether "the music itself" might be an actor in the set of activities, understandings, and ways of being that constitute trad. What if "the music itself" has agency—what if it is a collaborator rather than an object, and what if it operates in both everyday and supernatural realms, like the fairies whose music some musicians profess to have heard?

Readers familiar with actor-network theory will hear resonances of this idea with the work of Bruno Latour and others, but while I embrace the theory's construction of agency and actors as nonhierarchical, I am less concerned with the connectivity of actants or with the results of thinking about music and musicians as an assemblage.[11] Instead, I am interested in "the music itself" as subject rather than object as a way of expanding who (and what) has a claim to subjectivity in trad. I also want to explore how the idea of "the music itself" as an agent might change human perceptions and actions—how it might jar us out of the hierarchies and exclusions embedded in liberal humanism.[12] I follow this line of thinking to get at the mysteries of embodied action as a way humans create (or cocreate) entities that blend with human consciousness and then take on lives of their own as sound and discourse. By imaging "the music itself" as an actor (rather than a product) and the act of musicking as cocreation, we might move beyond the text-context binary in trad scholarship and begin to imagine our way past the self-other opposition that trad requires as an instrument of ethnic nationalism, in which Irishness is experienced only in its relation to not-Irishness. Finally, if we can understand music as an actor with its own predilections and desires, we might become more open to recognizing the predilections and desires (including the desire for recognition) of other human and nonhuman actors, especially those marked as nonnormative.

ITSELF

The phrase "the music itself" is well established in Irish traditional music, where it stands for more than just the texts of tunes or performance as text (the set of codified and legible embodied practices—sonic and not—labeled "traditional," including bodily gesture and the production of particular timbres and articulations). The particularly Hiberno-English resonances of "itself" in "the music itself" reinforce the idea that music is an actor that should be revered. Adding "self" to "him" or "her" indicates power (and often refers to the master or mistress of a house), even if that power is sometimes acknowledged only grudgingly or if the person referred to as "Himself" or "Herself" has claimed power that is not rightly his or hers. This intensification appears with "itself" in relation to poitín, as in the third verse of "Stick to the Craythur," a song about the delights of drink:

> Through my youthful aggression, and times of depression
> My childhood impression still clung to my mind
> And at school or at college the basis of knowledge
> I never could gulp 'til with whiskey combined
> And as older I'm growing, time's ever bestowin'
> On Erin's potation, a flavor so fine
> And howe'er they may lecture on Jove and his nectar
> Itself is the only true liquid divine.[13]

Applied to either poitín or music, "itself" denotes power, enchantment, and divinity—though it's worth noting that I have never heard anyone refer to trad as "itself," however common the shortened form "the music" might be.

Embedded in the phrase "the music itself" is a range of unspoken understandings about how one embodies "the tradition," because to reach the privileged position of playing or talking about "the music itself" with any authority, one must perform legibly as a traditional player. At the same time, some fear that talking about performance as text risks spoiling the magic: if I attempt to describe how "the music itself" operates, then I might seem to endanger the tradition by revealing the mechanisms we use to decide what counts as Irish traditional music—mechanisms that are routinely obfuscated through attention to "the music itself" as an object rather than an actor. That is not my intention. Instead, I hope to unveil a more exquisite magic by imagining that "the music itself" is a participant with agency—and that orienting oneself toward this conception of agentive sound is the experience of literally coming to one's senses (to echo the Joe Cooley quotation at the beginning of this chapter).

BRINGING US TO OUR SENSES: THE EXPERIENCE OF TRAD FLOW

Why might a musician turn toward trad? One recurring theme resonates with the Ursula Le Guin quotation that opens this chapter: the search for balance, invariably described in binary terms, between the Apollonian drive toward order and the Dionysian urge for release from the pressures of everyday responsibility.

In Irish traditional music, players talk about the hard work of learning tunes and techniques and speak of the pleasures of both exerting and relinquishing control, often in sensual or spiritual ways. Along with an appreciation for the community-focused aspects of the scene, this kind of pleasure seems to attract musicians from all genders, sexualities, ethnicities, and races (indeed, my interlocutors in this section represent a wide range of participants in trad, including heterosexual white men).

Most of my interlocutors do not separate the intellectual, spiritual, musical, and corporeal aspects of playing Irish traditional music, and indeed many talk about control (mainly through discussions of skill or technique) and the relinquishing of control in the same breath. Here, Thomas cites both intricacy and repetition as enticing aspects of trad performance: "My dad took me to [my first session] . . . and I was just . . . swept up in it, you know. It just sounded really meditative and spiritual, but also intellectual in some way—like, it's very intricate, and it takes a bit of skill to do, and . . . because of the repetition of tunes, there was a certain groove that made me feel good!"[14] Jacqueline also uses the concept of meditation to describe the kind of awareness that makes interaction with musical agency possible: "It's . . . like a meditation in some ways. Just noticing things, you know? Where the . . . heart of it is and how you can shift it just a little bit by this one little thing that you do."[15] In understanding trad performance through meditation, Thomas and Jacqueline—who both live in areas of the United States where "mindfulness" is used in common parlance—may be applying a particularly middle-class American framework to their experience of trad.

In connecting skills with repetition and a groove that "made [him] feel good," Thomas unwittingly echoes the conditions that the psychologist Mihaly Csíkszentmihalyi attributes to creating "flow," a state of "optimal experience" characterized by enjoyable concentration in activities that combine high challenge and high skill.[16] Quite a few musicians described flow states when I asked them how it feels when the music is going well. Juniper is the most explicit: "For me, it's this genre of music where I get into a flow state the easiest and the fastest and the most—most deeply. Like, it happens for me in classical, but it takes a lot of work to get there. . . . Sessions are like immediate flow if they're going well."[17] Jacqueline uses the words "floating" and "flowing" and talks about the pleasure of playing trad as an almost out-of-body experience: "When it's going really well, it's completely nonverbal. It's—it's like floating. . . . You're making choices but it's like they're obvious. . . . Things are just flowing out of you, through your fingers and your body—and I think I have moments of looking at it and seeing it and just reveling in it, but I don't think I have that much sense of who I am in that moment, you know? I'm just being."[18] Similarly, Jack describes playing tunes as something that can happen independently from conscious thought, though he also points out that experiences like these most often happen among musicians who know each other well and are at similar levels of proficiency: "You get the tune started and it just comes out of you, and it's like you're not even thinking. Your body is creating it and your mind is somehow shaping it, but it's happening before you can even grasp it. You know what I mean?"[19] Just as musicians sound out tunes in relation to each other and the acoustic space we play in, Jack bounces his description of flow back to me with "You know what I mean?" Perhaps this question is a pause in his train of thought, but perhaps he also seeks to locate his experience in relation to another person's in a way akin to echolocation.

Jack's qualifier about trad flow being more likely in certain company also reminds us that the pleasures of orientation toward "the music itself" are often shared pleasures. Flow tends to be framed as an individual experience, though studies of sports teams and music ensembles address the possibility of collective flow.[20] Stefan describes this kind of collective flow as "merging":

> STEFAN: There is a sense of losing yourself.... There are sometimes unexpected moments of beauty that stick with you, that you end up mythologizing later. When you really merge into the other person's playing—and it feels like it's a single instrument playing. I don't mean in the slavish identical sense.... When it happens, it feels right, it's great. I mean, I've had this happen with not great musicians, either.... It's just if you happen to be in sync, and you have a close enough setting of the tune, but mainly . . . it's all about the rhythm—when you've got the same sense of rhythm and expressing the same kind of phrasing, not necessarily exactly the same phrasing, but the same kind of phrasing, and the sense of—it's like, how would you read a poem. If you both have the same kind of idea of the poem, a harmonically compatible result will happen.
>
> AUTHOR: When I try to describe that feeling to my students, I call it "sharing a brain"—that you start sharing a brain with somebody, and you might not ever have met that person before.
>
> STEFAN: Yeah, and it's super exciting—the sparkles go off.[21]

Not all of my interlocutors framed their comments about community so positively. In a conversation about the extreme intolerance and sexism in her local session in Texas, Anne described her experience of playing trad as a mechanism for compartmentalizing negative social aspects to enjoy positive musical ones:

> The music . . . for me is so utterly different [from thinking about] gender or sexuality. I mean, I'm thinking about things like where's a really good place to put that slur, or where's a great place to put a roll, and how should we do this particular accent—and you know, it's almost like gender and sexuality are on the other side of my brain—I'm not in that side of the brain right now, I'm over here, in the opposite lobe. And it's just free of all that politics and all the power struggle, and just everything that goes along with it. To me, that's how it feels. It's like, okay, we're doing music now—that's what we're doing, and it has nothing to do with the other stuff.[22]

Interactions with other musicians—including social interactions—have the potential to interrupt or prevent flow states as well as to bring them on, and a recurrent theme in most of the interviews I conducted was the importance of choosing one's musical company well. This selectivity may seem obvious, though many trad musicians also tell stories about musically intimate exchanges with musicians they had never met previously.

HUMAN BARRIERS TO FLOW

For women musicians, LGBTQ+ musicians, and musicians of color, however, the potential for *craic*-destroying and flow-preventing interactions because of sexism, heterosexism, and racism is ever present.[23] In theory, flow is a state equally available to all, but in reality, entering that state depends on feeling physically and existentially safe enough to do so. Drawing on interviews with women traddies in Galway, the ethnomusicologist Helen O'Shea articulates the compound problem of male-dominated music scenes embedded in societies that objectify women and examines how this problem diminishes women's musical participation and threatens personal safety: "Because women are rarely session leaders, they are more likely to remain on the fringes of the session, however, where they are at a disadvantage musically (less able to hear, less supported if they lead a tune) and socially ('fair game' for the harassment of male drinkers)."[24]

Ellen describes pubs as enduringly male-dominated and cites her gender and status as a "foreigner" as reasons she sometimes feels uncomfortable in musical settings even though she has lived in rural Ireland for more than a decade:

> I still wouldn't feel 100% comfortable to go into a pub on my own even though I'm only going in for music, and people in the local area know me well enough at this stage, but somehow I feel I have to be brave to do so. And I know a big part of the reason is because I'm a woman. When you look around you in a pub, [the] majority of people are men. Pubs, especially pubs in rural Ireland stay this way in the 21st century! The other fact is probably because I'm foreign. I'm not even from [the] western world, so I suppose I get unnecessary attention at times. It depends on where you are, but it can be quite intense if you're standing in the middle of the floor on your own with your fiddle on your back, in a real local pub in a strange village!![25]

Most of the women musicians and musicians of color I talked to described at least one occasion where some form of gender- or race-based harassment or discrimination occurred, and some musicians (especially those whose identities intersect multiple oppressed categories) cited regular microaggressions and recurrent overt actions. For example, Clara, an Irish-born (and ethnically Irish) musician, discussed choosing to play the fiddle rather than her main instrument, the flute, at local gigs so as to avoid fielding sexually charged comments about a woman playing an instrument with phallic connotations:

> You know, I used to play a Saturday night gig for years .. . . . And less and less I would play the flute as time went on because I'd end up playing the fiddle. . . . And maybe that was the start of me being aware of something funny about the flute and me. . . . I could put money on it, someone was going to make a comment about me playing the flute or playing their flute or some other bloody comment.[26]

The relatively small size of Clara's hometown was no deterrent to harassment—men making suggestive comments was (and continues to be) accepted and, in some circles, embraced. Several women also reported receiving invitations to engage in sexual activities in traditional music contexts, most often—but not always—from punters (audience members) in pubs where sessions were happening.[27]

Local attitudes shape interactions around gender, sexuality, and race in trad settings, especially in places where musicians circulate less frequently and have less experience with the norms of aggregate settings like festivals where musicians from a number of localities congregate. Anne attributes the very closed, male-dominated nature of her scene to local, state, and regional politics:

> Well, Texas is a very [macho] place. For instance, there's this one learning session, and the first time I walked in there, it was so striking because the men were all in the center of the room—they were talking with each other. The women were all on the periphery. The men were not talking to the women. A couple of times I tried to sort of interject something—a little comment here and there—but they kept right on going like I hadn't said a word. And I was just, like, "Okay, this is pretty heavy-handed." And you know, my guess is that they had no idea that they were coming across that way, because it was just so automatic in this state, you know, that the women are in the back seat—the women are off to the side—don't pay them any mind. You know what I mean? ... That's just how you treat women. ... As I come out and identify more with women, then it becomes ever clearer just how much we're relegated to the back seat in this state. And I know it's not like that everywhere else, but here, that's kind of the pervasive attitude.[28]

While it's easy to just blame Texas (or Irish America, or rural Ireland, or a particular age group), displacing (hetero)sexism and racism onto certain people and places erases both the nuances of so-called conservative society and the discrimination that happens in more cosmopolitan spaces.

Reports of negativity toward trans people reinforce this point. My interlocutors have shared antitrans stories from as many so-called progressive locations as conservative ones. An example is an encounter that Frances (a cisgender lesbian) had in an American city generally known for its acceptance of nonnormative genders and sexualities:

> They've always been very welcoming to me. . . . [But one time] we were playing, and they started making some odd comments about trans people, which I felt was inappropriate. . . . And it was kind of out of the blue. And that . . . stuck with me because, you know, I've always felt—as long as I've been out, I've always felt comfortable being with the musicians I play with. And that was the first time that I'd ever been in a trad scene and thought, "Wow—I'm not entirely sure I feel comfortable here."[29]

Although my interlocutors mostly focused on exchanges within a circle of musicians or interactions initiated by listeners, Zeke wrote about commentary among musicians about an audience member in an Irish town with a thriving trad scene: "Most recently, some transphobia in [town]: a 'high ranking' player reacted to the presence of a person (I couldn't surmise what gender or genders the person identified as). Some uncomfortable giggling and use of the term 'he-she.' . . . The person was strikingly dressed in white robes, possibly Tibetan or Thai. [They were] fascinated by the pipes and very engaged in the music."[30]

In my experience, musicians' commentary about punters is so common as to be unremarkable—most of us make comments, and often they are fairly benign ("Wow—check out that sweater!" or "He's in here every week, isn't he?"). Zeke's and Frances's anecdotes represent the bevy of unexamined utterances that establish group norms: that it is acceptable to make lewd comments about a woman punter, stare at the only person of color in what will almost always be a predominantly white space, make gay jokes, and—as in these cases—dehumanize and ridicule trans people. Such norms shape the scene, either through attrition or by preventing interested people from learning the music, even if they are initially "fascinated by the pipes and very engaged in the music," like the listener Zeke described.

Sometimes harassment does not stop at verbal commentary, as shown in this conversation between Grace, an Asian American woman musician, and me. As work in critical race theory has amply demonstrated, oppressions do not operate independently but intersect and accumulate—and therefore, it is not surprising that Grace's space and integrity were invaded to a much greater extent than mine were, or that the perpetrator may have been motivated in part by Grace's perceived exoticism or submissiveness as someone of Asian descent:

> GRACE: I have many #metoo [stories] for Ireland alone, you know, including someone literally sticking their hand down my ass—like, *down* my pants while I was playing a tune.
>
> AUTHOR: That's worse than my ass-grab story!
>
> GRACE: Literally just—straight into my pants! And then I turned around and was, like, "I can't fucking believe that just happened!" Everyone else kept playing, and he was like, "Oh, what are you gonna do, hit me with your bow?" That's what he said to me. And I just sat there, and I was like, "Well, I'm gonna fucking get out of here anyway." And I—I, you know—no one did anything. No one reprimanded him; his friends didn't reprimand him. There was a woman who was just sort of shocked, and she was like, "What didja do that for?" And he was like, "I just wanted to feel—I wanted to see

what her ass felt like." That's what he said! [Sighs forcefully.] . . . I didn't go back to Ireland for, like, ten years.[31]

This conversation demonstrates women's simultaneous familiarity with sexual harassment and disbelief when we encounter it yet again, especially in musical settings. We know sexual harassment and discrimination are always possible—likely, even—but are disappointed anew each time it occurs and nobody confronts it. And the harasser is not always a stranger or a punter—sometimes, as in my own "ass-grab story," the aggressor is well known in the scene and to the person he harasses. The predictable power dynamics between teacher and student may also be amplified for nonnormative musicians or musicians from outside Ireland, whose gender, sexuality, race / ethnicity, and / or nationality can seemingly give license to behaviors that would not be tolerated otherwise.

Grace and I are not the only two traddies who have "ass stories." Rowan, an American transgender male musician, recounts a conversation with a man at the Catskills Irish Arts Week in which his perceived femininity during his transition seemingly offered license for harassment:

> I was looking for my flute workshop, and this guy (who turned out to be in the workshop) came up to me and asked me what my name was. I told him; evidently he decided that [Rowan] was a girl's name, because he said, "Good. I'm glad to know I'm allowed to look at your ass." And the rest of the week he kept calling me by female pronouns, even though my teacher and the rest of my flute class seemed reasonably clear on the point that I was a dude, or at least wanted to be treated like one.[32]

Hearteningly, the other people in Rowan's flute class respected his choice of gender pronouns—and, thus, his right to his own subjectivity.

Thus, musical conditions may be perfect for entering a flow state, but social conditions can consistently prevent certain musicians from enjoying flow. Given the social and musical pleasures of trad, it is not surprising that musicians—especially women and LGBTQ+ musicians and musicians of color—choose our sessions carefully. Both Clara (Irish) and Jacqueline (American) talk about needing to feel comfortable with their fellow musicians to play well and have a satisfying experience. Jacqueline muses about her tendency to keep certain musical company and avoid the kinds of fast sessions sometimes termed "laddish": "I've chosen to hang out with people where there isn't this strong male domination, you know?"³³ Although musicians in areas with larger trad scenes may have more choices about who they play with, those in smaller scenes sometimes find that the only way to find a reliably safe place is to only play at home with friends, as with the group of Galway women musicians that O'Shea discusses, who eventually abandoned pub sessions for the more congenial atmosphere of members' kitchens.³⁴ Over time, interactions like these can lead to disidentification with the trad scene and attrition from it. And unfortunately, it becomes very difficult to track many of those who have left, whether for other genres or for the peace of sessions in private houses.

"THE MUSIC ITSELF," SUBJECTIVITY, AND AFFECT

All the musicians I've quoted in this chapter speak of themselves as actors in the production of musical sound: "you're making choices," "your body is creating it and your mind is somehow shaping it," "I feel that I'm actually expressing myself properly," and so on. If flow in trad is the delicious simultaneity of control and not-control, or pleasant feelings of dissociation created through intense connection and concentration, then these states belong to human musicians. But what if we consider "the music itself" as another actor that might also have agency in asking for a note to be held out, demanding extra attention for a particularly tricky string crossing, or coyly revealing a trapdoor into a similar tune? In arguing that "the music itself" is an active force in trad performance—and in pointing out the pleasure many trad musicians experience through letting the tunes take control—I return to Suzanne Cusick's ecstatic description of playing Bach to which I alluded in chapter 3:

> I love feeling like I'm on top, controlling with skilled hands the articulation of climax because it is at that moment that the music gets away from me, at that moment that *she* is on top in the sense that because of my hands' work *she* has all the power, and I am reduced to rapture by that power's release. . . . Is there a lesbian, as I've defined her, in all this love? For me, yes: for when I play the fourth variation, a great deal of my pleasure derives from the jumbling of who's on top—am I playing "Vom Himmel hoch," or is she playing me? In all performances that give me joy, the answer is unclear—we are both on top, both on our backs, both wholly ourselves and wholly mingled with each other. Power circulates freely across porous boundaries; the categories player and played, lover and beloved, dissolve.³⁵

Cusick's description is familiar. When it's going well, playing trad is when I feel most like myself—and, paradoxically, least bound by the quotidian experience of having to be a self. In this momentary relief from subjectivity, I get to be something that's neither subject nor object, and in that moment, I can best experience playing with (and not merely next to) other musicians and with "the music itself," which also asks for our attention and rewards us when we do some of the many things it likes.

The whole thing falls apart when someone attempts to exert more than momentary control. One player's alpha nature might kick in to try to overpower others (many of us are guilty of this at times)—and in this moment, perhaps that player is trying to impose their idea about what the music likes onto the rest of us. And sometimes the music throws us something we can't handle—funnily, some of us call this "falling off" a tune (though I imagine falling off a moving train when I use this phrase).[36] The whole thing is more interesting and more complex than the simple expression of release that occasionally inspires traddies (almost always male) to invoke comparisons with sex at the finish of a particularly satisfying set of fast reels.

I believe this often worshipful attitude toward a repertoire that consists mostly of sixteen- to thirty-two-measure melodies in a handful of keys derives precisely from the capacity the tunes have for promoting the circulation of power among musicians and between musicians and "the music itself." The seat of this reverence is in performance, not text, and in the absolutely unreplicable relationships between music and musician(s) enacted in each moment of performance. As lived and often deeply felt experience, it also resists entextualization: although we can and do "read" bodies in performance to place people and to learn tunes, styles, and social cues, trad flow happens when our awareness of creating or reading performance as text seems most distant. Here, affect theory—in both its psychological and critical theory guises—is useful in framing some of my musings about what is happening when I feel most connected with the music and my fellow musicians.

Many psychologists and theorists understand affect as an autonomic response.[37] Without getting mired in nature-nurture debates or disagreements about whether or not affect is precognitive, I want to think about the connection between intention and flow in trad performance as dynamic—as neither the absence of intention nor its inexorable result. Mainstream affect theory claims that affective responses (facial expressions, outcries, and so on—"basic emotions," to use Ruth Leys's term) do not result from conscious intention and have no intrinsic connection to our interpretation of their meanings.[38] The cultural studies scholar Eric Shouse helpfully distinguishes among affect, feeling, and emotion: "A feeling is a sensation that has been checked against previous experiences and labelled.... An emotion is the projection / display of a feeling.... An affect is a non-conscious experience of intensity; it is a moment of unformed and unstructured potential."[39] Irish traditional musicians experience all three responses, of course, though I hold that as Shouse defines the terms, the intensity of the affective state—experienced as semiconscious—fuels both the moment of performance and feelings of addiction trad players talk about in relation to the music.[40] In the language of affect theory, the combination of intensity and intention (or perhaps the perceived dampening of intention that embodied skill enables) is what creates the pleasurable feelings musicians associate with trad flow: intensity of experience produces momentary relief from the effort of putting intention into verbal language, even to oneself. Without this intermediate step of verbalization, action feels effortless, magical—and the perception of a mind-body split seems entirely nonsensical in the midst of sensory feedback.

Elisabeth Le Guin marks this lack of "verbal mediation" and introduces the gaze of the audience: "[The amateur chamber music performer] is engaged in an activity that displays his body in its most exquisite capacity for interactive responsiveness, and without verbal mediation. There is potential here—one might suspect a deliberate invitation—for a listener's absorption to become an erotic one."[41] Such potential also exists in Irish traditional music, but unlike the *sensibilité* ("social performances of emotional hyperreactivity") that Le Guin discusses in the context of eighteenth-century France, trad operates on the level of affect and feeling rather than through overt displays of emotion.[42] While tradition-conscious players might occasionally project overt emotion, most are bound by an aesthetics of subtlety that privileges relatively unobtrusive performance choices like changes in bow pressure, the drawing of breath or bellows, or variations that might alter only two or three notes of a melody. Just as often, though, these choices are not entirely about expressing emotion—musicians are playing *with* the tune ("interactive responsiveness") rather than merely playing the tune. In that moment, "the music itself" is another participant in the proceedings, not just the material that allows a performance to proceed.[43]

For the humans sharing this experience, absorption becomes erotic in the Lordean sense—a reminder of our capacities for joy and the "power which comes from sharing deeply any pursuit with another person."[44] Here, the easy move is to personify "the music itself" so that it becomes capable of sharing pursuits as well as power with the humans in the session. If I were to argue for trad's personhood in the moment of performance, I would grant "the music itself" a place at the table rather than taking away its freedom, which Carolyn Abbate suggests overreliance on the gnostic (interpretive) mode does: "Why repay the freedom we are given by putting the gift-giver in a cage, doing so continuously or without regrets, without wondering what this activity may say? Such statements anthropomorphize musical works, making them into living things towards which we must develop an ethical position. They are not, of course, but the way we cope with them may reflect choices about how to cope with real human others or how not to.[45]

Abbate offers an orientation toward human and nonhuman actors alike that promises liberation from the confinements of binary formations like subject and object: if "the music itself" is a living thing, then everyday understandings of subjectivity as available only to human actors are suddenly suspect. If—suddenly—anything might occupy the condition we call "the subject position," then the binary between human and nonhuman becomes nonsensical, just as I argue that it does in the moment of trad flow.[46] By imagining "the music itself" as a participant in musicking, *what* and *who* (to hearken back to chapter 3's discussion of musician as an identity) become hopefully (rather than hopelessly) entwined in ways that expand possibilities rather than foreclose upon them.

In following this line of thinking to dismantle the subject-object binary (easier in theory but much harder in practice), we also take an approach that could structure a unified discipline of music and sound studies that would understand both its human and nonhuman participants in very different ways than do the current disciplines of musicology, music theory, and ethnomusicology. More important for my argument here, though, is that asking musicians to consider how they interact with "the music itself" begs the question of how they interact with other human trad musicians—especially those whose social identities are nonnormative within this very white, very male, and very heterosexual genre. But I resist Abbate's assumption that treating musical works (and, by extension, performance) as agential entities must also anthropomorphize them.

For me, the point is that "the music itself" is most emphatically not human—not just another human character in the cast of the session.[47] If, for example, it is a lover, it is unlike any human lover except in its penchant for giving and (we hope!) receiving pleasure through the circulation of power, embodied action, and sound. If we bind it by the same constraints and motivations as human musicians, "the music itself" becomes mundane—or, unfettered from these constraints and motivations, it becomes godlike, though still anthropomorphized and thus still subject to being understood through the same humanistic framework. Instead, I want to remind us all that "the music itself" is decidedly not human, so that in considering our interactions with it, we must begin to generate new questions—perhaps even strange ones. In imagining how a nonhuman (and possibly inanimate, depending on how we understand "animation") sonic agency might operate, we begin to imagine some questions we have not been asking about Irish traditional music. Which questions have been absent, and what experiences have these absences silenced or even prevented? Chapter 5 addresses some of these questions.

FIVE

Playing Right and the Right to Play

(Dis)identification Tactics Among Queer Musicians and Musicians of Color

Like the preceding chapters, this one begins from the premise that racism, sexism, homophobia, and other forms of exclusion are unacceptable in Irish traditional music. Some readers might ask why a genre tied to Christian whiteness played in societies still organized around reproductive heteropatriarchy should concern itself with race, sexuality, or gender. What, some may ask, does it matter if a predominantly white scene remains so? If, as emcees and cultural politicians and journalists assure us, the tradition is in the safe hands of the overwhelmingly white (and generally male) young musicians who reach prominence in each generation, what does it matter if a few women, LGBTQ+, or nonwhite musicians leave the scene—especially if those practitioners are *not even Irish* to begin with? Must Irish music welcome players who represent something other than the heterosexual and ethnically Irish national ideals that have been in place for centuries?

This chapter takes a postnationalist approach to the genre whose identifying adjective, "Irish," already does not adequately describe current practice and argues that trad's safety in perpetuity lies in its potential to transcend the boundaries of race and nation to reflect Irish cultural values like hospitality or community without requiring particular national or ethnic credentials. I begin by relating some of the challenges that musicians of color and queer and women musicians regularly face in the transnational Irish traditional music scene. Then

I discuss the need for transformation rather than mere assimilation, and I conclude by looking forward to a more equitable trad scene through the words of some of my interlocutors.[1]

INTERPELLATING NATIONAL TRAD SUBJECTS

One of the currents that runs through this book has been an attention to subjectivity, and I have argued in each chapter that recognition is one of the primary actions through which the subject position of "musician" is granted and embodied. By "recognition," I do not mean fame or other accolades. Instead, I mean the iterative process of being seen as a traditional musician, and thereby seeing oneself as a traddie—the sentiment represented by the well-known adage, "*athníonn ciaróg ciaróg eile* (one beetle recognizes another)." However neatly contained in this evocative phrase, the process of recognition is not always simple, clear, or even unreservedly positive. In the first two chapters, I traced instances in which recognition had been bestowed by a musician's contemporaries and then removed by later scholars and musicians, and in chapter 3, I showed the contrast between the recognition of Julia Clifford and that of other women trad musicians of her generation. In this chapter, I mobilize the experiences of queer and nonwhite musicians to expose what Louis Althusser calls "ideological state apparatuses"—ideologies that operate in trad and interpellate some musicians as good subjects and withhold recognition to others.[2] Following the work of José Esteban Muñoz, I then argue that nonnormative trad musicians use tactics of disidentification to "retain the problematic object [here, the trad scene] and tap into the energies that are produced by contradictions and ambivalences."[3] By pointing out these disidentificatory tactics, I hope to show a path toward transformation of the trad scene away from ethnic nationalism and toward the ethics of fairness already embedded in Irish culture and discourse (if not always in everyday life).

Althusser's expansion on Marxist theory holds that the conditions of production are reproduced with the help of both repressive state apparatuses (police, prisons, armies, and so on) and ideological state apparatuses (such as schools, religion, media, and the arts). Unlike the direct coercive action of repressive apparatuses, ideological apparatuses operate through the creation of subjects who both exert agency and are subject to the will of the state. The classic illustration of interpellation is the scenario in which a police officer yells, "Hey, you!" and a person turns. In that moment, the person is recognized as part of an ideological system that grants the police certain kinds of authority and simultaneously recognizes themself as subject to that authority and, by extension, to the ideology that legitimates and enlivens that authority. It is very important to note, however, that when it is working most effectively, interpellation as a way of instilling ideology is extremely decentralized: it relies on the effects of recognition on the subject being recognized.[4] Thus, in Irish traditional music, being interpellated as a good musician suggests that one belongs. Having experienced the feeling of belonging, however provisional, the interpellated musician is then more likely to uphold the rules relating to aesthetics and social practices that got them recognized in the first place. This system of trad interpellation operates within larger state systems—a point that will become important below in this chapter, when I discuss musicians' encounters with immigration officers and other representatives of states.

Applying this concept of interpellation to trad—exploring the process of subject formation through overtly and implicitly transmitted ideologies—helps us understand the belief systems that define the genre and practices of Irish traditional music. These ideologies did not emerge from thin air, and so the substance of this chapter is intricately tied to the ideologies of the Irish nationalist movement of the early twentieth century and to the early days of the Irish Republic that I discuss in the first several chapters of this book, as well as to present-day ideologies. I focus here on trad's position in Ireland and the United States for two reasons: first, most of my interlocutors are from one of these two places. Second, the differences in the enactment of state ideologies provides a meaningful contrast for the musicians I interviewed and also for my larger argument that dissociating Irish traditional music from ethnic nationalism offers a model for social and political transformation in an era characterized by white supremacist and right-wing nationalism. Aesthetics—specifically, the value placed on understatement and certain kinds of silence—provides an excellent place to begin outlining this complicated interplay between individual artistic desire and the ideological and discursive tethering of Irish traditional music to heterosexual reproductive whiteness as reinforced through ethnic nationalism.

AESTHETICS, RECOGNITION, AND FANTASIES OF PASSING

Chapter 4 discusses issues of affect and aesthetics and suggests that "the music itself" might have something to say about these topics. In the human realm, the deep appreciation of understatement in trad—including the actual silences between notes and the metaphorical silence of the unadorned long note—reflects a range of social practices in which almost imperceptible movements, sounds, and utterances convey meaning and affect. A head lifted millimeters from the chin rest of a fiddle signals other musicians to start the next tune; a quiet click of the tongue against the hard palate expresses deep sympathy; and the utterance "Ah, but sure—what can you do?" gives the participants in a conversation the companionability of collectively "offering up" hardship or perhaps just expressing resigned exasperation about a well-meaning but inept session player.[5] In music and dance performance, the subtleties of repertoire choice, phrasing, ornamentation, and variation can reveal a player's personality, influences, and sometimes point of origin to an enculturated listener or viewer.

As a traddie myself, I am torn between my appreciation of the aesthetic of understatement and my dismay at the extended silencing effects it often has on certain voices in a predominantly white, male, and heterosexual genre. My enjoyment of trad's subtleties are reminiscent of the delight that pre-Stonewall queers took in producing and reading the codes that proved their existence even as they offered a modicum of protection in an unfriendly society.[6] I love trad's understatement for what it doesn't have to say out loud and for the range of expression that a single note can convey, as in the high G that I describe Julia Clifford playing in chapter 3. Although Vladimir Jankélévitch writes about Western art music, I quote him here because he articulates the delights of "contained expression" and, more important for my argument, demonstrates the problematic connection between understatement and "quality": "Understatement proves the independence of quality in relation to quantity, and makes manifest, paradoxically, the expressive effectiveness of contained expression: the inexpressive, and a fortiori the least expression, suggest meanings, and do so more powerfully than complete, direct expression."[7] Both Jankélévitch and Irish traditional music discourse thus foreclose nonnormative understandings and practices in connecting the aesthetic of understatement (framed as indirectness) with quality.

When musical aesthetics merge with social practices, understatement becomes dangerously close to "decorum" (invariably understood as white and upwardly mobile) and "blending in" (impossible for people of color in such a white scene, and usually complicated for white women and queer musicians). Such personal understatement may not be possible for people who look, speak, or act significantly different from the norm, however adept they might be at producing aesthetically appropriate sounds or movements.[8] For example, Laoise has recently begun to think about her own orientation toward understatement:

> Now I end up emphasizing "understatement" to prove my place to the people whose opinion matters most to me. . . . [I have] recently start[ed] to question and explore what my dancing would be stripped of striving to prove myself and "belong." [I am] thinking about how I now am embarking on being more embodied and more seen—to make space for others who are not white cishet [cisgendered and heterosexual] men. A different statement. Which maybe depends on 20 years of proving myself and making connections. I have earned the social capital to take a risk on being more visible.[9]

To argue that understatement (or indirectness) is synonymous with quality, as Jankélévitch does here and Irish traddies do everywhere, stealthily joins musical practice with more pervasive cultural imperatives around "not sticking out" that only some bodies can—or wish to—obey. The politics of obeisance is particularly fraught when understatement becomes a de facto closet for nonnormative traddies.

SILENCE AS A MORAL IDEAL

Visibility—and perhaps more to the point, audibility—have been the aims of the civil rights, feminist, and gay liberation movements since the mid-twentieth century, and audibility is at the heart of today's Black Lives Matter, #metoo, and transgender rights movements. I intend this book to eliminate the weight of silence around topics like (hetero)sexism and racism in the Irish traditional music scene that white, heterosexual, and male participants often deem too uncomfortable to discuss—or even irrelevant. The almost mystical power attributed to the space between notes in Irish traditional music aesthetics reinforces an ideal of extramusical silence and understatement and brings us to a path well trod in musicology: can music have meaning? Here, I do not aim to rehash this argument, but I turn briefly to Carolyn Abbate's and Jankélévitch's argument for the primacy of the drastic over the gnostic, since this dynamic also operates in Irish traditional music.[10]

In trad, musicians frequently uphold the drastic (the act of playing) over the gnostic (the interpretation of musical texts, which I expand to include historical commentary and conversation about social context). The practitioner-scholar divide is not as pronounced in trad as it is in Western art music (many trad scholars also play at a high level), and the importance of the drastic is so embedded in the genre that arguing for it would be nonsensical—indeed, one might instead profitably argue for renewed attention to interpretation (albeit in the broader sense that I outline above). Here, though, my purpose is to think through the kind of silencing that the drastic-gnostic binary engenders.

Silence—or rather, the absence of speech about music—figures largely in both Jankélévitch's and Abbate's efforts to make sense of live, unrecorded performance: "Jankélévitch's argument acknowledges music's precious humanity and social reality, not by insisting that musical works trace historical facts or release specific sanctioned cultural associations, but by emphasizing an engagement with music as tantamount to an engagement with the phenomenal world and its inhabitants. For instance, playing or hearing music can produce a state where resisting the flaw of loquaciousness represents a moral ideal, marking human subjects who have been remade in an encounter with an other."[11] Trad's common refrain, "shut up and play" (and the nonverbal version—simply starting a new set of tunes to cut off an overenthusiastic musician who is offering a detailed history of a tune), indexes just such a "moral ideal," and as with other ideals, it may guide, liberate, or constrain. In its wake, we focus again on playing—on the feeling of strings under fingers, the edge of the embouchure hole on the lip, the bag of the pipes firm beneath the elbow. We are reminded that we are here to produce sounds together that alternately hang in space and get lost in the tumble and jumble of heterophony, never quite the same but altogether together. We seek what "the music itself" likes, even though we may never know what it wants. Producing silence through music is a glorious state, and exalting sound lifts up those who produce it.

Except when this silence through music is a gag order. In playing music, we may be engaged with the phenomenal world and its inhabitants, but the "moral ideal" of silence supposes that every player has equal access to musical and verbal speech. Moreover, "shut up and play" may result in sound, but like "don't ask, don't tell" and "thoughts and prayers," it is an utterance that substitutes silence (or another kind of sound that functions as silence) for speech. Though "shut up and play" is not always aimed at those who would start "difficult" conversations about gender, sexuality, or race, the "moral ideal" of silence-as-music in Irish traditional music has had the effect of limiting critical discourse, especially about the experiences of musicians in the scene. As work in sound studies has demonstrated, both sound and silence are tools wielded by the powerful, and the politics of imposing silence can be devastating.[12]

For example, several of my interlocutors talk about the silence of the closet and the implicit and explicit "don't ask, don't tell" messages sent by fellow traddies. Anne, who lives in the American South, describes the "intolerant atmosphere" generated by restrictive state laws.[13] Despite this societal intolerance, she says that she is open about her sexuality everywhere except in her local trad scene, in part because its members have signaled that they are unwilling to accept nonheteronormative players. Kate, a resident of a large city in the Northeast, reenacts the kind of silencing conversation she has experienced around the simple topic of transportation from the pub: "They just—in the words 'my husband is coming to pick me up'—it means nothing. And they don't think that they're saying the thing that if we were saying it, it, like, outs you. And people are, like, 'Why are you mentioning your lover? Why do I have to know that your partner is the same gender as you? Can't you say 'someone' is coming to pick you up?'"[14]

Juniper, the one genderqueer musician I talked to for this project, points out that being correctly gendered isn't the "hill [they are] gonna die on," because it would limit their choice of sessions so greatly.[15] Juniper continues:

> And this is a thing that I appreciate about [my current session leaders], . . . that they don't run it in any sort of authoritarian way. Or like, I don't know, with a sharp edge of masculinity that is sometimes there. They are pretty great, but I've been to sessions where . . . my MO is generally to sit down and shut up, and that [serves] me well . . . because the session leader is a guy who likes power. And that has kind of sucked.[16]

"Sitting down and shutting up" does not provide the promised liberation of the drastic because the feeling of being silenced gets in the way of fully engaging with the music. It also does not allow space for critical conversations about power in traditional music contexts.

PASSING AND / AS DISIDENTIFICATION

This tension around musical understatement and embodied excess (the "too much" of marked bodies against the backdrop of straight white masculinity) emerges in conversations with queer musicians and musicians of color—with the profound difference that white musicians from outside Ireland can speak of choosing, or refusing to try, to pass as Irish (or of Irish descent) through performance practice and social behavior. For example, the sean-nós dancer Laoise describes her notably traditional dance style as partly an attempt to minimize the difference her queer American body presents in the west of Ireland. Indeed, my decision to dig deeply into the Sliabh Luachra style and repertoire came from a desire to be taken seriously despite my decidedly un-Irish surname, as well as from my identification with the style's sounds and rhythms. Muñoz locates passing as a tactic of disidentification: "Passing is often not about bold-faced opposition to a dominant paradigm or a wholesale selling out to that form. Like disidentification itself, passing can be a third modality where a dominant structure is co-opted, worked on and against. The subject who passes can be simultaneously identifying with and rejecting a dominant form."[17]

Indeed, some musicians who come closer to passing through their performance practice do work on and against dominant structures. For example, Laoise uses her respected position in her local scene and her white privilege to begin conversations about race in trad by wearing Black Lives Matter T-shirts to Irish cultural events in the Pacific Northwest.[18] In trad, however, the stakes for passing as Irish are much lower than they are for the kinds of race and gender passing that Muñoz describes. Elsewhere, authors have framed the incorporation of non-Irish musicians into the genre through the concept of affinity, but I maintain that using passing and disidentification in this context helps us understand some of the dynamics that drive ethnic nationalism and calls the racialized, gendered, and sexed assumptions of seemingly neutral terms like "affinity" into question.[19]

Here, it is helpful to distinguish among identification, counteridentification, and disidentification. When we identify with something, we accept it as right and natural and incorporate it into our sense of self. Counteridentification, in contrast, is the refusal to identify with one set of ideologies and practices (often socially dominant ones) in favor of opposing ones. And disidentification, Muñoz writes, is "a way of negotiat[ing] a phobic majoritarian public sphere that constantly elides or punishes the existence of subjects who do not conform to the phantasm of normative citizenship."[20] While I acknowledge that the risks for queer people of color are infinitely higher than they are for white queer people, I believe that passing and disidentification are tactics that white musicians also use, and thinking about how they operate can give clues about how to dismantle racist and (hetero)sexist paradigms in the Irish music scene and beyond. For example, participation in trad (which is a subculture even in Ireland) can be an act of counteridentification or disidentification from normative citizenship, whether one is Irish, American, Japanese, or something else.[21] Anecdotally, for some white American musicians, seeking to pass as Irish seems to be a counteridentification with being American—a disavowal of American exceptionalism and cultural imperialism. Combined with a selective identification with aspects of Irish culture (including values like hospitality and community mindedness) and disidentificatory ambivalence about other aspects (like gossip and social conservatism), this complicated interplay of identifications, counteridentifications, and disidentifications demonstrates the constructed nature of national (and racial and gender) identification.

Passing is always a performance with an audience, and here, successful passing brings recognition that an outsider has become an honorary Irish person—or perhaps that they cease to be not-Irish, even if they have not exactly become Irish. This not-not-Irishness is a result of the repetition of musical, social, and sometimes sartorial behaviors, and it is generally much more readily available to people who look Irish and have attributes (gender, sexuality, complexion, and so on) that match accepted norms. The parameters of passing in the trad scene include musical style, repertoire choice, and social connections, so a wider variety of people might gain acceptance there than can manage to successfully pass as Irish on the street. It is important to note, however, that acceptance and passing are not synonymous. No matter how successful a nonwhite person's performance of Irish mannerisms and musical style is, visual difference will be a barrier as long as Irishness and whiteness are inextricably linked, and as long as ethnically non-Irish citizens of Ireland are not recognized as legitimately Irish by the country's ethnically Irish citizens and members of the diaspora.[22] The fallacy of ethnic nationalism is all the more apparent when passing results in a change of status.

THE THREAT OF MUSICAL BLACKNESS (AND QUEERNESS)

But what about musicians who do not identify with the aesthetic of understatement and who choose not to attempt sonic or embodied passing? The conscious choice of musical excess is one form of refusal that is often enacted through a combination of performance practice and repertoire choice (including the performance of newly composed tunes), as well as participation in fusion projects that connect elements of trad with other genres. More conservative members of the Irish traditional scene, as well as many of the institutions that support trad, are quick to distinguish these players and their music from the core of the tradition. Though sometimes presented as neutral aesthetic judgments, these distinctions often reflect anxieties about ethnicity / race, gender, and sexuality.

Here, I focus on race and, to a lesser extent, sexuality, but I point readers to chapter 2's exposition of the connection between gender and classical music, with its connotations of effeminacy.

Laoise and I have chosen more traditional performance styles in part to attempt to pass. Zeke, however, articulates his sartorial and musical choices as a conscious choice to not blend in, despite the silencing effects of the trad scene's "don't ask, don't tell" mentality: "A prominent [musician]—a prim and proper sort, raised Catholic—would sometimes compare my hair to Oscar Wilde's and wink. We have never once discussed things. I believe she is uncomfortable with the gay issue but accepting—at the very, very least, on the 'hate [the] sin, not [the] sinner' path."[23] Michel Foucault, of course, would say that the proliferation of discourse around not talking about sexuality exposes a foundational concern with it.[24] Zeke identifies his aesthetic choices as acts of "defiance": "There's a certain musical defiance that colors my persona in the trad community. It's an 'outsider' thing. Gay, Italian, adult-learner-of-the-tunes; I study good old music but I dig in, rail it up, add harmonies. . . . Being a gay man does somehow license—at least in my generational paradigm—a guy to be more unabashedly expressive than the prototypical single-syllable straight dude."[25] Here, Zeke mobilizes stereotypes to explain his choice to express himself musically in ways that are typically not considered traditional, particularly the addition of harmonies. Unlike other gay traddies, who cite their disidentification with stereotypically gay modes of presentation like camp and flamboyance as reasons they identify with Irish traditional music, Zeke embraces the challenge to heterosexual masculinity that "unabashed express[ion]" presents.

Perhaps because blackness poses a greater threat to normative white Irish (and diasporic Irish) identities, the aesthetics Zeke identifies as gay are more often racialized in trad. These racial anxieties have been embedded in Irish culture and in rationales for ethnic nationalism and self-determination in Ireland since at least the nineteenth century. British discourses of race assigned colonized peoples to subordinate positions and portrayed Irish people (especially men) as apes, in cartoons and elsewhere.

The history of Irishness as a flawed, not-quite-white category in comparison with so-called Anglo-Saxon whiteness in Britain and the United States helps explain Irish (and especially Irish diasporic) anxieties around race, even if it does not excuse them. Likewise, the discrimination Irish immigrants faced in the United States in the nineteenth and early twentieth centuries proved a powerful

FIGURE 5.1 "A Great Time For Ireland!" *Punch*, 14 December 1861.
Used by permission of Punch Cartoon Library/TopFoto.

motivator for distancing Irishness from blackness in ways that included aligning with proslavery groups before the US Civil War.[26] And in the early twenty-first century, unsubstantiated white supremacist claims that the Irish were enslaved attempt to mobilize histories of anti-Irish discrimination and economic hardship to deny the existence of institutionalized antiblack racism in the United States. The popular argument goes something like this: How can the Irish (and Irish

Americans, and so on) possibly be racist when we faced so many centuries of hardship at the hands of colonial and imperialist powers ourselves?

But racism is unavoidably embedded in the discourses and aesthetics of Irish traditional music, especially in its use of the adjective "jazzy" to denigrate nontraditional performance styles. More complicated is the use of "soul" in the African American sense to describe Irish musics. The term is most frequently heard from Irish people, but one of my African American interlocutors, Missy, also cited trad's "soul" as one of the reasons she was drawn to the Irish song tradition.[27] Nevertheless, claims that the Irish are the "blacks of Europe" in *The Commitments* and elsewhere frame Irish economic struggles through metaphorical blackness in ways that obscure racism in Ireland (including anti-Traveller racism) and decenter the contexts and concerns of transnational black cultural forms like jazz and soul, as well as the musical lives of migrants from sub-Saharan Africa.[28]

Of all foreign musical genres, jazz has long been targeted as the source of a host of threats to nationalist Catholic morality in Ireland and, by extension, to Irish traditional music in its role as an instrument of cultural nationalism. These threats can all be traced back to anxieties about cultural contamination and sexuality, and thus to race through jazz's roots in African American culture and long-standing stereotypes of sexualized black bodies—especially dancing or musicking bodies. Irish responses to jazz have included legislation like the Public Dance Halls Act of 1935, which was designed to shield Ireland's youth from the ostensible dangers of premarital sex even as it regulated dance halls in the interest of capitalist endeavor. Although a modified version of the act remains on the books and jazz performance has entered the Irish mainstream, jazz—or rather, "jazz"—continues to function as shorthand for trad performance that falls outside the parameters of what is considered traditional practice.

The sounds that get called "too jazzy" in trad bear very little resemblance to actual jazz. Instead, "jazzy" is an adjective used to neutralize perceived threats to both traditional performance practice and the ideal of trad as an embodied expression of Irishness unmarked by diasporic, gender, sexual, or ethnic / racial difference. "Jazzy" sounds are often produced by bodies that are outside the ideal of Irish nationalism—often second-generation performers raised in the cities of Britain and the United States and / or women, queer, or nonwhite musicians. This connection between idealized Irish whiteness and sounds implicitly labeled "black" is one tactic used in policing ethnicity, sexuality, gender, and race as demonstrated in the sonic breach of so-called traditional sounds, even though the players called jazzy are usually white. Other kinds of gatekeeping happen even more intensely when nonwhite players enter the picture.

"HOW DID *YOU* GET INTO THIS?": THE AGGRESSION OF DISBELIEF

As I demonstrated in the early chapters of this book, women musicians have not always been granted equal access to educational and performance opportunities in Irish traditional music, and assessments of style and traditionality derive in part from nonmusical attributes like gender and perceived social class. Furthermore, disbelief about the possibility that women traditional musicians of the past were publicly active has resulted in their disappearance from the historical record in Irish music scholarship. Similarly, disbelief in the presence of queer musicians has reinforced the perception that heteronormative traddies need not concern themselves about homophobia within the scene. But nowhere is this issue more pronounced than in the experiences and reception of musicians of color, where manifestations of majoritarian gatekeeping can adversely affect nonnormative musicians by withholding access to trad contexts and denying recognition of their place as legitimate participants in Irish traditional music.[29]

On the surface, trad is an extraordinarily accessible genre: several of its common instruments are widely available, and participating on a basic level does not require years of practice or musical literacy. With the advent of the internet, the establishment of undergraduate and graduate programs in Irish traditional music, and the proliferation of festivals and camps around the world, tunes and tuition are more available than ever before. Online forums provide opportunities for communication with other aficionados, and many Irish traditional musicians are active on social media. Sessions abound in Ireland, Britain, the United States, Canada, Australia, Germany, France, Japan, and elsewhere, yet the scene remains close-knit enough to maintain a strong transnational sense of community. While financial concerns and work and home obligations limit some musicians' activities, and trad participation both inside and outside Ireland tends to be a middle-class pastime, it is still possible to be part of a trad scene without extensive means.

But despite the seeming openness of the trad scene, access is not guaranteed or easy for everyone. Earlier chapters described the difficulties women in Ireland and its diasporic enclaves have historically faced in entering pubs, and chapter 4 discussed sexual harassment in musical contexts as an enduring problem for women and queer musicians who play trad. Women of all colors are also disproportionately affected by safety concerns related to getting to and from music venues in a variety of locations, and musicians of color (especially black musicians) report additional barriers to accessing the overwhelmingly white spaces where trad happens. Subject to institutionalized and structural racism in their points of origin—whether in Ireland, Britain, the United States, or elsewhere—musicians of color must also navigate the additive effects of different and differently enacted racisms in the transnational scene. For example, white Australians bring their feelings about Aboriginal people to bear on their encounters with African Americans in the trad scene, while South Africans experience racial difference through apartheid and postapartheid politics, and fears of Asian economic domination and memories of US military involvements feed some Americans' anti-Asian racism.

Whatever the cultural circumstances, these racisms all contribute to a mentality in the trad scene that sees "white" as "us" and "not white" as "not us." White musicians are thus understood as Irish or of Irish descent until proved otherwise (and sometimes even if proved otherwise) while musicians of color are not, whatever the realities of each person's genetic heritage.[30] For white musicians from outside Ireland, Irishness can be slippery, claimed by descent but often presumed based on musical style and associations. For example, people in the trad scene tend to assume that my mother must be Irish or Irish American, and the Irishness of white, nonethnically Irish women who take their husbands' Irish surnames generally goes unquestioned. This set of "presumed Irish" judgments, which benefit white musicians tremendously in smoothing social relationships and getting gigs, are never bestowed on musicians whose racial difference is visible. For musicians of color with Irish heritage, claiming Irish ethnicity in public can feel like acquiescing to the racist assumption that a musician must have a direct genetic connection with Ireland to play "right" or even to have the right to play, as Henry, an Asian American musician, points out: "I will say to people often that my mother's Irish [American]—sometimes just to defuse the conversation, because I just don't want to have it. Sometimes just to see, like, what's the reaction going to be? Like, 'oh, okay! That suddenly now makes sense—so you play Irish music!'"[31] The intelligibility that results from pointing out Irish heritage demonstrates the extent to which whiteness, perceived musical ability, and one's right to musical and sonic space are enmeshed.

But emphasizing the existence of an Irish parent to avoid being silenced musically (literally or rhetorically) can do epistemic and ontological damage.[32] By inviting others to see one as part white, one's experience of living in the world and in the trad scene as a person of mixed race is rendered either unspeakable or the topic of speculation, as is shown in this conversation between the American fiddler and singer Rhiannon Giddens, winner of a MacArthur Foundation fellowship, and Renee Montagne, a reporter for National Public Radio:

> Montagne: Well, I know you've recorded songs in Gaelic. Is that in your tradition? I mean, your name Rhiannon is a Welsh name from mythology.
> Giddens: Yeah, my mother was reading the *Mabinogion*, the Welsh mythological epic, when I was born . . . and decided to name me Rhiannon. That definitely got me interested in sort of Celtic culture and stuff, but, you know, that whole idea of, "Is it my culture?" It gets asked of me in a way that white people who do blues don't get asked.
> Montagne: I actually thought it might be actually your culture—there might be a connection.
> Giddens: Well, that's the thing. Whether I am or not, like, that's my point. . . . I don't know all of my genealogy, but my point is that if music speaks to you, I think that you have the ability to do that.[33]

Giddens gently points out the inequity inherent in asking nonwhite musicians about their "cultural" (read: genetic) connections to a genre when white musicians are not subject to the same kind of questioning. Moreover, although there are many reasons a person might not be able to trace their genealogy, white listeners are obliged to remember that enslavement and the sexual violence of oppression often result in gaps in genealogical knowledge and / or complicated identifications with genetic heritage. But trad's connection with ethnic nationalism implicitly suggests that nonethnically Irish musicians should disidentify with part or all of their family heritage to identify with the genre.

Given trad's appeal to listeners of many backgrounds, it may surprise some readers that nonwhite musicians are constantly asked to explain their presence in ways that range from curious to hostile. Every single nonwhite musician I interviewed talked about the predictable and incessant expressions of disbelief they face from new people: "How did *you* get into this?" Missy, an African American fiddle player who now focuses on other genres, emphasizes the inevitability of the question, which she attributes to curiosity: "Playing [Irish] music was always interesting—no matter where I was, eventually somebody would ask me, 'What's a black girl like you doing playing this music?' And, like, okay, I could be offended, but I'm not gonna be, because I know you really just want to know [laughs]."[34]

Playing Right and the Right to Play **167**

Other traddies of color experience this question as microaggression because it feels inescapable, a constant reminder that some see trad as the property of ethnically Irish people. Henry talks about a live radio spot he did with one of his bands when the host voiced this kind of race-based disbelief: "It was myself and . . . three clearly white guys, but none of them Irish, either. But [the host] did the whole thing of—'I know why *you* three guys [play trad]—but why do *you* play Irish music?' and like, you're on the air, and so it [was] that particular kind of infuriating."[35] However harmless such questions might seem to the person asking them, they expose the essentialist fantasy that only certain bodies might be able to produce appropriate sounds and social behaviors. Sometimes race policing happens in more menacing ways. For example, Henry was confronted by an Irish American listener who asked, "What gives you the right to play *our* music?" And a group of skinheads wrote his band (which included Henry and a Jewish musician) a menacing "cease and desist" note at a gig in the Pacific Northwest.[36]

This belief that music and dance are expressions of genetic heritage might seem harmless when audience members ask white musicians about their family backgrounds, but it represents a dangerous illogic that drives white supremacy—the idea that skin color, religion, sexuality, and other aspects of identity determine one's abilities and aptitudes and, thus, one's humanity. Disbelief (as opposed to curiosity) that a non-Irish person might be a skilled trad musician can masquerade as a more socially acceptable form of this kind of racism, which emerges more overtly in the African American fiddler Esmi's story about searching for a teacher in a large metropolitan area in the United States with a vibrant trad scene:

> There are just people who have prejudices. So, let's take an Irish person who comes to [the US] who's a marvelous musician—like, he has prejudices. He starts . . . teaching a lot of students, and he passes on his prejudices and says, "There are certain people who cannot learn this music, and there are certain people who can." And he begins to share his music with the people who he feels he can share it with, and he won't share it with others. So those students take those ideas with them to the session.[37]

Despite a great deal of effort, Esmi never found a local teacher willing to take her on as a student. She was driven and lucky enough to be able to address this problem in part by attending classes at festivals elsewhere in the United States and by going to Ireland—solutions that require resources and time. And like other musicians of color, she reports a warmer reception among musicians in Ireland than she has experienced at home.

Traddies of East Asian descent face essentialist discrimination when others assert that where they belong is in classical music. As with other manifestations of racism, external factors drive this presumption: in addition to widespread education in Western art music worldwide, the West has long fetishized Asian bodies—especially women's bodies—in its consumption of virtuosic classical performance. Grace, an Asian American musician, connects gender and ethnicity in describing her experience in the trad scene:

> One of the most depressing things about Irish music to me is, like, you go to these things, and it's 99 percent white people, and . . . they treat me like I'm a cute little girl—"Oh, your feet! It looks like you're a dancer!" . . . And then it's always, "How did you get involved in blah blah blah blah blah." You know, I get it, because--you never would've said that if I was playing Beethoven, for some reason. Like, you never would have said that, because Midori happened.[38]

Grace is an established performer with decades of experience as a professional musician, and to her chagrin, being perceived as "cute" (complete with this stereotypical and creepy attention to her feet) generates approval at the cost of being taken seriously.

Henry turns the stereotype of the Asian classical musician around to express wonder at the universalism attached to Western art music and the particularity ascribed to Western vernacular musics when he asks, "Do people ask Yo-Yo Ma why he plays Italian music, or German music? Would they ever ask that? Like, what is it about Irish music that makes it so race-based?"[39] This double critique reminds us that the roots of art music in Western imperialism are deep, and that the importance of nationalist sentiment in musics from Europe's fringes (including the music of composers like Jean Sibelius and Antonín Dvořák) is a result of imperialist power relationships that continue to shape music performance, composition, reception, and scholarship. The assumption that musicians of Asian descent must be classical musicians also obscures the imperialism that brought Western art music to Japan, China, Korea, and elsewhere and continues to complicate the position of scholars of non-Western composers of "Western" music.[40] Indeed, if childhood exposure to Irish, Scottish, and English folk melodies grants any legitimacy as an Irish traditional musician, Japanese musicians have as valid a claim to this familiarity as many white traddies, since songs like "Believe Me If All These Endearing Young Charms" and "Auld Lang Syne" were incorporated into standardized music education during the Meiji period in the late nineteenth and early twentieth centuries.[41]

Disbelief that nonwhite people might be passionate and valued members of traditional music scenes in Ireland and elsewhere does material as well as epistemic and ontological damage to both nonnormative musicians and the scene more generally. Althusser's concept of interpellation provides a useful framework for thinking about recognition as an external force that can enable or prevent access to the scene. The African American fiddler Esmi and I both have had encounters with Irish police and immigration officials, and the contrast between our experiences demonstrates how racism operates in determinations of who can and cannot be a traddie—how local and national attitudes toward race threaten access, create material hardship, and ultimately jeopardize individual subjectivity, since—as I argued in my discussion of Julia Clifford in chapter 3—traditional musicians are often *who*, rather than merely *what*, we are.

By now, the excessive policing of nonwhite (and especially black) bodies in white spaces is well established, and ease of access is not a given in the predominantly white spaces where sessions and concerts are usually held in majority-white countries. Esmi, who grew up in an affluent white neighborhood in the United States and attended schools where she was the only black student, experienced frequent and intrusive police attention. She describes encounters with police officers who assumed that she was an interloper in her own neighborhood—someone who, even as a child and teenager, ostensibly posed a threat to the white residents of her town for such nefarious activities as riding her bike and waiting for the bus. In contrast, she finds the Irish Gardaí much more subtle: even though she says she knows she is being watched, Irish municipal police rarely approach her in subjectivity-damaging ways.

Gaining entry into Ireland has not been easy for Esmi, however—even after she had been accepted into a graduate music program in Ireland. Her way of telling the story demonstrates how an immigration officer's blatant refusal to recognize her as a musician and a human struck a deep blow to her senses of bodily integrity and personhood:

> I got accepted, and had all my paperwork—I had all my banking statements, and . . . I put it all in a big folder, and I got on a plane, and I landed [in Ireland]. The [immigration officer] asked me, "So, what are you here for?" and I said, "Well, I've been accepted to university," and he just said, "I don't believe you." And I literally started trembling, and my mouth started watering. Like, the lights all started to go out. And he said, "Go sit over there." And I sat there until every single plane landed that day before he came over—or anyone came

over—and assisted me. And then he said, "I need all your paperwork." So I was just fortunate enough that I even had it stuffed in my violin case pocket—that it wasn't in my suitcase. Because I'm telling you—he would have sent me home. And . . . he went through every single paper. I sat there for an hour . . . and then he came back and started asking me questions: "So you play Irish music?" He said he was a flute player, and he would be watching me. He would be watching me. Yeah. And so he stamped my passport that I had to leave the country four days after the last class—four days. I had four days to leave the country after the course ended.[42]

Already undone by having been interpellated as an illegitimate presence in Ireland by an agent of the state, Esmi's subjectivity as a traditional musician was even more devastatingly undone when the immigration officer identified himself as a flute player. The immigration officer's disbelief in the legitimacy of a black woman playing fiddle at a high enough level to be admitted to an Irish graduate program was enough for him to choose to use his power to change the routine procedure of issuing a student visa to cut Esmi's stay in Ireland from the standard two years she was entitled to under the law to one year and eleven days.[43] Esmi left Ireland at the end of her course and returned at considerable expense to attend her graduation—but not before additional soul-, time-, and money-consuming abuse at the hands of another immigration officer, who said, "You expect me to believe that you're here for graduation?" Understandably, Esmi experienced this interpellation as a "bad subject" as another physical assault: "I'm telling you, it was like a complete loss of blood—everything in my body was draining out of me. And I couldn't even speak, it was just such a desperate experience."[44]

My own immigration story is very different. While my student visa for a course of similar length was issued before the imposition of time limits on student visas in 2010, I was treated cordially and granted a stay several months longer than the duration of the course "to sightsee," according to the immigration officer who processed my paperwork at the same airport where Esmi was later denied the time she was legally entitled to. During my official check-ins with the immigration office in the same city where Esmi was in school, officials overtly hailed me as a fellow white person in their diatribes against the Nigerian clients in the waiting room. This privilege meant that my visits to the immigration office were brief and uncomplicated, however uncomfortable I was as a young foreign student who did not feel able to speak up on behalf of my African counterparts. This kind of race-based interpellation (made even easier by my vaguely Scots-Irish appearance) has benefited me in countless ways, and despite occasional quizzings by cranky immigration officers, I have never doubted that I would be admitted to Ireland. Esmi's run-ins with these immigration officers, however, have resulted in "limited entry" stamps in her passport that she worries may jeopardize her admittance to other countries.

WHY ASSIMILATE WHEN YOU CAN TRANSFORM?

The question of assimilation is central to this chapter: interpellation is a process designed to inculcate ideologies and create "good subjects" who follow the rules of the state apparatus. As these stories from musicians of color demonstrate, access to trad contexts—whether finding a teacher in the diaspora, gaining admittance to Ireland, or simply having one's right to play trad taken as a given—depends on being interpellated as a "good subject," someone deemed an appropriate player of this music. Thus, recognition as a traddie can depend on skin color and other factors that uphold essentialist understandings of Irishness. Once in a trad setting—assuming one has been granted entry—appropriate aesthetic and social behaviors can bring a form of recognition that seeks to assimilate those who are recognized. And sometimes that is exactly what we want—the embrace of belonging.

But some musicians find that the costs of assimilation are far too great and resist interpellation where once they might have welcomed the feelings of belonging and approval that recognition as a good subject can bring. Grace articulates these costs as a burden carried by her female Asian body:

> In my younger days, first getting out into the world, my interface was Irish music. And it was mainly a white society I was dealing with, and I was only there because I loved the music. I actually did not like being around so much whiteness, but I was just being a musician, you know. And it's one of those things that carries a lot of weight, and you don't really realize that you're under all of that weight until you get out, and then you're like, "God, this is so much better!" [Laughs.] And then everything changes—your colleagues change—like, how much you can relate to your colleagues changes, and how much you can relate to your audience changes.[45]

Grace voices the reason most people—especially non-Irish people—get into trad: "I was only there because I loved the music." Love of the music is powerful indeed, and many of us talk about "the music itself" as a beloved and a source of never-ending awe. But part of this lovely discourse are sentiments like "all you need is love" and "love conquers all," which are just as problematic in trad as they are elsewhere—if indeed there *is* an elsewhere: after all, a remarkable number of heterosexual trad musicians find romance within the scene, although queer traddies sigh wistfully about the nigh impossibility of finding another queer traddie to date. The specter of miscegenation also looms for nonwhite traddies: one of my interlocutors was asked how a guy with a name like his wound up with a "nice Irish girl," and another was asked if interracial dating was even legal.

Thus, exclamations like "All that matters is the music!" cloak social practices within exhortations to attend to the sounds of "the music itself," effectively shutting down conversation about those same social practices. With statements like these in play, the problem is framed as a flaw in the individual for whom love of the tunes may not conquer all. Moreover, the tactics of disidentification and passing that some musicians of color, queer traddies, and women musicians use to navigate the scene may mask intolerance and discrimination when it occurs: calling attention to a group's problems is not a recommended way to assimilate into it. But as my interlocutors attest, the Irish traditional music scene does have problems, and we do not know who has left the scene because its benefits were not great enough to offset recurrent instances of racism, sexism, or heterosexism.[46]

The majority of normative Irish traditional musicians may not find their experiences represented in these pages. A heterosexual white male traddie reading this volume may feel dismay that women, queer musicians and musicians of color have negative experiences and may assert that these experiences must be outliers—that the people who have talked about negative experiences have just been unlucky, because this is not the trad scene the reader knows, in which musicians are judged solely on their playing abilities and whether they are good company. While I reassure such readers that most of the nonnormative musicians I have talked to describe wonderful, warm, inspiring relationships within the trad scene and to "the music itself," and that they say the benefits far outweigh the problems, I implore readers not to minimize the problems we describe or chalk them up to the disaffections of a group of mostly non-Irish outsiders. These problems will remain as long as the members of the scene with the most power continue to claim that discrimination occurs only on the fringes of the scene—when, for example, the socially and politically conservative leadership of Comhaltas Ceoltóirí Éireann undercuts broader Irish rhetorics of fairness in upholding the premises around race, gender, and reproductive sexuality that inform ethnic nationalism.[47]

FORWARD

> Some will say that all we have are the pleasures of this moment, but we must never settle for that minimal transport; we must dream and enact new and better pleasures, other ways of being in the world, and ultimately new worlds. Queerness is a longing that propels us onward, beyond romances of the negative and toiling in the present. Queerness is that thing that lets us feel that this world is not enough, that indeed something is missing.
>
> José Esteban Muñoz, Cruising Utopia

I conclude this book by looking toward a future where today's pleasures of trad make space for "new and better pleasures"—the joys of a postnationalist genre built upon community and the shared love of the sounds we will probably always call "Irish," but without the limitations of static, essentialized identity, whether that is ethnic, gendered, sexed, or otherwise. It is fitting that I conclude by pointing toward the idea of futurity or utopia, because if we're not working toward better futures, then what are we doing? In many of my conversations with nonnormative traddies, my final question was about outcomes—what, in a perfect world, do you hope might be the result of a study like this? Most expressed the desire to see one's own identities more widely represented in the scene and to help younger women musicians, queer musicians, and musicians of color feel more like they belong in the scene.

Almost all the queer musicians and musicians of color I talked to mentioned the homogeneity of the Irish trad scene within and outside Ireland and expressed an interest in coalition building with other nonnormative traddies. While many were quick to talk about the overall warmth of trad communities, most also talked about feeling isolated and yearning for more contact with fellow queer musicians or musicians of color. For example, Anne—a lesbian who experiences her local scene as both sexist and homophobic—says, "I would love to connect with whoever else is out there for support and just . . . to know that I'm not the only person, because it definitely feels very isolated where I'm sitting."[48] Similarly, Theo talks about the loneliness of being "the only one" despite having grown up in a large city: "When I was playing around a lot and being gay, I was the only one, and I kind of felt like I was in pretty much total isolation."[49] Several musicians wished that the LGBTQ+ population in Irish traditional music was large enough to constitute a functional dating pool—in part because trad is a subculture that often operates around couples, and participation in it can be time- and energy-consuming enough that maintaining relationships with "civilians" can be challenging. Increased visibility is one way of addressing these gaps, although it requires enough mainstream acceptance to ensure individuals' safety.

For obviously nonwhite traddies and women, visibility presents other kinds of issues and leads to the desire to be seen as oneself, not merely as a representative of a category homogenized by the assumptions of dominant white and / or male society. This set of issues relates to my discussion in chapter 3 about the importance of being seen as a musician as well as a marginalized person, and as in the case of Julia Clifford, this form of recognition plays out in different ways for different musicians.[50] For example, Henry feels that musicians in Ireland relate to him as a musician first—a reversal he finds relieving after confronting racism at home in the United States:

> My experience in Ireland has been . . . one of the things that I've grown to sort of need now once a year—not for some weird spiritual journey, or, like, some ethereal mystic "woo." But I need to go play music with people who don't give a shit who you are, what your name is, that you are a brown person. At least, that's been my experience—like, I haven't had to deal with that in Ireland. And yet [who] still play at a really high level, you know. It's in North America where I've had all the problems in the world.[51]

For Henry, positive action would include "any step towards bringing down the idea of Irish music being inherently attached to Irishness."[52] While Esmi's experiences as a black woman have been more mixed, she describes a similar feeling of acceptance while playing music in some circles in Ireland.[53]

Ellen, a musician of color who has lived in Ireland for over a decade, tells a story that suggests that the seeming embrace of foreign musicians in Ireland may have as much to do with upholding an Irish self-image of tolerance as it does welcoming individual musicians:[54]

> People love seeing and having foreign people in the Irish music scene. They love it, they feel good with themselves, and it makes them proud. Some people get excited and treat you well. They tell you that you're a brilliant fiddle player. Even though you know you're not in the same league as the other Irish lot, they still tell you that you're brilliant! This often bothers me. To me, it sounds like [they're saying], "You're brilliant [for] playing our music even though you're

a foreigner." I don't find it genuine, and it makes me tired listening to them sometimes. Discrimination is far too strong a word for it, but they certainly don't treat you as if you're from Ireland![55]

While she is quick to point out that living and playing music in Ireland is her "perfect world," Ellen identifies the negative effects of positive attention, including being praised for musicianship that would go without remark if she were Irish. Being recognized as "good for a foreigner" acknowledges the hard work and time a non-Irish musician has put in to learn skills and repertoire—but it also reinforces a hierarchy based on the myth of inborn ethnic talent. This sort of tokenistic "A for effort" praise can also perpetuate the infantilization of women and / or nonwhite players.

Being seen and heard for oneself is vital—for one's individuality, musicality, and place in the larger community, as well as for the shared flaws of humanity. Theo muses about his younger self in existential terms that echo the quotation from Judith Butler about recognition at the end of chapter 1: "I think it would be interesting if there were an awareness that gay people exist in Irish music . . . maybe an awareness that I existed at that time would be—I don't know, I don't know—it's hard to put into words."[56] Theo's difficulty putting this thought into words demonstrates the confusion and loneliness of not seeing one's subjectivity mirrored back—it is like calling out into a canyon without getting an echo in response. Several queer musicians and dancers talked about feeling out of place both as queer in the trad scene and a traddie in queer scenes—both positions suggest impossibility based on group norms, as does the experience of being a person of color in an overwhelmingly white music scene (a feeling reinforced by the expressions of disbelief I discussed above in this chapter).

And in a genre that concerns itself tremendously with generational continuity, many of the women, queer musicians, and musicians of color I interviewed expressed hopes that attention to racism and (hetero)sexism in Irish traditional music would help smooth the path for younger musicians in the scene. Many are also working to help effect change. For example, Clara mentors young Irish women traddies: "I have a few good flute players that come to me. Girls—and I think that's something that's been happening in the last couple of years, that they're more inclined [to] travel over to me once a month maybe from somewhere else because I'm a girl [laughs]. And I give them stuff, and seeing them develop and actually beginning to start to develop their own style . . . it's also very rewarding when you see that happening."[57] She also has been working on scholarship about women flute players and spreading the word about women instrument makers like the Brittany-based flute maker Solen Lesouef.

And at the end of the day, sometimes presence itself is an activist effort. It can be an act of defiance, an attempt to claim musical space, or a conscious decision to show up and be a role model. Anne muses that the presence of queer trad musicians gives kids coming up the opportunity to say, "'You know, maybe it *is* okay if I get into this really funny little music off to the side over here, that everybody else doesn't seem to get.' I mean, it gives them the permission. And I think that's a very good thing."[58] Frances echoes this wish and also points out that despite its flaws, the trad scene is not always as homophobic as one might think: "I think visibility is important, because there's a kid out there somewhere who needs to see that you can play trad music and be queer, and present however you present, and be accepted by the community at large. I think there's also sort of an image thing for the trad community, because I think that it's far more accepting as a whole than people give it credit for." She continues with humorous defiance: "Because, you know, I'm here, this is my girlfriend, and I hope that's cool! [Laughs.] I'm still gonna be here with my girlfriend!"[59]

After musing on the exchange of cultural material between Irish people and black people, Missy also expresses hope that bringing attention to issues of race, gender, and sexuality in trad will help demonstrate that "we [Irish traditional musicians] have a lot more in common, and I think that's the hope—that through these conversations, we realize that working together is in our best interests, you know, for subverting the—whatever it is—that's happening around us—the thing that feels completely insurmountable, but at the same time, feels doable if we all can connect."[60] While some traddies may not feel that changes in governments and policies in the United States and Europe present a threat, Missy's point about working together directs our attention back to contemplating the differences between what we do and what we think we are doing. Even if Irish trad generally understands itself as tolerant, accepting, and inclusive, its connections with ethnic nationalism position it as intolerant and exclusive.

This book has taken an explicit stance on politics in the early twenty-first century—a stance that some readers may find uncomfortable, and one that is at odds with the idea that Irish traditional music should serve primarily as an escape from quotidian concerns. While I exhort readers and musicians to think deeply and fearlessly about music's powers to separate or unite, I close by invoking the joys of Irish traditional music and its potential to bring people together. In this spirit, I end with words from two of my interlocutors. In our conversation about how the trad scene could change for the better, Marie, an Irish-born lesbian, exclaimed, "Let people be who they are—for me, that's the joy of music. It connects people—that's what it should be. It's connection, you know."[61] Similarly, Esmi points toward shared humanity and the delights of musicking by hoping that readers will begin to recognize that "all people, everywhere, and in all cultures are equally intelligent, creative, and curious beings looking for new and exciting ways to express their world to others."[62]

NOTES

Introduction

1. This story is told in full in Isak Dinesen [Karen Blixen], *Out of Africa*, 201. By citing Blixen here, I foreshadow chapter 3's discussion of feminist biography and Adriana Cavarero's idea of life stories as gifts we give to each other.

2. "Two in the trap and one in the box" refers to catching mice; the deceased was someone in the community.

3. See, for example, Christopher J. Smith, *The Creolization of American Culture*; Fiona Ritchie and Doug Orr, *Wayfaring Strangers*; Emily Gale and Bonnie Gordon, "Sound in Jefferson's Virginia."

4. It could also easily appear on the dust jacket for books like Ciaran Carson's *Last Night's Fun* or Henry Glassie's *Passing the Time in Ballymenone*.

5. I am referring to Christopher Small's concept of "musicking," which broadens our focus to include a range of personnel (including listeners and the workers who support performances) in the act of making music (*Musicking*). For general information about Irish traditional music, see Sean Williams, *Focus*, and Gearóid Ó hAllmhuráin, *O'Brien Pocket History of Irish Traditional Music*.

6. A full treatment of singing traditions in Ireland is beyond the scope of this study. See Sean Williams and Lillis Ó Laoire, *Bright Star of the West*.

7. Una Crowley, Mary Gilmartin, and Rob Kitchin, "'Vote Yes for Common Sense Citizenship,'" 6.

8. Leith Davis, *Music, Postcolonialism, and Gender*; Helen O'Shea, "'Good Man, Mary!'" and *The Making of Irish Traditional Music*; Tes Slominski, "'Pretty Young Artists' and 'The Queen of Irish Fiddlers'" and "Queer as Trad." John O'Flynn begins to take up questions of race in *The Irishness of Irish Music*, as do some of the contributors to Mark Fitzgerald and John O'Flynn, eds., *Music and Identity in Ireland and Beyond*.

9. Joe Cooley, interview with Cathal O'Shannon.

10. My thinking here is influenced by Sara Ahmed's *On Being Included*, especially chapter 2, where she describes diversity as an "empty container" (ibid., 80).

11. For example, the presence and increasing popularity of African American musicians like the members of the Carolina Chocolate Drops in American old-time music exposes long-standing but unasked questions about race and ethnicity in a genre long considered the domain of rural white Southerners.

12. Kimberle Crenshaw, "Demarginalizing the Intersection of Race and Sex."

13. Clan-na-Gael, "Ballylongford Echoes."

14. Karen Fishman and Jan McKee, "It's Scandalous!"; Richard Killeen, *A Short History of Modern Ireland*.

15. This argument is central to Noel Ignatiev's *How the Irish Became White*.

16. Ronit Lentin, "Ireland," 11.

17. European Network against Racism, "Racism and Discrimination in Employment in Europe," 31; Crowley, Gilmartin, and Kitchin, "'Vote Yes for Common Sense Citizenship,'" 15–16.

18. Ibid., 2.

19. Eben E. Rexford, "The Boy Who Loves His Mother." The original title was "A Manly Boy."

20. Republic of Ireland, "Constitution of Ireland," art. 41.2 and 42.1. At the time of this writing, a movement is under way to remove the "woman in the home" clause.

21. Irish Archives Resource, *The Present Duty of Irishwomen*, 11.

22. Douglas Dalby, "Gay Activists Hail Vote" Nick Duffy, "Ring Your Granny Campaign Aims to Mobilise Elderly Vote for Ireland's Marriage Referendum."

23. Michel Foucault and Robert Hurley, *The History of Sexuality*. Alexander Weheliye rightly critiques both biopolitics and Giorgio Agamben's concept of "bare life" (*Homo Sacer*) for "placing racial difference in a field prior to and at a distance from conceptual contemplation" (Weheliye, *Habeas Viscus*, 7). By erasing considerations of identity from "theory," Weheliye argues, Western scholars have ignored the role of liberal humanism in creating hierarchies of humanness, and in moving toward posthumanism, they have failed to take race or enduring racial violences into account.

24. Matthew Gelbart, *The Invention of "Folk Music" and "Art Music"*; Benjamin R. Teitelbaum, *Lions of the North*.

25. European Network against Racism, "Racism and Discrimination in Employment in Europe," 30–33.

26. See Mick Moloney, "Irish Music in America"; Gearóid Ó hAllmhuráin, *Flowing Tides*.

27. O'Shea, *The Making of Irish Traditional Music*, 3.

28. Moloney, "Irish Music in America," 445.

29. The fallacy of inborn talent based on genetics has an inescapable opposite, inborn

unfitness, which is the driving force behind eugenics and the evils its exponents have perpetrated. While Ireland never wholly embraced practices of negative eugenics like birth control and sterilization because of its relationship with the Catholic Church, its sex/gender system is based on natalism—state support for the reproduction of new ethnically Irish citizens. See Greta Jones, "Eugenics in Ireland."

30. "That the Age of Nationality Is Gone."

31. See Helen O'Shea, "Defining the Nation and Confining the Musician."

32. Here, my use of "postnationalism" focuses on the elements of cosmopolitanism that Richard Kearney discusses in *Postnationalist Ireland*.

33. I include the full quotation here because my reading is somewhat against the authors' original: "Today the hegemonic 'soft focus' construction of Ireland is one of a pluralistic, multicultural, liberal, cosmopolitan, open society. However, this construction is not as diametrically opposed to the rhetoric of conservative 'old' Ireland as it may first appear and occludes as much as it includes" (Crowley, Gilmartin, and Kitchin, "'Vote Yes for Common Sense Citizenship,'" 20).

34. Moloney, "Irish Music in America," 449.

35. In *Flowing Tides*, Ó hAllmhuráin invokes the term "glocal" (9 and 17) to describe connections between Irish localities and places outside Ireland, but like other Irish scholars, he tends to treat non-Irish places as undifferentiated other than by nation and the origins of Irish immigrants to them. This smoothing out of geographic difference limits what can be said about the connections among musicians, music, and sociabilities in these places. I resist the term "glocal" because it conveniently slides over the problem of nationalism, and instead prefer "postnational." Daithí Kearney takes a region-based approach in "Towards a Regional Understanding of Irish Traditional Music."

36. Chain migration has been a notorious part of Irish diasporic life, of course, as the story about how the Kerry accordion player Terry Teahan got the nickname "Cuz" demonstrates (he told new immigrants to Chicago to tell employers he was their cousin).

37. Comhaltas Ceoltóirí Éireann is a complex organization that teaches (and employs) a wide variety of Irish traditional musicians worldwide.

38. Despite his positive treatment of non-Irish musicians elsewhere in his work, Ó hAllmhuráin also writes about visiting musicians with the language of invasion—"music tourists scaled the battlements" (*Flowing Tides*, 37). And indeed anyone in the vicinity of Doolin, County Clare, in the summertime can attest to the onslaught of musicians and listeners from outside Ireland.

39. See Anthony McCann, "All That Is Not Given Is Lost."

40. See, for example, Sylvia Wynter, "Human Being as Noun?"; Angela Davis, *Abolition Democracy*; Vanessa Watts, "Indigenous Place-Thought and Agency Amongst Humans and Non Humans"; Hortense Spillers, *Black, White, and in Color*; and Weheliye, *Habeas Viscus*.

41. The image of reused parchment comes from Michel Foucault, "Nietzsche, Genealogy, History."

42. Janet L. Beizer, *Thinking through the Mothers: Reimagining Women's Biographies* (Ithaca: Cornell University Press, 2009). Shanachie Records' 1985 recording projects Cherish the Ladies (79053) and Fathers and Daughters (79054) embody this conceptual problem within Irish traditional music, and the continuing and essentialized connection between women musicians and their fathers (and sometimes husbands) confounds attempts to imagine a truly nonpatriarchal Irish music scene.

43. Philip Bohlman articulates the category of the voiceless tradition bearer in a larger explication of the contrasts between notions of *das Volk* as a collective and the reality of individual creativity within traditional musics (*The Study of Folk Music in the Modern World*, especially 70–72). The phrase "tradition bearer" is disappearing from the mission statements of organizations like the Irish Arts Council and the US-based National Council for the Traditional Arts, but it still appears frequently in brief biographies of musicians funded by such organizations. For more on liquid metaphors in Irish traditional music, see Anthony McCann, "A Tale of Two Rivers."

44. This project could be pigeonholed as historical ethnomusicology, but rather than contributing to the Balkanization of music and sound studies, I call for relaxing the boundaries between ethnomusicology and historical musicology.

45. See, for example, E. Patrick Johnson, "'Quare' Studies."

ONE *Mother Ireland and the Queen of Irish Fiddlers*

1. Eavan Boland, *Object Lessons*, 66.

2. Ibid., 66–67.

3. These laws limited the rights of Catholics to own land, practice the Roman Catholic faith, and hold political office.

4. See R. F. Foster, *Modern Ireland*; Robert Kee, *The Green Flag*; Alvin Jackson, *Home Rule*; Diarmaid Ferriter, *The Transformation of Ireland*.

5. Adriana Cavarero, *Relating Narratives*.

6. Nira Yuval-Davis, *Gender and Nation*, 21–23.

7. Marina Warner, *Monuments and Maidens*, 46.

8. Anne McClintock, *Imperial Leather*, 35 and 218. See also John Tenniel's cartoon from *Punch*, 3 March 1866, reproduced in Catherine Lynette Innes, *Woman and Nation in Irish Literature and Society*, 13. The character of John Bull comes from *The History of John Bull*, a political allegory published by John Arbuthnot in 1712 (see Miles Taylor, "John Bull and the Iconography of Public Opinion in England c. 1712–1929"; Jeannine Surel, "'John Bull.'"

9. See Maurice Agulhon, *Marianne into Battle*.

10. Charu Gupta, "The Icon of Mother in Late Colonial North India," 4291.

11. Adele Dalsimer and Vera Kreilkamp, "Re/Dressing Mother Ireland," 37. See also James MacKillop, *A Dictionary of Celtic Mythology*, 192.

12. See Innes, *Woman and Nation in Irish Literature and Society*; Richard Kearney, *Postnationalist Ireland*; Gerardine Meaney, *Sex and Nation*. This body of work parallels the scholarly attention to women as embodied symbols of nation elsewhere, particularly in India, as Suruchi Thapar-Bjorkert and Louise Ryan point out in "Mother India/Mother Ireland."

13. McClintock, *Imperial Leather*, 28.

14. Ania Loomba, *Colonialism-Postcolonialism*, 98.

15. See John Tenniel's cartoons in *Punch*, 8 June 1867 and 3 March 1866, reproduced in Innes, *Woman and Nation in Irish Literature and Society*, 12–16. For critical work on the portrayal of Irish men as apes or children, see L. Perry Curtis, *Apes and Angels*; Richard Haslam, "'A Race Bashed in the Face.'"

16. Innes, *Woman and Nation in Irish Literature and Society*, 14.

17. Luke Gibbons, *Transformations in Irish Culture*, 21.

18. Nancy Curtin argues that by gendering their nation female, male Irish nationalists sexualized England as an amoral violator ("A Nation of Abortive Men," 49).

19. Gerry Kearns, "Mother Ireland and the Revolutionary Sisters," 444.

20. See William H. A. Williams, *'Twas Only an Irishman's Dream*. For more information on British street ballads, see Reg Hall, comp., *The Voice of the People*.

21. H. Halliday Sparling, *Irish Minstrelsy*, 18–20 (emphasis in the original). The book is available online at the American Libraries Internet Archive, accessed 10 December 2008, http://www.archive.org/details/irishminstrelsyboospar.

22. "Shan Van Vocht" is a phonetic spelling of the Irish *an t-seanbhean bhocht* ("the poor old woman") and was inspired by one of two unsuccessful French attempts to invade Ireland in support of its rebellion against England.

23. A. M. Sullivan, *New Ireland*, 439. See also Guy Beiner, *Remembering the Year of the French*, 92–94.

24. Georges Denis Zimmermann, *Songs of the Irish Rebellion*, 10.

25. Julie Mostov, "Sexing the Nation/Desexing the Body," 93.

26. Gupta, "The Icon of Mother in Late Colonial North India," 4292.

27. Richard Kearney, *Postnationalist Ireland*, 119.

28. Recently, Irish women writers—including the poets Nuala Ní Dhomhnaill and Eavan Boland—have challenged this construction and pointed out its destructive aspects.

29. Dipesh Chakrabarty, *Provincializing Europe*, 149.

30. MacKillop, *A Dictionary of Celtic Mythology*, 69–70.

31. Sara Ahmed, *The Cultural Politics of Emotion*, 123.

32. Ibid., 124.

33. Pádraig Pearse, "A Mother Speaks." Innes also discusses the connections between

Mother Ireland and the Virgin Mary (*Woman and Nation in Irish Literature and Society*, especially chapter 2).

34. Earnest Ball, "Mother Machree."

35. The use of "mo chroí" or "machree" as an epithet is common in older songs, including "Erin Machree."

36. By the late twentieth century, writers were beginning to ridicule this interpretive monomania. For a discussion of late twentieth-century literary refiguration of the Mother Ireland metaphor, see Nicholas Grene, "Black Pastoral."

37. Zimmermann, *Songs of the Irish Rebellion*, 52–53.

38. See John William Cousin, "Thomas Osborne Davis"; Blanche Mary Kelly, "James Clarence Mangan."

39. In Irish epithets like "Dark Rosaleen," colors generally refer to hair rather than skin.

40. James Clarence Mangan, "My Dark Rosaleen," in James Clarence Mangan, *James Clarence Mangan*, 115.

41. Zimmermann, *Songs of the Irish Rebellion*, 85.

42. "Kathaleen Ny-Houlahan" is one variant of the more common name Kathleen Ní Houlihan. Mangan's poem foreshadows William Butler Yeats's transformation of the character into an old woman in his play *Cathleen Ní Houlihan*.

43. James Clarence Mangan, "Kathaleen Ny-Houlahan," in Mangan, *James Clarence Mangan*, 173.

44. Innes, *Woman and Nation in Irish Literature and Society*, 22.

45. Marina Warner, *Alone of All Her Sex*, 336.

46. Rosemary Cullen Owens, *Smashing Times*, 16–17. Owens points out that this idea largely comes from the unpublished work of Eibhlín Breathnach.

47. Maria Luddy, *Women in Ireland*, 5 and 7. These figures are based on statistics from W. E. Vaughan and A. J. Fitzpatrick, *Irish Historical Statistics*, 87–89. The percentages break down as follows: 35 percent of women were over the age of fifteen and single, 9 percent were widowed, 26 percent were married, and 30 percent were under the age of fifteen at the time of the census.

48. Joseph Guinan, *Scenes and Sketches in an Irish Parish*, 45.

49. Luddy, *Women in Ireland*, 6. Luddy draws these statistics from Robert E. Kennedy, *The Irish*, 78. Kennedy shows that 86,294 men emigrated, and according to the 1901 census, the Irish population numbered 4,443,370 in that year (Library Ireland, "Ireland's Loss of Population".

50. Luddy, *Women in Ireland*, 8.

51. Ibid., 10. Luddy draws on Tony Fahey, "Nuns and the Catholic Church in Ireland in the Nineteenth Century," 7.

52. For a discussion of social class distinctions within convents, see Catriona Clear, "Walls within Walls."

53. Lucy Farr, interview with Reg Hall, 24 February 1988.

54. Roly Brown, "Lucy Farr: Heart and Home."

55. For a further discussion of the Travellers, see below in this chapter. For a description of the masculinization of the Traveller population and the subsequent erasure of women's work in that population, see Jane Helleiner, *Irish Travellers*, 161–73.

56. See Owens, *Smashing Times*; Cliona Murphy, *The Women's Suffrage Movement and Irish Society in the Early Twentieth Century*.

57. The Cumann na mBan (Irishwomen's Council), discussed below, was originally founded to assist the Irish Volunteers primarily through fund-raising. For extensive and sometimes contradictory accounts of the organization, see Margaret Ward, *Unmanageable Revolutionaries*; Cal McCarthy, *Cumann na mBan and the Irish Revolution*.

58. Catherine Cox, "Elizabeth O'Farrell." O'Farrell and Julia Grenan, another revolutionary, lived together until O'Farrell's death in 1957 and are buried next to each other. See also Mary McAuliffe and Liz Gillis, *Richmond Barracks 1916*.

59. See Jackson, *Home Rule*.

60. Quoted in Declan Kiberd, *Inventing Ireland*, 142.

61. Oireachtas na Gaeilge, "Stair an tOireachtas."

62. David P. Moran coined the term "Irish Ireland" in 1898 and later published *The Philosophy of Irish Ireland*.

63. Frank Biletz, "Women and Irish-Ireland, 61.

64. For a comprehensive breakdown of Gaelic League membership, see Timothy G. McMahon, *Grand Opportunity*, chapter 3.

65. "Champion Chatter."

66. Timothy G. McMahon reckons that Pearse's estimate of 50,000 Gaelic League members isn't far off, but membership numbers may have been higher in some years ("'All Creeds and All Classes'?").

67. Ibid., 135.

68. Biletz, "Women and Irish-Ireland," 64. Many historians identify "Máire" as the novelist Mary Butler.

69. Quoted in ibid. Newspaper accounts from Counties Clare and Kerry demonstrate that even though factory and production opportunities for women had decreased, they did still exist in the early 1900s.

70. For information about women's technical education, the diversification of the Irish diet, and traveling home economics teachers, see Joanna Bourke, *Husbandry to Housewifery*.

71. Biletz, "Women and Irish-Ireland," 64.

72. "Lilting" is the practice of singing the melodies of dance tunes using nonsense syllables. Some Irish musicians today—mostly men—cite their mothers' lilting as the source for the tunes they now play.

73. Quoted in Margaret Ward, *Unmanageable Revolutionaries*, 51.

74. Women won these rights in 1898. See Owens, *Smashing Times*, 30; Myrtle Hill, *Women in Ireland*, 37.

75. Unlike the "living statuary" displays in the United States in the mid-nineteenth century, these tableaux seem not to have drawn the extensive criticism for perceived breaches of morality Gillian M. Rodger describes in *Champagne Charlie and Pretty Jemima*, 24–25.

76. Margaret Ward, *Unmanageable Revolutionaries*, 59; see also 52–55.

77. Quoted in Margaret Ward, "Marginality and Militancy," 59.

78. See Cal McCarthy, *Cumann na mBan and the Irish Revolution*, 45; Margaret Ward, *Unmanageable Revolutionaries*, 102–6. Not all branches or members of Cumann na mBan engaged in these activities, and the organization's membership was limited to women with family connections to the Volunteers or with enough income to withstand familial disapproval of their participation in the increasingly militant organization. Therefore, to say that Cumann na mBan armed Ireland's women would be a vast exaggeration.

79. The uilleann ("elbow") pipes are often referred to in early twentieth-century sources as the union pipes.

80. The extensive scholarship on women's history includes foundational works by Gerda Lerner (*The Majority Finds Its Past*), Joan Wallach Scott (*Gender and the Politics of History*), Joan Kelly (*Women, History, and Theory*), and others.

81. Joan Wallach Scott, introduction, 3.

82. Ó hAllmhuráin, *Flowing Tides*.

83. The concertina player Molly Morrissey, whose more customarily used surname was O'Connell (according to her grand-nephew Joe Gerhard, Morrissey may have been her mother's maiden name), was the mother of the Sliabh Luachra fiddler Maurice O'Keeffe. Margaret O'Callaghan (who played the fiddle and concertina) was the mother of the Sliabh Luachra fiddler Pádraig O'Keeffe.

84. Fintan Vallely, *The Companion to Irish Traditional Music*, 285. See also Caoimhín MacAoidh, *The Scribe*; Nicholas Carolan, *A Harvest Saved*; Francis O'Neill, *The Dance Music of Ireland*.

85. Francis O'Neill, *Irish Minstrels and Musicians*.

86. Irish, American, and English reprinted editions of *Irish Minstrels and Musicians* appeared in 1973, 1987, and 1997 and are available in many public and university libraries in the Irish diaspora.

87. While *Irish Minstrels and Musicians* is remarkable for including women musicians at all, the proportion of men to women in this work is woefully unbalanced.

88. Francis O'Neill, *Irish Minstrels and Musicians*, 389.

89. Ibid., 387.

90. See, for example, the advertisement for "Limerick Irish Pipers' Club at Kilkee," *Clare Champion*, 18 July 1903.

91. This possibility is supported, however thinly, by the prevalence of the surname McDonough (and variants of the name) in the 1953 Schools Questionnaire, where Travellers were counted (see Meath Travellers Workshops, "1953 Names by Locality").

92. Micheál Ó hAodha, *Irish Travellers*, 11–13. The Celtic revival of the late nineteenth and early twentieth centuries tended to see Travellers as "embodiments of the pre-colonial past" even as the Traveller population was popularly perceived as immoral, promiscuous, and dirty (Helleiner, *Irish Travellers*, 41).

93. For a discussion of the effects of the emerging bourgeois Catholic nationalist class on perceptions and treatment of Travellers during the Irish nation building of the early twentieth century, see Helleiner, *Irish Travellers*, 46–50.

94. Francis O'Neill, *Irish Minstrels and Musicians*, 387.

95. See Jürgen Habermas, *The Structural Transformation of the Public Sphere*.

96. "An Interrupted 'Soiree,'" *Kerry People*, 7 February 1903. The fiddler in this case had been hired to play for a house dance that was broken up by police for being unlicensed.

97. Siamsa Gaedheal Céilí Band, *The High Road to Galway*. See also Reg Hall, *Irish Dance Music* (a compilation that includes a remastered version of this recording).

98. Social class may have dictated that Kenny's instrument always be called the fiddle rather than the violin, since the latter word did have specifically middle- and upper-class connotations.

99. Just as the highland bagpipes are considered quintessentially Scottish, the uilleann pipes are inextricably linked with Ireland and the Irish.

100. For information about Hall, née Fielding (1800–81), see "Mrs. S. C. Hall (Anna Maria Fielding)." "Kelly the Piper" first appeared in Mrs. S. C. Hall, *Sketches of Irish Character*. For more information on pattern days, see Helen Brennan, *The Story of Irish Dance*, 19.

101. See Francis O'Neill, *Irish Folk Music*.

102. Plain Piper [pseud.], "The Irish Pipes."

103. O'Neill describes the post-Famine situation of pipers this way: "Changed conditions, lack of patronage, and other well-understood causes, forced this class of minstrels, many of them blind, to take to the highways for support—a form of mendicancy which brought their once honored calling into disrepute" (*Irish Minstrels and Musicians*, 153). He continues, defending the collective reputation of traditional musicians: "Indeed, the musicians of Ireland are as harmless and inoffensive a class of persons as ever existed, and there can be no greater proof of this than the very striking fact that in the criminal statistics of the country the name of an Irish piper or fiddler has scarcely if ever been known to appear" (ibid., 155).

104. Ibid., 342. O'Neill does not supply a date, but Kitty Hanley seems to have been active in the 1830s and 1840s.

105. Ibid., 268. Again, O'Neill does not supply a date, but his profile of "Nance the Piper" appears in a section about pipers from the late nineteenth century.

106. "Warpipes" are akin to the Scottish highland pipes—another instrument whose exponents are almost all male. But in the 1913 Oireachtas, three of the four listed winners in the warpipes competition were women. All of the winners in the uilleann pipes competition were men ("Oireachtas").

107. This portrayal of Morrissey as the musical equivalent of a bean counter echoes Catherine Lutz's critique that women's writing is "more often seen as description, data, case, personal, or as in the case of feminism, 'merely' setting the record straight" ("The Gender of Theory," 251).

108. "Fideogist" remains mysterious. Given the context, most likely the word is a misspelled neologism based on the Irish for tin whistle, "feadóg." Perhaps the author of the *Ladies' Pictorial* article meant "feadógist," or perhaps the typesetter, more familiar with Latin roots than with Irish nouns, altered the word. It's also possible, though less likely, that "fideogist" is an unwitting contraction of "fideologist," which would suggest that Morrissey's devout faith was her most important characteristic. Thanks to Ivan Goff for pointing out the similarity between "fideo" and "feadóg."

109. Quoted in Francis O'Neill, *Irish Minstrels and Musicians*, 334–36.

110. Ibid., 334.

111. Jonathan Allison coined the term "magical nationalism," and only a few others have taken it up ("Magical Nationalism, Lyric Poetry and the Marvellous," 230).

112. Francis O'Neill, *Irish Minstrels and Musicians*, 334.

113. O'Neill remarks upon the novelty of including women in musical clubs in his discussion of the Cork Pipers' Club, formed in 1898: "In precept and example it was an inspiration, and not only that but convention was disregarded, barriers were broken down, and the musical franchise conferred on the fair sex" (*Irish Minstrels and Musicians*, 330).

114. O'Neill cites Manchester's *Daily Sketch*, which reports that "at the concert in Birmingham last night, those who met to celebrate St. Patrick's Day heard a performer who is probably without an equal, as far as the Union bagpipes are concerned" (ibid., 334).

115. Mervyn Busteed, *The Irish in Manchester c.1750–1921*, 257. According to contemporary accounts, both the Manchester and London branches of the Gaelic League were remarkably active in the early twentieth century.

116. Mary Mitchell-Ingoldsby, "Cork Pipers Club: Club History."

117. "Limerick Irish Pipers' Club at Kilkee."

118. Cal McCarthy, *Cumann na mBan and the Irish Revolution*, 105.

119. These phrases appear in numerous songs and poems and in colloquial speech. Poetic sources include Aogán Ó Rathaille's "Gile na Gile" (from the late seventeenth or early eighteenth century), Mangan's "Kathaleen Ny-Houlahan" (nineteenth century), and Pádraig Pearse's "Renunciation" (twentieth century).

120. Quoted in Francis O'Neill, *Irish Minstrels and Musicians*, 334. For a biographical sketch of Edward Cronin, see ibid., 413.

121. Compare the first two lines of "Gile na Gile": "Brightness of brightness lonely met me where I wandered, / Crystal of crystal only by her eyes were splendid."

122. O'Neill, *Irish Musicians and Musicians*, 334.

123. Mangan, *James Clarence Mangan*, 179 and 184 (the poems are "The Dream of John MacDonnell" and "Leather Away the Wattle O," respectively).

124. Ibid., 182 and 201.

125. Bernadette McCarthy, interview with author.

126. Mitchell-Ingoldsby, "Cork Pipers Club."

127. Marie McCarthy, *Passing It On*, 86.

128. "Violin Class for Ballinasloe." These classes were connected with the local temperance society.

129. Lucy Farr gives an anecdotal account of fife and drum bands near Ballinakill (interview with Reg Hall, 1983). For a brief but salient discussion of temperance bands, see Marie McCarthy, *Passing It On*, 48–51. Contemporary news items about brass and fife and drum bands abound.

130. Farr, interview with Reg Hall, 1987 (emphasis in the original).

131. In avoiding the normative reproductive role of women, Kilcar and other single women inhabited a different and potentially queer temporal space. For an explication of this idea of "queer time," see Judith Halberstam, *In a Queer Time and Place*.

132. Gayle Rubin, "The Traffic in Women."

133. Farr, interview with Hall, 24 February 1988.

134. Farr, interview with Hall, 23 April 1988.

135. Cavarero, *Relating Narratives*, chapter 5.

136. Judith Butler, *Undoing Gender*, 58. Elizabeth Povinelli's *The Cunning of Recognition* also informs my thinking about recognition, identity, and diversity here and throughout this book.

TWO *The Not-So-Strange Disappearance of Treasa Ní Ailpín (Teresa Halpin)*

1. I use the Irish version of Treasa Ní Ailpín's name to recognize her lifelong contributions to the maintenance of the Irish language, though I retain "Halpin" where it appears in sources and when referring to members of her family or the family in general.

2. "Grand Benefit Concert and Pictures in Aid of the Sufferers in the Recent Fire"; "Concert in Cooraclare."

3. Reg Hall, notes to *Past Masters of Irish Fiddle Music*, 19–20.

4. For a nuanced treatment of Irish masculinities, including the dichotomy between the "rural, untamed masculinity" of male sean-nós singers like Joe Heaney and the feminization of Irish tenors, see Sean Williams and Lilis Ó Laoire, *Bright Star of the West*, 141.

5. The composer Seán Ó Riada (1931–71) is the most famous and respected of the Irish

composers who have blended traditional repertoire with Western art music composition. In the 1960s he founded Ceoltóirí Chualann—the group that would become the Chieftains. See Tomás Ó Canainn, *Seán Ó Riada*. Other more recent musical crossovers, like Bill Whelan's music for *Riverdance*, have been less well received by the majority of traditional musicians.

6. See Donal Joseph O'Sullivan and Bonnie Shaljean, *Carolan*; Leith Davis, *Music, Postcolonialism, and Gender*. For an insightful discussion of the metaphor of the pure drop, see Anthony McCann, "A Tale of Two Rivers."

7. Harry White, *The Keeper's Recital*, 110.

8. See Ruth Solie, *Music in Other Words*; Judith Tick, "Passed Away Is the Piano Girl"; Davis, *Music, Postcolonialism, and Gender*, especially chapter 6.

9. Marie McCarthy, *Passing It On*, 56–63.

10. Quoted in ibid., *Passing It On*, 95. This ruling was reversed in 1903.

11. Ibid., 66–68.

12. Incorporated Society of Musicians, "About Us." See also Marie McCarthy, *Passing It On*, 106.

13. "Incorporated Society of Musicians Local Practical Examinations." Of the three boys who passed, two played violin and one piano.

14. Quoted in "Concert." See also "Concert at St. John's"; "Rathkeale Gaelic League Annual Concert."

15. Feis Ceoil Association, *Feis Ceoil Syllabus of Prize Competitions*. In the Irish fiddle competition, women won all the prizes, while in the Irish pipes competition, no women placed. In the rest of the art music competitions, the gender breakdown is predictable based on gendered patterns of art music performance: few women placed in the organ or woodwinds competitions, and none in the brass.

16. *HMS Pinafore*, *The Mikado*, *The Gondoliers*, and *The Pirates of Penzance* were all staged in Limerick in 1911–13. See "Special Orchestra of 25"; "Limerick Opera Society," 28 November 1911 and 18 March 1913; "Limerick Operatic Society."

17. Clan-na-Gael, "Ballylongford Echoes."

18. Feis Ceoil Association, *Feis Ceoil Syllabus of Prize Competitions*.

19. More research on Irish women's art music performance is necessary to determine whether women musicians were steered away from works by certain composers before the 1920s, as happened in the ladies' orchestras of late nineteenth-century Britain and the United States (see Tick, "Passed Away Is the Piano Girl"; Margaret Myers, "Searching for Data about European Ladies' Orchestras, 1870–1950."

20. Quoted in Breandán Breathnach, "The Feis Ceoil and Piping," in Breathnach, *The Man and His Music*, 139.

21. Arthur Darley and Patrick Joseph McCall, *Feis Ceóil Collection of Irish Airs Hitherto Unpublished*; Fintan Vallely, *The Companion to Irish Traditional Music*, 313.

22. Quoted in Marie McCarthy, *Passing It On*, 75.

23. Carl Hardebeck, "Traditional Singing: Its Value and Meaning," *Journal of the Ivernian Society* 3 (January–March 1911), 93, quoted in Marie McCarthy, *Passing It On*, 75.

24. Breandán Breathnach, "The Feis Ceoil and Piping," 149. See also Harry White, *The Keeper's Recital*, 111–17.

25. Barry O'Neill, "Piping Contests at the Feis, 1897–1935."

26. Feis Ceoil Association, *Feis Ceoil Syllabus of Prize Competitions*. The most widely available recording that features the playing of Mrs. Sheridan and Mrs. Whelan is Reg Hall, *Irish Dance Music*. The fiddler Tommy Potts later cited Mrs. Sheridan as an influence on his playing.

27. Marie McCarthy, *Passing It On*, 56–63.

28. For an extended discussion (and critique) of attempts to create a truly "Irish" art music, see Harry White, *The Keeper's Recital*.

29. For an account of the interplay between class and (proto)nationality in the romanticizing of Irish music as lower class, see Davis, *Music, Postcolonialism, and Gender*, 164–85.

30. A survey of newspapers from 1903–25 supports this assertion. See, for example, "Notes from Kilrush": "Ladies' Warfare. At the Kilrush Petty Sessions on Monday, a woman named Kate Coughlan was fined 5s[hillings] for giving an uninvited lesson in the manly arts to Mrs Anne Gormley, of Chapel Street. One third of the fine was awarded to the latter to appease her wounded feelings for the very wanton atrack [sic] made upon her."

31. Francis O'Neill, *Irish Minstrels and Musicians*, 387.

32. "The rising step" is a movement in Irish step and céilí dance.

33. Gerald Griffin, *The Collegians*, 5.

34. Diarmuid Breathnach and Máire Ní Mhurchú, *Beathaisnéis a Cúig*, 149.

35. National Archives of Ireland, "Census of Ireland, 1911: Residents of a house 28 in Garryowen East." Two children had died by the time of the census.

36. S. J. Barrett, *The Proceedings of the Third Oireachtas*. See also Diarmuid Breathnach and Ní Mhurchú, *Beathaisnéis a Cúig*. Because of the political valences of the Irish language at the time, we cannot assume that everyone who claimed to be bilingual on the 1911 census was. The Halpins, however, also listed Irish as a household language in the 1901 census, and Treasa's activities later in life support the claim that the family was fluent in both languages.

37. Diarmuid Breathnach and Ní Mhurchú, *Beathaisnéis a Cúig*, 149; "Limerick Irish Pipers' Club at Kilkee."

38. Ibid., 150.

39. "Great Challenge Contest in Irish Dancing."

40. Diarmuid Breathnach and Ní Mhurchú, *Beathaisnéis a Cúig*, 150.

41. Quoted in Helen Brennan, *The Story of Irish Dance*, 40.

42. Ibid., 40–42.

43. Ibid., 41.

44. Laurel Hill Secondary School, F.C.J., "Laurel Hill." See also Faithful Companions of Jesus, "Who We Are."

45. Kate O'Brien, *The Land of Spices*. The novel was initially banned in Ireland.

46. Quoted in Anne V. O'Connor, "Influences Affecting Girls' Secondary Education in Ireland, 1860–1910," 86.

47. See ibid., 88.

48. Diarmuid Breathnach and Ní Mhurchú, *Beathaisnéis a Cúig*, 149.

49. The most explicit source for this claim is Diarmuid Breathnach and Ní Mhurchú's biography of Seán Ó Cuirrín (ibid.), but Francis O'Neill's sketch of Teresa Halpin states that she already had an "extensive repertoire of old tunes" by 1907 (*Irish Minstrels and Musicians*, 402)—an unlikely accomplishment had she picked up the violin only at school. Moreover, it is possible Laurel Hill did not offer violin lessons at that time.

50. Francis O'Neill, *Irish Minstrels and Musicians*, 391.

51. National Archives of Ireland, "Census of Ireland, 1911: Form A." See also the acknowledgments in Frank Roche, *The Roche Collection of Traditional Irish Music*, unnumbered page.

52. "A Brilliant Success."

53. Francis O'Neill, *Irish Minstrels and Musicians*, 391–92.

54. A documented family relationship between Joseph and William would also complicate evidence indicating that Joseph was a member of the lower classes.

55. Dermot Hanifin, *Pádraig O'Keeffe: The Man and His Music* (self, 1995), unnumbered page. According to the 1911 census, Martin Clancy was a widower and lived alone (National Archives of Ireland, "Census of Ireland, 1911: Form A.").

56. Francis O'Neill, *Irish Minstrels and Musicians*, 402.

57. Paddy Canny, P. J. Hayes, Peadar O'Loughlin, and Bridie Lafferty, *An Historic Recording of Traditional Irish Music from County Clare and East Galway*.

58. Other such volumes published in the early 1900s include collections by George Petrie, Frank Roche, and of course, Francis O'Neill.

59. Darley and McCall, *Feis Ceóil Collection of Irish Airs Hitherto Unpublished*.

60. Breandán Breathnach, "The Feis Ceoil and Piping," 138–50.

61. Robert Young, "The Pipers' Competition at the Feis Ceoil," 6. He also supplies information about plans to transcribe the recorded tunes (as far as we know, subsequent competitions for unpublished Irish airs proceeded in similar fashion).

62. Breandán Breathnach, "The Feis Ceoil and Piping," 143. The recorded tunes were "The High Road to Galway," "The Boys of Wexford," "Bathing in the Boyne," and "The Groves." The first two have been digitized and are available at the National Folklore

Collection at University College Dublin; the second two were not included in the 1914 published collection, and presumably the recordings have not survived.

63. These Feis results are compiled in Jackie Small, "Feis Ceoil Results," 8.

64. We know that her rendition of "'The Ennistymon Jig" was recorded in 1907 and can probably safely assume that the tunes printed in Darley and McCall's *Feis Ceóil Collection of Irish Airs Hitherto Unpublished* were likewise recorded then. If they weren't recorded in 1907, they were most likely recorded in 1909.

65. "Feis Ceoil," 4.

66. "Wednesday Violin Competitions." Ní Ailpín later praised Kelly's playing when asked about it by Tony Linneen for *Treoir*, CCÉ's magazine. Linneen writes: "When I first heard of Luke, he was coming towards the end of his days, and to establish how great he was in his hey-day, as the expression goes, I had to make a number of enquiries from people who knew him in his earlier days. I made sure the people I questioned were discerning people. . . . I then asked Bean Uí Chuirín [sic], better known as Treasa Halpin, for years an Oireachtas adjudicator, if I was right in thinking that Luke was a master, and she replied: 'Oh, yes; he was really great; he was a great stylist.' I need not have gone any further than that" (Tony Linneen, "Had Wicklow Its Own Michael Coleman?," unnumbered page). This quotation suggests that Ní Ailpín remained well regarded into the 1960s.

67. Harry White points out a similar link between the early twentieth-century nationalist valuation of ancient Irish music and idealized notions of a precolonial self-governing Ireland (*The Keeper's Recital*, 20).

68. "An Buachaill Caol Dubh" ("The Dark Slender Boy") is a well-known song about the tragic love affair between a man and his bottle of stout.

69. Vallely, *The Companion to Irish Traditional Music*, 165.

70. Harry Bradshaw, "Michael Coleman, 1891–1945," 37.

71. Diarmuid Breathnach and Ní Mhurchú, *Beathaisnéis a Cúig*, 149.

72. Ibid., 150; Coláiste na Rinne, "Brief History."

73. Treasa Ní Ailpín and Seán Ó Cuirrín, *Teagosc-Leabhar na Bheidhlíne* (Dublin: Oifig Díolta Foillseachám Rialais, 1923). The original Irish reads, "Oideas cuinn coir ar bheartú an bhogha agus na méar; dréimrí ceoil agus liacht chleachtadh in órd is in oireagar oireamhnach, maille le cnuasach toghta taithneamhach de suantraidhe, goltraidhe, agus geantraidhe na nGaedheal." Thanks to Deirdre Ní Chonghaile for help with the finer points of this translation.

74. The book includes forty airs, twelve jigs, ten reels, six hornpipes, five slip jigs, three marches, and two set dances.

75. Ní Ailpín and Ó Cuirrín, *Teagosc-Leabhar na Bheidhlíne*, 73.

76. Philip O'Leary, *Gaelic Prose in the Irish Free State, 1922–1939*, 177. Ní Ailpín's husband contributed an arithmetic book to this nationalist effort in 1922.

77. Matt Cranitch, *The Irish Fiddle Book*.

78. My clues about the existence of a second book are that not all the test pieces listed in the feis program are included in *Teagosc-Leabhar* and that the titles are in English—which could be a translation for the feis program, or it could indicate a book in English. *Teagosc-Leabhar* was reprinted at least once.

79. Senior competitors were responsible for "Ned of the Hill," "The Dear Irish Boy," "The Flannel Jacket," "The Sporting Pitchfork," and "Thomond Bridge." Entrants in the under-sixteen competition prepared "The Coulin," "The Flowers of Donnybrook," "The Rocky Road [to Dublin]," and "The Job of Journeywork."

80. Feis Ceoil Association, *Feis Ceoil Syllabus of Prize Competitions*, 32 (emphasis in the original). Today, competitors in Comhaltas Ceoltóirí Éireann's All-Ireland choose their own pieces, which must be demonstrably traditional (usually meaning old tunes with unknown composers).

81. Halpin Trio, *Over the Moor to Maggie*; Alan Ng, "Irish Traditional Music Tune Index."

82. Geoff Wallis, "Past Masters of Irish Fiddle Music."

83. A very few tunes are played AABBC or AABC, or otherwise vary the form—but all maintain the eight-measure structure.

84. Halpin Trio, *Rogha an Fhile*. This was reissued in the compilation *Past Masters of Irish Fiddle Music* (see Reg Hall, liner notes to *Past Masters of Irish Fiddle Music*). At that time both Parlophone and HMV were based in London, and presumably both companies hoped to sell records to Irish emigrants in the United Kingdom as well as to consumers in Ireland.

85. Diarmuid Breathnach and Ní Mhurchú, *Beathaisnéis a Cúig*, 150.

86. Perhaps Ní Ailpín wrote the dance tune "Rogha an Fhíle" to match the limitations of recording—or, more likely, the dance involved repeated patterns that could be done one, two, or ten times, depending on the taste and stamina of the dancers and the availability of someone to move the record needle back to the beginning of the side.

87. A survey of newspapers from the period 1903–35 shows that gramophone records were available in shops in "county towns" like Ennis and Tralee, as well as in cities like Limerick, Galway, Cork, and Dublin. Immigrants to America also often sent home gramophones and albums—a practice well documented in oral history accounts (see Hilary Bracefield, "Let Erin Remember"; Bradshaw, "Michael Coleman, 1891–1945." See also Mick Moloney, "Irish Ethnic Recordings and the Irish-American Imagination." In an excellent review article, Johanne Trew also identifies several Irish theses and dissertations on early recordings of Irish music and Irish American record labels ("Treasures from the Attic"), and Philippe Varlet's and Reg Hall's liner notes for various albums remain excellent sources for information about specific recordings (see, for example, Varlet, liner notes to *Milestone in the Garden* and Hall, liner notes to *Past Masters of Irish Fiddle*

Music). The consumption of nontraditional records in Ireland in 1900–1950 has received little attention, unfortunately.

88. Francis Roche, "Note on Irish Dancing," in *The Roche Collection of Traditional Irish Music*, 3:v.

89. Victoria White, "Will the Real Irish Dancing Please Stand Up?"

90. Some musicians are hostile to attempts to incorporate the Irish language into everyday speech, as occasionally demonstrated on the listserv IRTRAD-L ("Irish trad list"), a primarily Anglophone internet forum most active in the 1990s and early 2000s.

91. In at least one case, ignorance about Ní Ailpín's married name has meant that Teresa/Treasa/Bean Uí Chuirrín has been treated in print as two distinct people, as in Seán Donnelly's review of Terry Moylan's *Toss the Feathers: Irish Set Dancing*: "The claim that 'The Walls of Limerick' and 'The Siege of Limerick' [*sic*] were composed by the secretary of the Gaelic League in Munster also needs examining. Theresa [sic] Halpin, a well known musician and dancer in Gaelic League circles at the start of the century, is also claimed to have composed 'The Walls of Limerick'" ("Rise upon the Sugawn, Sink upon the Gad," 73). Of course, Ní Ailpín *was* the secretary of the Gaelic League in Limerick at one time.

92. Ibid. The question of the composition of dances is fraught, and complicated by the common view that older dances (and tunes) are inevitably more valuable.

93. Ibid.

94. Brennan, *The Story of Irish Dance*, 55.

95. Ibid., 29.

96. This is very similar to a turn but usually played so that the separate notes of the ornament are not audible. Here, the notes would be GAGF-sharpG. A short roll on B begins on the upper note of the roll: DBAB.

97. Tomás Ó Canainn, *Traditional Music in Ireland*, 101.

98. Quoted in ibid., 133.

99. Ibid., 74–75.

100. Harry White, *The Keeper's Recital*, 8; see also 125–50.

101. Sean Williams and Lilis Ó Laoire make a similar point in reference to sean-nós singing in *Bright Star of the West*, 56–57 and 147.

102. See Frederick Neumann, *Ornamentation in Baroque and Post-Baroque Music*, 511–22; Greta Moens-Haenen, "Vibrato."

103. Bradshaw, "Michael Coleman, 1891–1945," 71–72. In *Capturing Sound*, Mark Katz argues that the extensive use of vibrato in early recorded violin performance helped ensure a full sound, covered slight inaccuracies in intonation, and helped establish a performer's acoustic "presence." While I believe that recorded performances influenced some Irish fiddlers, exact intonation and a full, rich sound in traditional music are of much less importance than rhythm in identifying "traditional" style. No evidence exists

that record producers directed Irish traditional fiddlers to use vibrato, and other fiddlers recorded during the 1929 Parlophone session did not use it extensively.

104. Eugene O'Donnell is the notable exception here, and his one album (Mick Moloney and Eugene O'Donnell, *Slow Airs and Set Dances from Ireland*), specifically focuses on a subset of the repertoire that is usually ignored.

THREE Biography, Musical Life, and Gender

1. Stroh violins were invented in the early twentieth century to produce a more directed sound for mechanical recording: the violin's horn was designed to be directed toward the horn of the recording device. As recording technology improved, the Stroh violin—with its notoriously thin and tinny sound—fell into disuse. See Hugh Davies, "Stroh Violin." Clifford did not always play a Stroh violin.

2. Adriana Cavarero, *Relating Narratives*, 1–2.

3. Here, I invoke Judith Butler's *Gender Trouble*.

4. James Clifford coined the term "ethnobiography," a concept that would anticipate and perhaps help bring about anthropology's reflexive turn in the 1980s ("'Hanging Up Looking Glasses at Odd Corners'"). Ethnobiography, however, seems to have had a short life as a named genre.

5. Daniel Aaron, preface, v.

6. Stanley Brandes, "Ethnographic Autobiographies in American Anthropology," 2.

7. Gayle Wald, *Shout, Sister, Shout!*; Susan Cheever, *A Woman's Life*. The unquestioned specificity of the "ordinary" woman's race, class, and sexuality in the latter monograph raises questions about whether a biography can ever be truly exemplary.

8. Richard Dyer, *White*, 9.

9. Here, I use first names to emphasize the individuality of each musician, as well as to convey a sense of familiarity between Pádraig O'Keeffe and the Murphy family.

10. Suzanne G. Cusick, "On a Lesbian Relationship with Music," 74–78.

11. Helen O'Shea, *The Making of Irish Traditional Music*, 119–40.

12. Cusick, "On a Lesbian Relationship with Music," 72.

13. For more about identification, see Nancy Miller, *But Enough about Me*. Janet Beizer reformulates the question of identification in her coinage of "bio-autography" (*Thinking through the Mothers*, 3). In chapter 5 I investigate disidentification through the work of José Muñoz.

14. Cavarero, *Relating Narratives*, 57–58 (emphasis in the original).

15. To my knowledge, Clifford and Maureen O'Carroll Cronin (a fiddle, concertina, and melodeon player) are the only women whose autobiographies appear in the *Journal of Cumann Luachra*.

16. Sonny Riordan, "My Life and Music," 21.

17. Maurice O'Keeffe, "My Life and Music," 20.

18. Jimmy Doyle, "My Life and Music," 6.

19. Paddy Cronin, "My Life and Music," 33.

20. Mike Duggan, "My Life and Music," 13.

21. Pádraig O'Keeffe is a classic example: he quit his job as a National School principal in large part because it conflicted with his preferred pastime of playing music. Today, many traditional musicians are schoolteachers because the academic calendar gives them freedom to travel to summer festivals. And it is worth noting that teaching was not an option for married women during the mid-twentieth century, when the marriage ban required women to leave public service jobs upon marrying.

22. O'Shea, *The Making of Irish Traditional Music*, 107.

23. Most of the male musicians who contributed their life stories to the *Journal of Cumann Luachra* mentioned their mothers' musical activity in the home.

24. Alan Ward, "Music from Sliabh Luachra," 7.

25. Julia Clifford, "My Life and Music," 22. Denis died in 1974, only hours after returning home from a night of making music in Knocknagree with the accordion player Johnny O'Leary.

26. Ibid., 20.

27. Quoted in Alan Ward, "Music from Sliabh Luachra," 7. In his account of Julia's early life, Ward goes into some detail about her father, known locally as Bill the Waiver (weaver), who organized the fife and drum band in Lisheen, and whom Julia's son Billy remembers as an early musical influence. In keeping with Irish naming custom, the name Waiver persisted after that branch of Murphys left the weaving trade in the late nineteenth century, and Denis and Julia were known at times as "Denis the Waiver" and "Julia the Waiver."

28. Julia Clifford describes practicing at home, where her father would correct her from another room if he heard her making any mistakes ("My Life and Music," 20).

29. Rosemary Cullen Owens, *A Social History of Women in Ireland*, 174.

30. Conrad Arensberg and Solon Kimball, *Family and Community in Ireland*, 208–9. Domestic violence was also common. See Owens, *A Social History of Women in Ireland*, 176–77.

31. Quoted in Francis O'Neill, *Irish Minstrels and Musicians*," 334. This is the only time O'Neill uses the word "artiste" in this book.

32. Julia Clifford, "My Life and Music," 20.

33. Ibid.

34. Ron Kavana, liner notes to *The Rushy Mountain*, 5.

35. Julia Clifford, interview with Reg Hall.

36. Maurice O'Keeffe, "My Life and Music," 18; Dermot Hanifin, *Pádraig O'Keeffe*, unnumbered page.

37. Pádraig O'Keeffe, Julia Clifford, and Denis Murphy, *Kerry Fiddles*. The recording

was originally made by Seamus Ennis on 9 September 1952 in Charlie Horan's bar in Castleisland, County Kerry.

38. Julia Clifford, "My Life and Music," 20.

39. Ibid.

40. Excessive (20 percent) duties placed on exports between Ireland and Britain during the economic war of the 1930s compounded the effects of worldwide economic depression. See Diarmaid Ferriter, *The Transformation of Ireland*, 368.

41. Louise Ryan, "Irish Female Emigration in the 1930s," 273.

42. Julia Clifford, "My Life and Music," 21.

43. Julia Clifford, interview with Hall. See also Julia Clifford, "My Life and Music," 21. Again, Julia's accounts in these two sources differ slightly: in the interview with Hall, she says, "I had a sister-in-law, a nun . . . she was teaching in Scotland, and she took me out there." Thus, the family connection is unclear.

44. Julia Clifford, interview with Hall.

45. Connie O'Connell, interview with author.

46. Alan Ward, "Music from Sliabh Luachra," 13.

47. Ryan, "Irish Female Emigration in the 1930s," 280–81. In his "My Life and Music" account, Julia's son Billy mentions that his mother met some of the big film stars of the day, including Edward G. Robinson and Errol Flynn ("My Life and Music," 103). This relative proximity to the supposed immorality of Hollywood and the acting profession surely rendered hotel jobs even less appropriate for young Catholic girls.

48. Quoted in Alan Ward, "Music from Sliabh Luachra," 13.

49. Lucy Farr, interview with Reg Hall, 1987. For most of her early career, Farr lived in nurses' accommodations in the hospitals where she worked. Clifford also seems to have lived in the hotels where she worked, at least during her early years in London.

50. Quoted in Alan Ward, "Music from Sliabh Luachra," 13.

51. Ibid., 14; Julia Clifford, interview with Hall.

52. Alan Ward, "Music from Sliabh Luachra," 15.

53. Ibid., 13. Julia's account of John's exact job in Bristol is vague, but he may have been employed by an airplane manufacturer or in a chemical plant.

54. Ibid.

55. Alan Ward, liner notes.

56. Billy Clifford recalls them learning new tunes together by combining the phrases that each remembered (interview with author, 19 August 2009).

57. Alan Ward, "Music from Sliabh Luachra," 8.

58. Ibid., 14.

59. Julia Clifford, interview with Hall.

60. Today, most Irish box players' instruments have two rows of buttons on the melody side, with each row pitched in a different key. The most popular tunings are C-sharp/D,

which is usually associated with the Sliabh Luachra style, and B/C, which is considered more versatile. Both generally have a range of two and a half octaves. Therefore, most button accordions are chosen for ease of playing in the keys most in use in Irish music—D, G, A, and their relative minors. By contrast, the saxophones in use in London in the 1930s and 1940s were most likely pitched in B-flat or E-flat, and song keys were the singer's choice, so musicians needed to adapt accordingly.

61. Alan Ward, "Music from Sliabh Luachra," 14. See also Reg Hall, "Irish Music and Dance in London, 1890–1970: A Socio-Cultural History" (PhD dissertation, University of Sussex, 1994).

62. Quoted in Peter Browne, "Julia Clifford." This quotation does not elaborate on what those things might have been, but Denis may have been referring to Julia's ability to play in any key.

63. Lucy Farr, quoted in Julia Clifford, interview with Hall.

64. Julia Clifford, interview with Hall.

65. Ibid.

66. Julia Clifford, "My Life and Music," 21–22.

67. Alan Ward and Tony Engle, liner notes to *Kerry Fiddles*, 2.

68. Preface to Seán MacRéamoin, liner notes, 1.

69. Julia Clifford, interview with Hall.

70. It is possible that Catherine was the first woman drummer in a céilí band in Ireland.

71. Alan Ward, "Music from Sliabh Luachra," 18.

72. Although equating Irish ornamentation with Western art music ornamentation is a dangerous prospect, a roll is similar to a turn, while a cut is roughly equivalent to an unsounded grace note—a flick of the finger that adds more to the rhythm than to the melody. Triplets or trebles are as usually notated, but played on one note with separate bows, with a dig on the first of the three notes. Crans—a piping ornament sometimes adapted for other instruments—add an eighth note to a triplet, with some articulation between the notes provided through the use of cuts. Martin Tourish's 2013 PhD dissertation begins the work of identifying and cataloging a wider range of ornaments, although the trad scene at large has not adopted the terminology he uses to distinguish techniques ("In Process and Practice").

73. The melody of "The Home Brew" plays with the distinction between modality and tonality more generally—is it in D major, or in D mixolydian? Although I could have notated this pitch by more conventional means, I have chosen to indicate the difference between it and C-sharp with a downward-pointing triangle so that the "C-supernatural" stands out as something closer to an ornament than an essential part of the melody. Most musicians would play a C-natural on these notes.

74. Julia Clifford and Billy Clifford, *Ceol as Sliabh Luachra*.

75. Browne, "Julia Clifford."

76. See Georgina Boyes, *The Imagined Village*; Michael Brocken, *The British Folk Revival, 1944–2002*; David Harker, *Fake Song*; Britta Sweers, *Electric Folk*.

77. Lucy Farr, interviews with Reg Hall, 24 February and 23 April 1988 (emphasis in the original).

78. Donal O'Connor remembers Julia's drink preferences from playing sessions with her in Ireland (interview with author). More ladylike drinks included port and sherry, and as late as the late 1990s, many women would not order pints of beer for themselves but would instead request "glasses" (half-pints).

79. Billy Clifford, interview with author, 19 August 2009.

80. Peter Browne, liner notes.

81. Julia Clifford, interview with Hall.

82. Pirkko Moisala, "Gender Negotiation of the Composer Kaija Saariaho in Finland," 172.

83. Bruce Turnbull, "Girl on Film," 52.

84. Quoted in O'Shea, *The Making of Irish Traditional Music*, 110. O'Shea cites Bergin's quotation as from Mairéid Sullivan, *Celtic Women in Music*, 28–29.

85. This quandary plays out in the reception of the women who have played fiddle in *Riverdance*.

86. For information on the Magdalen laundries (Catholic institutions where pregnant and other ostensibly wayward women were sent and held, often against their will), see Owens, *A Social History of Women in Ireland*, 174–76.

87. O'Shea tells the story of "Anna," a pseudonymous Australian fiddle player who worked as a paid session leader in Doolin, County Clare, in the late 1990s. Anna reports that she was harassed by men in the pub and censured by the women of the community until she changed her demeanor to approximate that of "the lovely girl": she lowered her gaze, sat with her knees together, and avoided smiling at anyone (*The Making of Irish Traditional Music*, 113). My own research partially supports O'Shea's argument that all women must adopt the pose of "the lovely girl" or be seen as sexually available, but this binary oversimplification cannot quite account for the acceptance of Julia Clifford.

88. Billy Clifford, "My Life and Music," 104.

89. O'Connell, interview with author (emphasis in original).

90. Ibid.

91. For example, Clifford was not shy about discussing her health problems and including details that many women would reserve for close female friends (ibid).

92. Donal O'Connor, interview with author.

93. O'Connell, interview with author.

94. Bernadette McCarthy, interview with author.

95. Cross-culturally, women beyond childbearing age often take on different musical roles or positions in hierarchies at events where music is performed. See Susan Auer-

bach, "From Singing to Lamenting"; Patricia Shehan, "Balkan Women as Preservers of Traditional Music and Culture"; Ellen Koskoff, "The Sound of a Woman's Voice"; Jane Sugarman, *Engendering Song*. In Irish music, the living women now most respected in traditional music—including Josephine Keegan, Mary Bergin, Maeve Donnelly, and Liz Carroll—are all in their fifties or older.

96. Donal O'Connor, interview with author.

97. Bernadette McCarthy, interview with author.

98. O'Connell, interview with author. He then points out that even though Clifford didn't start many tunes at these sessions, she was the guest of honor, and everyone responded by starting tunes they associated with her—a sign of respect for older and established musicians that continues today, no matter what the honored guest's sex.

99. John Clifford, Julia Clifford, and Reg Hall, *The Humours of Lisheen*.

100. Julia Clifford, John Clifford, and Billy Clifford, *The Star of Munster Trio*.

FOUR Subjectivity, Flow, and "the Music Itself"

1. This exhortation not to do ethnographic work may also derive from the Irish traditional music scene's collective (and transnational) weariness of the endless stream of eager student ethnographers practicing their skills on the members of local sessions.

2. For an early and influential appearance of "the music itself" in print, see Annie W. Patterson, "The Characteristic Traits of Irish Music."

3. Harry White, "The Invention of Ethnicity," 86.

4. For a helpful and thought-provoking account of musicology's use of the term "the music itself," see Rachel Mundy, "Evolutionary Categories and Musical Style from Adler to America."

5. For an example of the use of trad in nationalist rhetoric, see statements from Comhaltas Ceoltóirí Éireann's director Labhrás Ó Murchú, including the one cited in John O'Flynn, *The Irishness of Irish Music*, 100.

6. Jonathan Allison, "Magical Nationalism, Lyric Poetry and the Marvellous," 230.

7. David A. Wilson, *Ireland, a Bicycle, and a Tin Whistle*, 141. Also see Tom Sherlock and Ríonach Uí Ógáin, *The Otherworld*.

8. Beliefs in the supernatural persist. For example, in the late 1990s, the motorway bypass around Ennis was delayed and eventually slightly rerouted to avoid cutting down a whitethorn bush believed to be a fairy tree—a gathering place for otherworldly beings. See Donal Hickey, "Piseogs Abound for the Whitethorn Plant." A piseog is a curse or superstition.

9. Quoted in Matthew Everett, "Irish-American Fiddler Martin Hayes Explores the Boundaries of Traditional Music."

10. Bill Margeson, "The Tune's the Thing," 18.

11. See Bruno Latour, "On Actor Network Theory," and *Reassembling the Social*.

12. My thinking here is most immediately influenced by Alexander Weheliye's *Habeas Viscus* and his framings of the work of Sylvia Wynter and Hortense Spillers.

13. The Green Fields of America, *Live in Concert*, 1993.

14. "Thomas," interview with author.

15. "Jacqueline," interview with author.

16. Mihaly Csikszentmihalyi, *Flow: The Psychology of Optimal Experience* (New York: Harper Collins, 1990), 53. A longer version of the quotation reads: "When all a person's relevant skills are needed to cope with the challenges of the situation, that person's attention is completely absorbed by the activity. . . . As a result, one of the most universal and distinctive features of optimal experience takes place: people become so involved in what they're doing that the activity become spontaneous, almost automatic; they stop being aware of themselves as separate from the actions they are performing."

17. "Juniper," interview with author, 10 February 2018.

18. "Jacqueline," interview with author.

19. "Jack," interview with author.

20. See R. Keith Sawyer, *Group Genius: The Creative Power of Collaboration* (New York: Basic Books, 2017); Janet A. Young and Michelle D. Pain, "The Zone."

21. "Stefan," interview with author.

22. "Anne," interview with author.

23. Craic (pronounced "crack" and meaning "fun") is a relatively new addition to the Irish lexicon from the English "crack," as in "a cracking good time." Although some Irish language speakers have objected to its inclusion in the Irish language, by 2019 craic has become the preferred spelling. See Nelson McCausland, "The Irish Word 'Craic.'"

24. Helen O'Shea, "'Good Man, Mary!,'" 59.

25. "Ellen," response to author's questionnaire.

26. "Clara," interview with author.

27. Helen O'Shea, "'Good Man, Mary!,'" 59, and *The Making of Irish Traditional Music*, 112–14.

28. "Anne," interview with author.

29. "Frances," interview with author.

30. "Zeke," email conversation with author.

31. "Grace," interview with author (emphasis in the original).

32. "Rowan," response to author's questionnaire, 18 June 2013.

33. "Jacqueline," interview with author.

34. O'Shea, "'Good Man, Mary!,'" 60.

35. Suzanne G. Cusick, "On a Lesbian Relationship with Music," 78 (emphasis in the original).

36. Here, I am reminded of the classic quotation from *Monty Python's Flying Circus*:

"I object to all this sex on the television—I mean, I keep falling off!" (Ian McNaughton, "The Ant").

37. For a synopsis of psychologists' and theorists' views on affect, see Ruth Leys, "The Turn to Affect," especially 437–78.

38. Ibid., 438–39.

39. Eric Shouse, "Feeling, Emotion, Affect."

40. Anecdotally, musicians use "addiction" frequently to describe their drive to play trad. Other common links between mental health and trad are the phrases "stone mad for the music" or "mad for the tunes"—a playful way to describe participation in a subculture viewed as somewhat strange by the mainstream.

41. Elisabeth Le Guin, "'One Says That One Weeps, but One Does Not Weep,'" 212.

42. Ibid., 207.

43. In this passage, Le Guin leaves interpretation open: "interactive responsiveness" could refer to the performer's relationship with the audience or with the music. In the context of her work more generally, it seems logical to retain both referents.

44. Audre Lorde, "Uses of the Erotic," 56.

45. Carolyn Abbate, "Music—Drastic or Gnostic?," 517.

46. This is a notion that would change the social order altogether, since if human consciousness were able to dismantle the subject-object binary, institutions like slavery and the objectification of certain bodies would become literally unthinkable.

47. Thanks to Kitty Preston for thoughts about music as a character in films like *The Red Violin* and *Blue*.

FIVE *Playing Right and the Right to Play*

1. "Transformation rather than assimilation" consciously echoes Angela Davis's exhortation (untited speech).

2. Louis Althusser, *On the Reproduction of Capitalism: Ideology and Ideological State Apparatuses*.

3. José Esteban Muñoz, *Disidentifications*, 71.

4. See Althusser, *On the Reproduction of Capitalism*, especially chapter 12.

5. "Offering [something] up" is shorthand for the idea of redemptive suffering in Catholicism: in suffering hardships, people share the burden of Christ's suffering and thus help redeem others from sin.

6. See Wayne Koestenbaum, *The Queen's Throat*.

7. Vladimir Jankélévitch, *Music and the Ineffable*, 50.

8. Irish society and the trad scene sanction certain kinds of excess, particularly related to alcohol consumption and energetic displays of local and national pride at sporting events.

9. "Laoise," email correspondence with author.

10. Carolyn Abbate, "Music—Drastic or Gnostic?"

11. Ibid., 530. See also Jankélévitch, *Music and the Ineffable*, chapter 4.

12. People and groups in less privileged positions have long known this—which is one reason various "ethnic" cultural festivals are in the business of making noise, as Deborah Wong points out (*Speak It Louder*). By using the word "wield" in this context, I mean to invoke the work of Suzanne Cusick, Martin Daughtry, Jonathan Pieslak, and others on music in the Global War on Terror of the early 2000s.

13. "Anne," interview with author.

14. "Kate," interview with author.

15. "Genderqueer" is defined as "of, relating to, or being a person whose gender identity cannot be categorized as solely male or female" ("Genderqueer").

16. "Juniper," interview with author.

17. Muñoz, *Disidentifications*, 108.

18. "Laoise," email correspondence with with author.

19. Mark Slobin discusses affinity groups in *Subcultural Sounds*, and I used this framework to think about queer musicians' participation in a chapter in *The Oxford Handbook of Queerness and Music* (Tes Slominski, "Queer as Trad"). Recent events have led me to question the positive valences of the word "affinity" as a way to describe the behaviors of groups, however.

20. Muñoz, *Disidentifications*, 4.

21. Mick Moloney talks about trad as countercultural in the United States context, albeit somewhat dismissively: non-Irish musicians "are not expressing an Irish ethnic identity by performing Irish music. They may, however, be consciously identifying themselves with some kind of counter culture ideology" ("Irish Music in America," 448).

22. For a discussion of racialized assemblages as visual phenomena, see Alexander Weheliye, *Habeas Viscus*, 5–6.

23. "Zeke," questionnaire from author.

24. Michel Foucault, *The History of Sexuality*. For an in-depth study of sex and sexuality in Ireland, see Diarmaid Ferriter, *Occasions of Sin*.

25. "Zeke," questionnaire from author.

26. Noel Ignatiev, *How the Irish Became White*.

27. "Missy," interview with author. The politics of what seems to be at least a somewhat mutual recognition of "soul" between African Americans and Irish people bears more investigation. John O'Flynn addresses the topic of "Irish soul" (*The Irishness of Irish Music*), and Noel McLaughlin discusses the appropriation of African American musical forms ("Post-Punk Industrial Cyber Opera?"). Annie Randall's work on Dusty Springfield also addresses such questions in depth in the context of Irish diasporic identity in Britain (*Dusty!*).

28. Alan Parker, *The Commitments*. See also Matteo Cullen, "Positive Vibrations."

29. Many of the arguments I make in this chapter also apply to Ireland's itinerant Traveller population, but a full treatment of Traveller issues is beyond the scope of this book.

30. Even Barack Obama's celebrated Irish heritage and roots in County Offaly have not managed to shift this paradigm.

31. "Henry," interview with author.

32. In what follows, I consciously use the term "nonwhite" to emphasize that the "lack" of whiteness leads to a lack of respect (among other things).

33. Rhiannon Giddens, "Push It Further."

34. "Missy," interview with author.

35. "Henry," interview with author.

36. Ibid.

37. "Esmi," interview with author.

38. "Grace," interview with author.

39. "Henry," interview with author.

40. See Gavin Lee, "A Home at Disciplinary Margins."

41. Sean Williams, "Irish Music and the Experience of Nostalgia in Japan," 106–8.

42. "Esmi," interview with author.

43. Irish Council for International Students, "Third Level Graduate Scheme."

44. "Esmi," interview with author.

45. "Grace," interview with author.

46. This question about attrition and silence echoes a blog post from Sara Ahmed: "Silence enables the reproduction of the culture of harassment and abuse. When we don't speak about violence we reproduce violence. Silence about violence is violence. There were many students who left in silence. We still do not know not what they would have said if they could have stayed. Missing documents; missing people. We don't know how much we are missing" ("Speaking Out").

47. Members of Comhaltas Ceoltóirí Éireann at the branch level often disagree with the stances of the organization's leaders—especially those of Director-General Labhrás Ó Murchú, who was vocal in opposition to the same-sex marriage referendum in 2015. Nativist language is embedded in the organization's constitution. O'Flynn discusses Comhaltas's and Ó Murchú's "nativist-essentialist" view of Irish traditional music (*The Irishness of Irish Music*, chapter 5). For a more extensive account of Comhaltas, see Lauren Stoebel, "Comhaltas Ceoltóirí Éireann (The Irish Musicians' Association) and the Politics of Musical Community in Irish Traditional Music."

48. "Anne," interview with author.

49. "Theo," interview with author.

50. For a consideration of issues of recognition, being asked to speak for one's race (or sex or gender) and expectations of being seen as an individual (or not), see Peggy

McIntosh's classic "White Privilege." This concept has been adapted to address male and heterosexual privilege. See, for example, Caity Stetner, "From Straight-Identified to Queer."

51. "Henry," interview with author.
52. Ibid.
53. "Esmi," interview with author.
54. In *Orientalism*, Edward Said calls attention to this problem in his articulation of "the Orient" as a construction of the West rather than an entity with intrinsic meaning outside this dyadic relation. Frank H. Wu eloquently articulates the disjuncture between white individuality and stereotypes of other racial identities: "We Americans believe in an heroic myth from the nineteenth century, whereby moving to the frontier gives a person a new identity. Even if they do not find gold, silver, or oil, men who migrate to the West can remake their reputations. But moving to California works only for white men. Others cannot invent themselves by sheer will, because no matter how idiosyncratic one's individual identity, one cannot overcome the stereotype of group identity" (*Yellow*, 8).
55. "Ellen," response to author's questionnaire.
56. "Theo," interview with author.
57. "Clara," interview with author.
58. "Anne," interview with author.
59. "Frances," interview with author.
60. "Missy," interview with author.
61. "Marie," interview with author.
62. "Esmi," interview with author.

BIBLIOGRAPHY

Aaron, Daniel. Preface to *Studies in Biography*, edited by Daniel Aaron. Cambridge, MA: Harvard University Press, 1978.

Abbate, Carolyn. "Music—Drastic or Gnostic?" *Critical Inquiry* 30, no. 3 (2004).

Agamben, Giorgio. *Homo Sacer: Sovereign Power and Bare Life*. Stanford, CA: Stanford University Press, 1998.

Agulhon, Maurice. *Marianne into Battle: Republican Imagery and Symbolism in France, 1789–1880*. Translated by Janet Lloyd. New York: Cambridge University Press, 1981.

Ahmed, Sara. *The Cultural Politics of Emotion*. New York: Routledge, 2004.

———. *On Being Included: Racism and Diversity in Institutional Life*. Durham, NC: Duke University Press, 2012.

———. "Speaking Out." *Feminist Killjoys* (blog). 2 June 2016. https://feministkilljoys.com/2016/06/02/speaking-out/.

Allison, Jonathan. "Magical Nationalism, Lyric Poetry and the Marvellous: W.B. Yeats and Seamus Heaney." In *A Companion to Magical Realism*, edited by Stephen M. Hart and Wen-chin Ouyang. Rochester, NY: Boydell and Brewer, 2005.

Althusser, Louis. *On the Reproduction of Capitalism: Ideology and Ideological State Apparatuses*. London: Verso, 2014.

"Anne." Interview with author. 22 June 2013.

Arensberg, Conrad M., and Solon Toothaker Kimball. *Family and Community in Ireland*. Cambridge, MA: Harvard University Press, 1968.

Auerbach, Susan. "From Singing to Lamenting: Women's Musical Role in a Greek Village." In *Women and Music in Cross-Cultural Perspective*, edited by Ellen Koskoff, 25–43. Urbana: University of Illinois Press, 1989.

Ball, Earnest. "Mother Machree." Accessed 14 January 2009. www.ingeb.org/songs/theresai.html.

"Ballinasloe Violin Classes." *Loughrea Nationalist*, April 6, 1905.

Barrett, S. J., ed. *The Proceedings of the Third Oireachtas*. Dublin: Gaelic League, 1899.

Beiner, Guy. *Remembering the Year of the French: Irish Folk History and Social Memory*. Madison: University of Wisconsin Press, 2007.

Beizer, Janet L. *Thinking through the Mothers: Reimagining Women's Biographies*. Ithaca, NY: Cornell University Press, 2009.

Biletz, Frank A. "Women and Irish-Ireland: The Domestic Nationalism of Mary Butler." *New Hibernia Review* 6, no. 1 (2002): 59–72.

Bohlman, Philip. *The Study of Folk Music in the Modern World*. Bloomington: Indiana University Press, 1988.

Boland, Eavan. *Object Lessons: The Life of the Woman and the Poet in Our Time*. New York: W. W. Norton, 1995.

Bourke, Joanna. *Husbandry to Housewifery: Women, Economic Change, and Housework in Ireland, 1890–1914*. New York: Oxford University Press, 1993.

Boyes, Georgina. *The Imagined Village: Culture, Ideology, and the English Folk Revival*. Manchester, UK: Manchester University Press, 1993.

Bracefield, Hilary. "Let Erin Remember: The Irish-American Influence on Traditional Music in Ireland." *Writing Ulster* 5 (1998): 29–44.

Bradshaw, Harry. "Michael Coleman, 1891–1945." Liner notes to *Michael Coleman*. Dublin: Viva Voce, 1991.

Brandes, Stanley. "Ethnographic Autobiographies in American Anthropology." *Central Issues in Anthropology* 1, no. 2 (1979).

Breathnach, Breandán. *The Man and His Music: An Anthology of the Writings of Breandán Breathnach*. Dublin: Na Píobairí Uilleann, 1996.

Breathnach, Diarmuid, and Máire Ní Mhurchú. *Beathaisnéis a Cúig: 1882–1982*. Baile Átha Cliath, Ireland: An Clóchomhar, 1997.

Brennan, Helen. *The Story of Irish Dance*. Dingle, Ireland: Brandon, 2004.

"A Brilliant Success." *Limerick Echo*, 17 January 1911.

Brocken, Michael. *The British Folk Revival, 1944–2002*. Aldershot, UK: Ashgate, 2003.

Brown, Roly. "Lucy Farr: Heart and Home." *Musical Traditions* 12 (1994). http://www.mustrad.org.uk/articles/farr.htm.

Browne, Peter. "Julia Clifford—Obituary." *Irish Music Magazine*, July 1997, 5.

———. Liner notes to *Denis Murphy: Music from Sliabh Luachra*. Dublin: Raidió Teilifís Éireann, 1995.

Busteed, Mervyn A. *The Irish in Manchester c. 1750–1921: Resistance, Adaptation and Identity*. Manchester, UK: Manchester University Press, 2016.

Butler, Judith P. *Gender Trouble: Feminism and the Subversion of Identity*. New York: Routledge, 1990.

———. *Undoing Gender*. New York: Routledge, 2004.

Canny, Paddy, P. J. Hayes, Peadar O'Loughlin, and Bridie Lafferty. *An Historic Recording* of *Traditional Irish Music from County Clare and East Galway (All-Ireland Champions: Violin)*. Reissue. New York: Shanachie 76001, 2001.

Carolan, Nicholas. *A Harvest Saved: Francis O'Neill and Irish Music in Chicago*. Cork, Ireland: Ossian, 1997.

Carson, Ciaran. *Last Night's Fun: In and out of Time with Irish Music*. New York: North Point Press, 1998.

Cavarero, Adriana. *Relating Narratives: Storytelling and Selfhood*. Translated by Paul A. Kottman. New York: Routledge, 2000.

Chakrabarty, Dipesh. *Provincializing Europe: Postcolonial Thought and Historical Difference*. Princeton, NJ: Princeton University Press, 2000.

"Champion Chatter." *Clare Champion*, 19 September 1903.

Cheever, Susan. *A Woman's Life: The Story of an Ordinary American and Her Extraordinary Generation*. New York: William Morrow, 1994.

Clan-na-Gael. "Ballylongford Echoes." *Kerryman*, 8 November 1913.

"Clara." Interview with author. 11 January 2018.

Clear, Catriona. "Walls within Walls: Nuns in Nineteenth-Century Ireland." In *Gender in Irish Society*, edited by Chris Curtin, Pauline Jackson, and Barbara O'Connor, 134–51. Galway: Officina Typographica, 1987.

Clifford, Billy. "My Life and Music." *Journal of Cumann Luachra* 1, no. 13 (2009).

———. Interview with author. Audio recording. Tipperary Town, County Tipperary, Ireland, 18 May 2005.

———. Interview with author. Audio recording. Tipperary Town, County Tipperary, Ireland, 19 August 2009.

Clifford, James. "'Hanging Up Looking Glasses at Odd Corners': Ethnobiographical Prospects." In *Studies in Biography*, edited by Daniel Aaron. Cambridge, MA: Harvard University Press, 1978.

Clifford, Julia. Interview with Reg Hall. Audio recording. 1990. C903/43 CI, British Library, London.

———. "My Life and Music." *Journal of Cumann Luachra* 1, no. 4 (1987).

Clifford, Julia, and Billy Clifford. *Ceol as Sliabh Luachra*. Dublin: Gael Linn, 1982.

Clifford, Julia, John Clifford, and Billy Clifford. *The Star of Munster Trio*. London: Topic, 1977.

Clifford, Julia, John Clifford, and Reg Hall. *The Humours of Lisheen*. London: Topic, 1976.

Clifford, Julia, and Denis Murphy. *The Star above the Garter: Fiddle Music from Kerry*. Reissue. 1969. New York: Shanachie, 1992. CD 34002.

Coláiste na Rinne. "Brief History." Accessed 19 July 2019. https://www.anrinn.com/about-us/brief-history/.

"Concert." *Limerick Echo*, 17 October 1911.

"Concert at St. John's." *Limerick Echo*, 28 November 1911.

"Concert in Cooraclare." *Clare Champion*, 7 January 1904.

Cooley, Joe. Interview with Cathal O'Shannon, 29 November 1973. 10310-RTE-WAV. Irish Traditional Music Archive, Dublin.

Cousin, John William. "Thomas Osborne Davis." In John William Cousin, *A Short Biographical Dictionary of English Literature*. New York: E. P. Dutton, 1910. Accessed 16 December 2009. http://www.gutenberg.org/etext/13240.

Cox, Catherine. "Elizabeth O'Farrell: The Woman Airbrushed from History." *Irish Independent*, 4 February 2016.

Cranitch, Matt. *The Irish Fiddle Book*. Cork, Ireland: Ossian, 1988.

Crenshaw, Kimberle. "Demarginalizing the Intersection of Race and Sex: A Black Feminist Critique of Antidiscrimination Doctrine, Feminist Theory and Antiracist Politics." *University of Chicago Legal Forum* 1, article 8 (1989). https://chicagounbound.uchicago.edu/uclf/vol1989/iss1/8/.

Cronin, Paddy. "My Life and Music." *Journal of Cumann Luachra* [date unknown].

Crowley, Una, Mary Gilmartin, and Rob Kitchin. "'Vote Yes for Common Sense Citizenship': Immigration and the Paradoxes at the Heart of Ireland's 'Céad Míle Fáilte.'" National Institute for Regional and Spatial Analysis Working Paper no. 30, March 2006. http://mural.maynoothuniversity.ie/1541/1/WPS30.pdf.

Csikszentmihalyi, Mihaly. *Flow: The Psychology of Optimal Experience*. New York: Harper Collins, 1990.

Cullen, Mateo. "Positive Vibrations: Musical Communities in African Dublin." In *Music and Identity in Ireland and Beyond*, edited by Mark Fitzgerald and John O'Flynn. Farnham, UK: Ashgate Publishing, 2014.

Curtin, Nancy. "A Nation of Abortive Men: Gendered Citizenship and Early Irish Republicanism." In *Reclaiming Gender: Transgressive Identities in Modern Ireland*, edited by Marilyn Cohen and Nancy J. Curtin. New York: St. Martin's Press, 1999.

Curtis, L. Perry. *Apes and Angels: The Irishman in Victorian Caricature*. Washington: Smithsonian Institution Press, 1971.

Cusick, Suzanne G. "On a Lesbian Relationship with Music: A Serious Effort Not to Think Straight." In *Queering the Pitch: The New Gay and Lesbian Musicology*, edited by Philip Brett, Elizabeth Wood, and Gary C. Thomas, 67–83. New York: Routledge, 1994.

Dalby, Douglas. "Gay Activists Hail Vote, 3 Decades after a Fatal 'Queer Bashing' Hate Crime." *New York Times*, May 23, 2015.

Dalsimer, Adele, and Vera Kreilkamp. "Re/Dressing Mother Ireland: Feminist Imagery in Art and Literature." In *Re/Dressing Cathleen: Contemporary Works from Irish Women Artists*, edited by Jennifer Grinnell and Alston Conley. Chestnut Hill, MA: Boston College McMullen Museum of Art, 1997.

Darley, Arthur, and Patrick Joseph McCall, eds. *Feis Ceoil Collection of Irish Airs Hitherto Unpublished*. Dublin: Feis Ceoil Association, 1914.

Davies, Hugh. "Stroh Violin." In *Grove Music Online*. 1 January 2001. https://www.oxfordmusiconline.com/grovemusic/view/10.1093/gmo/9781561592630.001.0001/omo-9781561592630-e-0000047635.

Davis, Angela Y. *Abolition Democracy: Beyond Empire, Prisons, and Torture*. New York: Seven Stories Press, 2005.

———. Untitled speech in the University of Virginia's Excellence through Diversity Distinguished Learning Series. 27 March 2018, Paramount Theater, Charlottesville.

Davis, Leith. *Music, Postcolonialism, and Gender: The Construction of Irish National Identity, 1724–1874*. Notre Dame: University of Notre Dame Press, 2006.

Dinesen, Isak [Karen Blixen]. *Out of Africa*. New York: Random House, 1938.

Donnelly, Seán. "Rise upon the Sugawn, Sink upon the Gad: Recent Set Dance Books." *Ceol na hÉireann* 1, no. 3 (2001).

Doyle, Jimmy. "My Life and Music." *Journal of Cumann Luachra* [date unknown].

Duffy, Nick. "Ring Your Granny Campaign Aims to Mobilise Elderly Vote for Ireland's Marriage Referendum." *Pink News*, March 18, 2015. https://www.pinknews.co.uk/2015/03/18/ring-your-granny-campaign-aims-to-mobilise-elderly-vote-for-irelands-marriage-referendum/.

Duggan, Mike. "My Life and Music." *Journal of Cumann Luachra* 1, no. 2 (1983).

Dyer, Richard. *White*. London: Routledge, 1997.

"Ellen." Response to author's questionnaire. 4 April 2018.

"Esmi." Interview with author. 20 March 2018.

European Network against Racism. "Racism and Discrimination in Employment in Europe 2013–2017." 2017. http://www.enar-eu.org/IMG/pdf/20107_shadowreport_2016x2017_long_v8_hr.pdf.

Everett, Matthew. "Irish-American Fiddler Martin Hayes Explores the Boundaries of Traditional Music." *Knoxville Mercury*, 19 July 2017. http://www.knoxmercury.com/2017/07/19/irish-american-fiddler-martin-hayes-explores-boundaries-traditional-music/.

Fahey, Tony. "Nuns and the Catholic Church in Ireland in the Nineteenth Century." In *Girls Don't Do Honours: Irish Women in Education in the Nineteenth and Twentieth Centuries*, edited by Mary Cullen. Dublin: Women's Education Bureau, 1987.

Faithful Companions of Jesus. "Who We Are." Accessed 7 February 2010. http://www.fcjsisters.org/.

Farr, Lucy. Interview with Reg Hall. Audio recording, 10 December 1983. C903/374, British Library, London.

———. Interview with Reg Hall. Audio recording, 10 July 1987. C903/375, British Library, London.

———. Interview with Reg Hall. Audio recording, 24 February 1988. C903/381, British Library, London.

———. Interview with Reg Hall. Audio recording, 23 April 1988. C903/453, British Library, London.

"Feis Ceoil." *An Píobaire* 1, no. 33 (1978).

Feis Ceoil Association. *Feis Ceoil Syllabus of Prize Competitions, 1926*. Dublin: Feis Ceoil Association, 1926.

Ferriter, Diarmaid. *Occasions of Sin: Sex in Twentieth-Century Ireland*. London: Profile, 2009.

———. *The Transformation of Ireland*. Woodstock, NY: Overlook Press, 2005.

Fishman, Karen, and Jan McKee. "It's Scandalous! It's Immoral! It's the 'Turkey Trot'!" *Now See Hear!* (blog). 27 November 2014. https://blogs.loc.gov/now-see-hear/2014/11/its-scandalous-its-immoral-its-the-turkey-trot/.

Fitzgerald, Mark and John O'Flynn, eds. *Music and Identity in Ireland and Beyond*. Farnham, UK: Ashgate Publishing, 2014.

Foster, R. F. *Modern Ireland, 1600–1972*. New York: Penguin Books, 1989.

Foucault, Michel. "Nietzsche, Genealogy, History." In Michel Foucault, *Language, Counter-Memory, Practice: Selected Essays and Interviews*, edited by Donald F. Bouchard. Ithaca, NY: Cornell University Press, 1977.

Foucault, Michel, and Robert Hurley. *The History of Sexuality*. Vol. 1. New York: Vintage Books, 1990.

Foy, Barry. *The Field Guide to Irish Sessions*. Boulder, CO: Roberts Rinehart Publishers, 1999.

"Frances." Interview with author. 18 June 2013.

Gale, Emily, and Bonnie Gordon. "Sound in Jefferson's Virginia." *Encyclopedia Virginia*. 25 October 2016. https://www.encyclopediavirginia.org/Sound_in_Jefferson_s_Virginia#start_entry.

Gelbart, Matthew. *The Invention of "Folk Music" and "Art Music": Emerging Categories from Ossian to Wagner*. 1st paperback ed. Cambridge: Cambridge University Press, 2011.

"Genderqueer." Merriam-Webster.com. Accessed 27 July 2019. https://www.merriam-webster.com/dictionary/genderqueer.

Gibbons, Luke. *Transformations in Irish Culture*. Notre Dame, IN: University of Notre Dame Press, 1996.

Giddens, Rhiannon. "Push It Further: Rhiannon Giddens Takes a Turn on Tradition." *Morning Edition*. 10 February 2015. https://www.npr.org/2015/02/10/384943903/push-it-further-rhiannon-giddens-takes-a-turn-on-tradition.

Glassie, Henry. *Passing the Time in Ballymenone: Culture and History of an Ulster Community*. 1982. Reprint. Philadelphia: University of Pennsylvania Press, 2007.

"Grace." Interview with author. 26 January 2018.

"Grand Benefit Concert and Pictures in Aid of the Sufferers in the Recent Fire." *Limerick Echo*, 6 June 1911.

"Great Challenge Contest in Irish Dancing." *Nenagh Guardian*, 21 October 1911.

Green Fields of America. *Live in Concert*. Danbury, CT: Green Linnet Records, 1993.

Grene, Nicolas. "Black Pastoral: 1990s Images of Ireland." *Litteraria Pragensia* 20, no. 10 (2000).

Griffin, Gerald. *The Collegians; or The Colleen Bawn: A Tale of Garryowen*. New York: Century Company, 1906.

Guinan, Joseph. *Scenes and Sketches in an Irish Parish, or Priest and People in Doon*. Dublin: Gill, 1906. http://books.google.com/books?id=qMBDAQAAMAAJ.

Gupta, Charu. "The Icon of Mother in Late Colonial North India." *Economic and Political Weekly* 36, no. 45 (2001).

Habermas, Jürgen. *The Structural Transformation of the Public Sphere: An Inquiry into a Category of Bourgeois Society*. Translated by Thomas Burger. Cambridge, MA: MIT Press, 1989.

Halberstam, Judith. *In a Queer Time and Place: Transgender Bodies, Subcultural Lives*. New York: New York University Press, 2005.

Hall, Mrs. S. C. "Kelly the Piper." In Mrs. C. S. Hall, *Sketches of Irish Character*. London: Frederick Westley and A. H. Davis, 1829.

Hall, Reg, comp. *Irish Dance Music*. London: Topic Records, 1995.

———. "Irish Music and Dance in London, 1890–1970: A Socio-Cultural History." PhD diss., University of Sussex, 1994.

———. Liner notes to *Past Masters of Irish Fiddle Music*. London: Topic Records TSCD605, 2001.

———, comp. *The Voice of the People*. 20 compact discs. London: Topic Records, 1998.

Halpin Trio. *Over the Moor to Maggie*. London: Parlophone Records, 1929. E3627.

———. *Rogha an Fhile*, London: Parlophone Records, 1929. CE2529–1.

Hanifin, Dermot. *Pádraig O'Keeffe: The Man and His Music*. Casteleisland, Ireland: self-published, 1995.

Hardebeck, Carl. "Traditional Singing: Its Value and Meaning." *Journal of the Ivernian Society* 3 (January–March 1911).

Harker, David. *Fake Song: The Manufacture of British "Folksong," 1700 to the Present Day*. Milton Keynes, UK: Open University Press, 1985.

Haslam, Richard. "'A Race Bashed in the Face': Imagining Ireland as a Damaged Child." *Jouvert* 4, no. 1 (1999).

Helleiner, Jane Leslie. *Irish Travellers: Racism and the Politics of Culture*. Toronto: University of Toronto Press, 2000.

Henry." Interview with author. 13 March 2018.

Hickey, Donal. "Piseogs Abound for the Whitethorn Plant." *Irish Examiner*, 20 June 2016, https://www.irishexaminer.com/lifestyle/outdoors/donal-hickey/piseogs-abound-for-the-whitethorn-plant-405734.html.

———. *Stone Mad for Music: The Sliabh Luachra Story*. Dublin: Marino, 1999.

Hill, Myrtle. *Women in Ireland: A Century of Change*. Belfast: Blackstaff, 2003.

Hobsbawm, Eric John, and Terence Ranger. *The Invention of Tradition*. Cambridge: Cambridge University Press, 1983.

Ignatiev, Noel. *How the Irish Became White*. New York: Routledge, 2009.

Incorporated Society of Musicians. "About Us." Accessed 28 January 2010. http://www.ism.org/about/.

"Incorporated Society of Musicians Local Practical Examinations." *Limerick Echo*, 30 May 1911.

Innes, Catherine Lynette. *Woman and Nation in Irish Literature and Society, 1880–1935*. Athens: University of Georgia Press, 1993.

"An Interrupted 'Soiree.'" *Kerry People*, 7 February 1903.

Irish Archives Resource. *The Present Duty of Irishwomen: The Contribution of Irish Women as Documented in the Archival Record*. Accessed 18 April 2018. https://www.iar.ie/Docs/The%20Present%20Duty%20of%20Irishwomen.pdf.

Irish Council for International Students. "Third Level Graduate Scheme." Dublin: Irish Council for International Students. Accessed 8 May 2018. https://www.internationalstudents.ie/info-and-advice/immigration/third-level-graduate-scheme.

"Jack." Interview with author. 28 June 2017.

Jackson, Alvin. *Home Rule: An Irish History, 1800–2000*. New York: Oxford University Press, 2003.

"Jacqueline." Interview with author. 2 October 2017.

Jankélévitch, Vladimir. *Music and the Ineffable*. Translated by Carolyn Abbate. Princeton, NJ: Princeton University Press, 2003.

Johnson, E. Patrick. "'Quare' Studies, or (Almost) Everything I Know about Queer Studies I Learned from My Grandmother." *Text and Performance Quarterly* 21, no. 1 (2001): 1–25.

Jones, Greta. "Eugenics in Ireland: The Belfast Eugenics Society, 1911–15." *Irish Historical Studies* 8, no. 109 (1992): 81–95.

"Juniper." Interview with author. 10 February 2018.

"Kate." Interview with author. 18 June 2013.

Katz, Mark. *Capturing Sound: How Technology Has Changed Music*. Berkeley: University of California Press, 2004.

Kavana, Ron. Liner notes to *The Rushy Mountain: Classic Music from Sliabh Luachra 1952–1977*. London: Globestyle Records CDORBD 085, 1994.

Kearney, Daithi. "Towards a Regional Understanding of Irish Traditional Music." PhD diss., University College Cork, 2009.

Kearney, Richard. *Postnationalist Ireland: Politics, Culture, Philosophy*. London: Routledge, 1997.

Kearns, Gerry. "Mother Ireland and the Revolutionary Sisters." *Cultural Geographies* 11, no. 4 (2004): 443–67.

Kee, Robert. *The Green Flag: A History of Irish Nationalism*. London: Weidenfeld and Nicolson, 1972.

Kelly, Blanche Mary. "James Clarence Mangan." In *The Catholic Encyclopedia*. New York: Robert Appleton Company, 1910. Vol. 9. http://www.newadvent.org/cathen/09589a.htm.

Kelly, Joan. *Women, History, and Theory: The Essays of Joan Kelly*. Chicago: University of Chicago Press, 1986.

Kennedy, Robert E. *The Irish: Emigration, Marriage, and Fertility*. Berkeley: University of California Press, 1973.

Kiberd, Declan. *Inventing Ireland*. Cambridge, MA: Harvard University Press, 1996.

Killeen, Richard. *A Short History of Modern Ireland*. Dublin: Gill and Macmillan, 2003.

Kimmel, John. *John Kimmel, Virtuoso of the Irish Accordian* [sic]. Washington: Smithsonian Folkways, 2007.

Koestenbaum, Wayne. *The Queen's Throat: Opera, Homosexuality, and the Mystery of Desire*. New York: Poseidon Press, 1993.

Koskoff, Ellen. "The Sound of a Woman's Voice: Gender and Music in a New York Hasidic Community." In *Women and Music in Cross-Cultural Perspective*, edited by Ellen Koskoff, 213–23. Urbana: University of Illinois Press, 1989.

"Laoise." Email correspondence with author. 7 April 2018.

Latour, Bruno. "On Actor Network Theory: A Few Clarifications." 11 January 1998. http://www.nettime.org/Lists-Archives/nettime-l-9801/msg00019.html.

———. *Reassembling the Social: An Introduction to Actor-Network-Theory*. New York: Oxford University Press, 2005.

Laurel Hill Secondary School, F.C.J. "Laurel Hill: History." Accessed 7 February 2010. http://www.laurelhillsecondary.com/our-school/history.

Le Guin, Elisabeth. *Boccherini's Body: An Essay in Carnal Musicology*. Berkeley: University of California Press, 2006.

———. "'One Says That One Weeps, but One Does Not Weep': Sensible, Grotesque, and Mechanical Embodiments in Boccherini's Chamber Music." *Journal of the American Musicological Society* 55, no. 2 (2002).

Le Guin, Ursula K. *The Left Hand of Darkness*. New York: Ace Books, 2000.

Lee, Gavin. "A Home at Disciplinary Margins: Reflections of an Ethno/Musicologist from Elsewhere." *Sounding Board* (blog), *Ethnomusicology Review*, 4 March 2018. https://www.ethnomusicologyreview.ucla.edu/content/home-disciplinary-margins-reflections-ethnomusicologist-elsewhere.

Lentin, Ronit. "Ireland: Racial State and Crisis Racism." *Ethnic and Racial Studies* 30, no. 4 (2007).

Lerner, Gerda. *The Majority Finds Its Past: Placing Women in History*. Oxford: Oxford University Press, 1979.

Leys, Ruth. "The Turn to Affect: A Critique." *Critical Inquiry* 37, no. 3 (2011): 434–72.

Library Ireland. "Ireland's Loss of Population." Accessed 16 January 2009. http://www.libraryireland.com/articles/LossPopulationOutlookIrelandDunraven/index.php.

"Limerick Irish Pipers' Club at Kilkee, Sunday Next, Nineteenth July, 1903." *Clare Champion*, 18 July 1903.

"Limerick Opera Society." *Limerick Echo*, 18 March 1913.

"Limerick Opera Society." *Limerick Echo*, 28 November 1911.

"Limerick Operatic Society." *Limerick Echo*, 28 March 1911.

Linneen, Tony. "Had Wicklow Its Own Michael Coleman?" *Treoir*, July–August 1969.

Loomba, Ania. *Colonialism-Postcolonialism*. London: Routledge, 1998.

Lorde, Audre. "Uses of the Erotic: The Erotic as Power." In Audre Lorde, *Sister Outsider: Essays and Speeches*. Freedom, CA: Crossing Press, 1984.

Lucas, Bob. "The Road Is a Lover." Nashville, TN: Belly Boy Music, n.d.

Luddy, Maria. *Women in Ireland, 1800–1918: A Documentary History*. Cork, Ireland: Cork University Press, 1995.

Lutz, Catherine. "The Gender of Theory." In *Women Writing Culture*, edited by Ruth Behar and Deborah A. Gordon. Berkeley: University of California Press, 1995.

MacAoidh, Caoimhín. *The Scribe: The Life and Works of James O'Neill*. Manorhamilton, Ireland: Drumlin Publications, 2006.

MacKillop, James. *A Dictionary of Celtic Mythology*. Oxford: Oxford University Press, 2000.

Mangan, James Clarence. *James Clarence Mangan: His Selected Poems, with a Study by the Editor*. Edited by Louise Imogen Guiney. Norwood, MA: Norwood Press, 1897. https://books.google.com/books?id=Ej8UAQAAMAAJ&pg=PA3&source=gbs_toc_r&cad=4#v=onepage&q&f=false.

Margeson, Bill. "The Tune's the Thing." *Irish Music Magazine*, July 2004, 18–19.

"Marie." Interview with author. 28 March 2018.

McAuliffe, Mary, and Liz Gillis. *Richmond Barracks 1916: We Were There: 77 Women of the Easter Rising*. Dublin: Four Courts Press, 2016.

McCann, Anthony. "All That Is Not Given Is Lost: Irish Traditional Music, Copyright, and Common Property." *Ethnomusicology* 45, no. 1 (2001): 89–106.

———. "A Tale of Two Rivers: *Riverdance, A River of Sound*, and the Ambiguities of 'Tradition.'" *Ethnologie Française* 41, no. 2 (2011): 323–31.

McCarthy, Bernadette. Interview with author. Audio recording. Spanish Point, County Clare, Ireland, 5 June 2005.

McCarthy, Cal. *Cumann na mBan and the Irish Revolution*. Cork, Ireland: Collins Press, 2007.

McCarthy, Marie. *Passing It On: The Transmission of Music in Irish Culture*. Cork, Ireland: Cork University Press, 1999.

McCausland, Nelson. "The Irish Word 'Craic' . . . It Sure Isn't All That It's Cracked Up to Be!" *Belfast Telegraph*, 18 February 2016. https://www.belfasttelegraph.co.uk/opinion/columnists/nelson-mccausland/the-irish-word-craic-it-sure-isnt-all-that-its-cracked-up-to-be-34463086.html.

McClintock, Anne. *Imperial Leather: Race, Gender, and Sexuality in the Colonial Contest*. New York: Routledge, 1995.

McIntosh, Peggy. "White Privilege: Unpacking the Invisible Knapsack." *Peace and Freedom Magazine*, July–August 1989, 10–12.

McLaughlin, Noel. "Post-Punk Industrial Cyber Opera? The Ambivalent and Disruptive Hybridity of Early 1990s U2." In *Music and Identity in Ireland and Beyond*, edited by Mark Fitzgerald and John O'Flynn. Farnham, UK: Ashgate Publishing, 2014.

McMahon, Timothy G. "'All Creeds and All Classes'? Just Who Made Up the Gaelic League?" *Éire-Ireland* 37, nos. 3–4 (2002): 118–68.

———. *Grand Opportunity: The Gaelic Revival and Irish Society, 1893–1910*. Syracuse, NY: Syracuse University Press, 2008.

McNaughton, Ian, dir. "The Ant, an Introduction." *Monty Python's Flying Circus*. Aired 14 December 1969, on BBC.

Meaney, Gerardine. *Sex and Nation: Women in Irish Culture and Politics*. Dublin: Attic Press, 1991.

Meath Travellers Workshops. "1953 Names by Locality." Accessed 10 April 2018. http://www.travellerheritage.ie/information-resources/academic-research/1953-names-by-locality/.

Miller, Nancy K. *But Enough about Me: Why We Read Other People's Lives*. New York: Columbia University Press, 2002.

"Missy." Interview with author. 31 March 2018

Mitchell-Ingoldsby, Mary. "Cork Pipers Club: Club History." Accessed 16 December 2008. http://www.corkpipersclub.com/history/club-history/.

Moens-Haenen, Greta. "Vibrato." In *Grove Music Online*. Accessed 28 April 2010. https://www.oxfordmusiconline.com/grovemusic/abstract/10.1093/gmo/9781561592630.001.0001/omo-9781561592630-e-0000029287.

Moisala, Pirkko. "Gender Negotiation of the Composer Kaija Saariaho in Finland: The Woman Composer as Nomadic Subject." In *Music and Gender*, edited by Pirkko Moisala, Beverley Diamond, and Ellen Koskoff. Urbana: University of Illinois Press, 2000.

Moloney, Mick. "Irish Ethnic Recordings and the Irish-American Imagination." In *Ethnic

Recordings in America: A Neglected Heritage. Washington: American Folklife Center, 1982.

———. "Irish Music in America: Continuity and Change." PhD diss., University of Pennsylvania, 1992.

Moloney, Mick, and Eugene O'Donnell. *Slow Airs and Set Dances from Ireland*. 1978. Reissue. Oakhurst, NJ: Musical Heritage Society, 2000.

Moran, David P. *The Philosophy of Irish Ireland*. Dublin: University College Dublin Press, 2006.

Mostov, Julie. "Sexing the Nation/Desexing the Body: Politics of National Identity in the Former Yugoslavia." In *Gender Ironies of Nationalism: Sexing the Nation*, edited by Tamar Mayer. New York: Routledge, 2000.

"Mrs. S. C. Hall (Anna Maria Fielding)." *Dublin University Magazine* 16, no. 92 (January 1840). Accessed 12 December 2008. http://www.libraryireland.com/articles/Hall DUM16-92/index.php.

Mundy, Rachel. "Evolutionary Categories and Musical Style from Adler to America." *Journal of the American Musicological Society* 67, no. 3 (2014): 735–68.

Muñoz, José Esteban. *Cruising Utopia: The Then and There of Queer Futurity*. New York: New York University Press, 2009.

———. *Disidentifications: Queers of Color and the Performance of Politics*. Minneapolis: University of Minnesota Press, 1999.

Murphy, Cliona. *The Women's Suffrage Movement and Irish Society in the Early Twentieth Century*. Philadelphia: Temple University Press, 1989.

Murphy, Denis. *Music from Sliabh Luachra*. Dublin: Raidió Teilifís Éireann, 1995.

Myers, Margaret. "Searching for Data about European Ladies' Orchestras, 1870–1950." In *Music and Gender*, edited by Pirkko Moisala and Beverley Diamond. Urbana: University of Illinois Press, 2000.

National Archives of Ireland. "Census of Ireland, 1911: Form A." Accessed 24 July 2019. http://www.census.nationalarchives.ie/reels/nai001762247/.

———. "Census of Ireland, 1911: Residents of a house 28 in Garryowen East (Limerick No. 6 Urban (Pt. of), Limerick)." Accessed 22 February 2010. http://www.census.nationalarchives.ie/pages/1911/Limerick/Limerick_No__6_Urban__Pt__of_/Garryowen_East/627280.

Neumann, Frederick. *Ornamentation in Baroque and Post-Baroque Music: With Special Emphasis on J.S. Bach*. Princeton, NJ: Princeton University Press, 1978.

Ng, Alan. "Irish Traditional Music Tune Index." Accessed 14 February 2010. www.irishtune.info.

Ní Ailpín, Treasa, and Seán Ó Cuirrín. *Teagosc-Leabhar na Bheidhlíne*. Dublin: Oifig Díolta Foillseachám Rialais, 1923.

"Notes from Kilrush." *Clare Champion*, 11 April 1903.

Ó Canainn, Tomás. *Seán Ó Riada: His Life and Work*. Wilton, Cork, Ireland: Collins, 2003.

———. *Traditional Music in Ireland*. 2nd ed. Cork, Ireland: Ossian Publications, 1993.

Ó hAllmhuráin, Gearóid. *Flowing Tides: History and Memory in an Irish Soundscape*. New York: Oxford University Press, 2016.

———. *O'Brien Pocket History of Irish Traditional Music*. Dublin: O'Brien Press, 2003.

Ó hAodha, Micheál. *Irish Travellers: Representations and Realities*. Dublin: Liffey Press, 2006.

O'Brien, Kate. *The Land of Spices*. 1941. Reprint. London: Virago, 2007.

O'Connell, Connie. Unpublished interview with author. Audio recording. Tullamore, County Offaly, Ireland, 18 August 2009.

O'Connor, Anne V. "Influences Affecting Girls' Secondary Education in Ireland, 1860–1910." *Archivium Hibernicum* 41 (1986).

O'Connor, Donal. Interview with author. Audio recording. Raheen, Limerick, Ireland, 19 August 2009.

O'Flynn, John. *The Irishness of Irish Music*. New York: Routledge, 2017.

"Oireachtas." *Galway Observer*, 2 August 1913.

Oireachtas na Gaeilge. "Stair an tOireachtas [history of the Oireachtas]". Accessed 28 March 2007. http://www.antoireachtas.ie/an-toireachtas/stair.html.

O'Keeffe, Maurice. "My Life and Music." *Journal of Cumann Luachra* [date unknown].

O'Keeffe, Pádraig. *The Sliabh Luachra Fiddle Master*. Dublin: Raidió Teilifís Éireann, 1980.

O'Keeffe, Pádraig, Julia Clifford, and Denis Murphy. *Kerry Fiddles: Music from Sliabh Luachra 1977*. Reissue. Cork: Ossian Records, 1993.

O'Leary, Philip. *Gaelic Prose in the Irish Free State, 1922–1939*. University Park: Pennsylvania State University Press, 2004.

O'Neill, Barry. "Piping Contests at the Feis, 1897–1935." *Seán Reid Society Journal* 11 (March 1999).

O'Neill, Francis. *The Dance Music of Ireland: 1001 Gems*. 1907. Reprint. Fenton, MO: Mel Bay Publications, 2007.

———. *Irish Folk Music: A Fascinating Hobby, with Some Account of Allied Subjects Including O'Farrell's Treatise on the Irish or Union Pipes and Touhey's Hints to Amateur Pipers*. 1910. Reprint. Darby, PA: Norwood Editions, 1978.

———. *Irish Minstrels and Musicians: With Numerous Dissertations on Related Subjects*. 1913. Reprint. Cork, Ireland: Mercier, 1987.

O'Shea, Helen. "Defining the Nation and Confining the Musician: The Case of Irish Traditional Music." *Music and Politics* 3, no. 2 (Summer 2009).

———. "'Good Man, Mary!': Women Musicians and the Fraternity of Irish Traditional Music." *Journal of Gender Studies* 17, no. 1 (March 2008): 55–70.

———. *The Making of Irish Traditional Music*. Cork, Ireland: Cork University Press, 2008.

O'Sullivan, Donal Joseph, and Bonnie Shaljean. *Carolan: The Life, Times, and Music of an Irish Harper*. Reprint. Cork, Ireland: Ossian, 2005.

Owens, Rosemary Cullen. *Smashing Times: A History of the Irish Women's Suffrage Movement, 1889–1922*. Dublin: Attic Press, 1984.

———. *A Social History of Women in Ireland, 1870–1970*. Dublin: Gill and Macmillan, 2005.

Parker, Alan, dir. *The Commitments*. Beverly Hills, CA: Twentieth Century Fox Home Entertainment, 1991.

Patterson, Annie W. "The Characteristic Traits of Irish Music." *Proceedings of the Musical Association* 23 (1896): 91–111.

Pearse, Pádraig. "A Mother Speaks." Thomas MacDonagh Family Papers, 1848–1966, National Library of Ireland. Accessed 14 January 2009. http://catalogue.nli.ie/Record/vtls000588922.

Plain Piper [pseud.]. "The Irish Pipes." *Kerryman*, 1 June 1912.

Povinelli, Elizabeth. *The Cunning of Recognition: Indigenous Alterities and the Making of Australian Multiculturalism*. Durham, NC: Duke University Press, 2002.

Preface to Seán MacRéamoin, liner notes to Denis Murphy and Julia Clifford, *The Star above the Garter: Fiddle Music from Kerry*. Reissue. 1969. New York: Shanachie, 1992. CD 34002.

Randall, Annie J. *Dusty! Queen of the Postmods*. New York: Oxford University Press, 2009.

"Rathkeale Gaelic League Annual Concert." *Limerick Echo*, 23 May 1911.

Republic of Ireland. "Constitution of Ireland, Enacted by the People 1st July, 1937." 2015. http://www.irishstatutebook.ie/eli/cons/en.

Rexford, Eben E. "The Boy Who Loves His Mother." *Kerryman*, 17 May 1913.

Riordan, Sonny. "My Life and Music." *Journal of Cumann Luachra* [date unknown]

Ritchie, Fiona, and Doug Orr. *Wayfaring Strangers: The Musical Voyage from Scotland and Ulster to Appalachia*. Chapel Hill: University of North Carolina Press, 2014.

Roche, Frank. *The Roche Collection of Traditional Irish Music*. 3 vols. 1927. Reprint. Cork, Ireland: Ossian, 1993.

Rodger, Gillian M. *Champagne Charlie and Pretty Jemima: Variety Theater in the Nineteenth Century*. Urbana: University of Illinois Press, 2010.

"Rowan." Response to author's questionnaire. 18 June 2013.

Rubin, Gayle. "The Traffic in Women: Notes on the 'Political Economy' of Sex." In *Feminism and History*, edited by Joan Wallach Scott. New York: Oxford University Press, 1996.

Ryan, Louise. "Irish Female Emigration in the 1930s: Transgressing Space and Culture." *Gender, Place and Culture* 8, no. 3 (2001): 271–82.

Said, Edward. *Orientalism*. New York: Pantheon Books, 1978.

Sawyer, R. Keith. *Group Genius: The Creative Power of Collaboration.* New York: Basic Books, 2017.

Scott, Joan Wallach. *Gender and the Politics of History.* New York: Columbia University Press, 1988.

———. Introduction to *Feminism and History*, edited by Joan Wallach Scott. New York: Oxford University Press, 1996.

Shehan, Patricia K. "Balkan Women as Preservers of Traditional Music and Culture." In *Women and Music in Cross-Cultural Perspective*, edited by Ellen Koskoff, 45–53. Urbana: University of Illinois Press, 1989.

Sherlock, Tom, and Ríonach Uí Ógáin. *The Otherworld: Music and Song from Irish Tradition.* Dublin: Folklore of Ireland Council, 2012.

Shouse, Eric. "Feeling, Emotion, Affect." *M/C Journal* 8, no. 6 (2005). http://journal.media-culture.org.au/0512/03-shouse.php.

Siamsa Gaedheal Céilí Band. *The High Road to Galway/The Groves Reel/The Salamanca Reel.* London: Parlophone Records, 1931.

Slobin, Mark. *Subcultural Sounds: Micromusics of the West.* Hanover, NH: Wesleyan University Press, 2000.

Slominski, Tes. "'Pretty Young Artistes' and 'The Queen of Irish Fiddlers': Intelligibility, Gender, and the Irish Nationalist Imagination," *Ethnomusicology Ireland* 2, no. 3 (2013).

———. "Queer as Trad: LGBTQ Performers and Irish Traditional Music in the United States," in *The Oxford Handbook of Queerness and Music*, edited by Fred Everett Maus and Sheila Whiteley. New York: Oxford University Press, 2018.

Small, Christopher. *Musicking: The Meanings of Performing and Listening.* Middletown, CT: Wesleyan University Press, 1998.

Small, Jackie. "Feis Ceoil Results." *An Píobaire* 2, no. 37 (Summer 1987).

Smith, Christopher J. *The Creolization of American Culture: William Sidney Mount and the Roots of Blackface Minstrels.* Urbana: University of Illinois Press, 2014.

Solie, Ruth A. *Music in Other Words: Victorian Conversations.* Berkeley: University of California Press, 2004.

Sparling, H. Halliday, ed. *Irish Minstrelsy: Being a Selection of Irish Songs, Lyrics, and Ballads.* London: W. Scott, 1888.

"Special Orchestra of 25." *Limerick Echo*, 7 February 1911.

Spillers, Hortense J. *Black, White, and in Color: Essays on American Literature and Culture.* Chicago: University of Chicago Press, 2003.

"Stefan." Interview with author. 14 October 2017.

Stetner, Caity. "From Straight-Identified to Queer: Unloading the Invisible Knapsack of Privilege." *Medium*, 19 March 2017. https://medium.com/@caity.stet/from-straight-identified-to-queer-unloading-the-invisible-knapsack-of-privilege-a46e9c3aa13b.

Stoebel, Lauren. "Comhaltas Ceoltóirí Éireann (The Irish Musicians' Association) and the Politics of Musical Community in Irish Traditional Music." PhD diss., City University of New York, 2015.

Sugarman, Jane C. *Engendering Song: Singing and Subjectivity at Prespa Albanian Weddings*. Chicago: University of Chicago Press, 1997.

Sullivan, A. M. *New Ireland: Political Sketches and Personal Reminiscences of Thirty Years of Irish Public Life*. Glasgow: Cameron and Ferguson, 1882.

Sullivan, Mairéid. *Celtic Women in Music: A Celebration of Beauty and Sovereignty*. Kingston, ON: Quarry Press Books, 1999.

Surel, Jeannine. "John Bull." In *Patriotism: The Making and Unmaking of British National Identity*, edited by Raphael Samuel, 3:3–25. New York: Routledge, 1989.

Sweers, Britta. *Electric Folk: The Changing Face of English Traditional Music*. Oxford: Oxford University Press, 2005.

Taylor, Miles. "John Bull and the Iconography of Public Opinion in England c. 1712–1929." *Past and Present* 134 (February 1992): 93–128.

Teitelbaum, Benjamin R. *Lions of the North: Sounds of the New Nordic Radical Nationalism*. New York: Oxford University Press, 2017.

Tenniel, Sir John. "Two Forces." *Punch*, 29 October 1881.

Thapar-Bjorkert, Suruchi, and Louise Ryan. "Mother India/Mother Ireland: Comparative Gendered Dialogues of Colonialism and Nationalism in the Early 20th Century." *Women's Studies International Forum* 25, no. 3 (2002): 301–13.

"That the Age of Nationality Is Gone." *Galway Observer*, 4 April 1925.

"Theo." Interview with author. 19 June 2013.

"Thomas." Interview with author. 19 June 2017.

Tick, Judith. "Passed Away Is the Piano Girl: Changes in American Musical Life, 1870–1900." In *Women Making Music: The Western Art Tradition, 1150–1950*, edited by Jane Bowers and Judith Tick. Chicago: University of Illinois Press, 1986.

Tourish, Martin. "In Process and Practice: The Development of an Archive of Explicit Stylistic Data for Irish Traditional Instrumental Music." PhD diss., Dublin Institute of Technology, 2013.

Trew, Johanne. "Treasures from the Attic: Viva Voce Records." *Journal of American Folklore* 113, no. 449 (Summer 2000): 305–14.

Tuck, Raphael, and Sons. "Erin Go Bragh Series #177." Postcard postmarked 1911. Accessed 20 July 2019. https://tuckdb.org/items/53309.

Turnbull, Bruce. "Girl on Film." *Big Cheese Magazine*, August 2009.

Vallely, Fintan. *The Companion to Irish Traditional Music*. New York: New York University Press, 1999.

Varlet, Philippe. Liner notes to *Milestone in the Garden*. Cambridge, MA: Rounder Records, 1996.

Vaughan, W. E., and A. J. Fitzpatrick, eds. *Irish Historical Statistics: Population, 1821–1971.* Dublin: Royal Irish Academy, 1978.

"Violin Class for Ballinasloe." *Loughrea Nationalist*, 30 March 1905.

Wald, Gayle. *Shout, Sister, Shout! The Untold Story of Rock-and-Roll Trailblazer Sister Rosetta Tharpe.* Boston: Beacon Press, 2007.

Wallis, Geoff. "Past Masters of Irish Fiddle Music." 21 August 2001. http://www.mustrad.org.uk/reviews/pmifm.htm.

Ward, Alan. Liner notes to *The Star of Munster Trio*. London: Topic Records, 1977.

———. "Music from Sliabh Luachra: An Introduction to the Traditional Music of the Cork/Kerry Borderland with Notes on Topic Records 12T(S)309-311." London: Topic Records, 1976.

Ward, Alan, and Tony Engle. Liner notes to *Kerry Fiddles*. Cork, Ireland: Ossian Publications, 1993.

Ward, Margaret. "Marginality and Militancy: Cumann na mBan, 1914–36." In *The Irish Women's History Reader*, edited by Alan Hayes and Diane Urquhart. London: Routledge, 2001.

———. *Unmanageable Revolutionaries: Women and Irish Nationalism.* 1983. Reprint. London: Pluto, 1995.

Warner, Marina. *Alone of All Her Sex: The Myth and Cult of the Virgin Mary.* New York: Random House, 1976.

———. *Monuments and Maidens: The Allegory of the Female Form.* Berkeley: University of California Press, 2000.

Watts, Vanessa. "Indigenous Place-Thought and Agency Amongst Humans and Non Humans (First Woman and Sky Woman Go On a European World Tour!)." *Decolonization* 2, no. 1 (2013). https://jps.library.utoronto.ca/index.php/des/article/view/19145.

"Wednesday Violin Competitions." *Connaught Tribune*, 19 July 1913.

Weheliye, Alexander G. *Habeas Viscus: Racializing Assemblages, Biopolitics, and Black Feminist Theories of the Human.* Durham, NC: Duke University Press, 2014.

White, Harry. "The Invention of Ethnicity: Traditional Music and the Modulations of Irish Culture." *De musica disserenda* 2 (2009).

———. *The Keeper's Recital: Music and Cultural History in Ireland, 1770–1970.* Notre Dame, IN: University of Notre Dame Press, 1998.

———. *The Progress of Music in Ireland.* Dublin: Four Courts Press, 2005.

White, Victoria. "Will the Real Irish Dancing Please Stand Up?" *Irish Times*, 18 December 1996. http://www.standingstones.com/ceili.html.

Williams, Sean. "Irish Music and the Experience of Nostalgia in Japan." *Asian Music* 37, no. 1 (2006): 101–19.

Williams, Sean, and Lillis Ó Laoire. *Bright Star of the West: Joe Heaney, Irish Song-Man.* New York: Oxford University Press, 2011.

Williams, William H. A. *'Twas Only an Irishman's Dream: The Image of Ireland and the Irish in American Popular Song Lyrics, 1800–1920*. Chicago: University of Illinois Press, 1996.

Wilson, David A. *Ireland, a Bicycle, and a Tin Whistle*. Montreal, QC: McGill-Queens University Press, 2014.

Wong, Deborah. *Speak It Louder: Asian Americans Making Music*. New York: Routledge, 2004.

Wu, Frank H. *Yellow: Race in America beyond Black and White*. New York: Basic Books, 2002.

Wynter, Sylvia. "Human Being as Noun? Or *Being Human* as Praxis? Towards the Autopoetic Turn/Overturn: A Manifesto." August 25, 2007. https://s3.amazonaws.com/arena-attachments/1516556/69a8a25c597f33bf66af6cdf411d58c2.pdf.

Yeats, William Butler. "Sailing to Byzantium." In *W. B. Yeats: Selected Poetry*, edited by John Kelly. London: J. M. Dent, 1997.

Young, Janet A., and Michelle D. Pain. "The Zone: Evidence of a Universal Phenomenon for Athletes across Sports." *Athletic Insight* 1, no. 3 (1999).

Young, Robert. "The Pipers' Competition at the Feis Ceoil." *An Píobaire* 1, no. 20 (1975).

Yuval-Davis, Nira. *Gender and Nation*. London: Sage, 1997.

"Zeke." Email conversation with author, 14 October 2017.

———. Questionnaire from author. Spring 2013.

Zimmermann, Georges Denis. *Songs of the Irish Rebellion: Irish Political Street Ballads and Rebel Songs, 1780–1900*. Portland, OR: Four Courts Press, 2002.

INDEX

Note: "Irish traditional music" is shortened to "trad" throughout index. Page numbers of figures are *italicized*.

Aaron, Daniel, 101, 102
Abbate, Carolyn, 151, 157–58
accessibility of trad, 165–66
accordion, 116, 198n60
activism, 39–44, 177
Acts of Union, (1800), 27, 182n3
"addiction" to music, 150, 203n40
aesthetics, 24, 150, 155–57
affect theory, 149–50
affinity groups, 16, 160, 204n19
African American musicians, 164, 167–68, 170, 180n11, 204n27. *See also* blackness; musicians of color
Africans, enslaved, 3, 9, 163, 167, 203n46
Agamben, Giorgio, 180n23
Ahmed, Sarah, 33, 180n10, 205n46
aisling (vision or dream) genre, 31, 34, 54, 55, 137
All-Ireland (Fleadh Cheoil na hÉireann), 17, 73, 77, 121, 194n80
Allison, Jonathan, 137, 188n111
Althusser, Louis, 154, 170
"A Mother Speaks" (Pearse), 33
animal dances, 8
"Ant, The" (McNaughton), 203n36
anthropomorphism, 75–76, 151, 152

apes, Irish portrayed as, 9, 29, 162, *163*
appeal of trad, 104–6, 140, 141, 172, 177–78
Arbuthnot, John, 182n8
Arensberg, Conrad, 110
art music. *See* classical music/art music
"Asian American" term, 22
Asian musicians, 146–47, 166, 169, 172. *See also* musicians of color
assimilation, 9, 18, 172–73
audience members, 144, 146
"authenticity," 7, 23, 96–97, 103; and dance, 88; and ethnic nationalism, 11, 66; and Kenny, 49; and monetary value, 17; and Ní Ailpín, 96–97

Barry, Margaret, 45
bassing, 119
Bean Sheáin Uí Chuirrín (Treasa Ní Ailpín). *See* Ní Ailpín, Treasa
Beizer, Janet, 20, 196n13
Bergin, Mary, 127–29
Bharat Mata (personification of India), 26, 29
Bill the Waiver (Bill Murphy), 28, 197n27
biography, 23, 100–104, 106–7, 124, 179n1, 196n7
black musicians, 164, 167–68, 170, 180n11, 204n27. *See also* musicians of color

blackness, 8, 9, 161–65
Blixen, Karen, 2, 99–100, 179n1
Bohlman, Philip, 182n43
Boland, Eavan, 25
"Boys of the Town" ("The Ennistymon Jig"), 193n64
Brandes, Stanley, 101–2
Breathnach, Breandán, 77, 78, 192n62
Breathnach, Eibhlín, 184n46
Brennan, Helen, 73
Britain, 114, 116–18, 125, 194n84; Britannia, 26, 28–29, 56, 57; colonialism of, 26, 36; Gaelic League in, 188n115; and Ireland, 9, 11, 27–30, 70–71, 113, 162, 183n18, 188n115, 194n40; music education in, 67. *See also* England
Britannia (personification of Britain), 26, 28–29, 56, 57
"Buachaill Caol Dubh, An" ("The Dark Slender Boy") (Ní Ailpín recording), 81, 84, 93–96
Bunting, Edward, 46, 78, 83
Butler, Judith, 63, 176
Butler, Mary, 41, 185n68

cailleach, 26, 30–32, 183n22
Capturing Sound (Katz), 93, 195n103
careers for trad musicians, 114, 197n21, 198n47, 198n49
Cathleen Ní Houlihan (personification of Ireland), 30, 34–37, 184n42
Cathleen Ni Houlihan (Yeats), 184n42
Catholic Church, 40, 180n29, 182n3, 203n5; and Clifford, 129–30; and dance, 90, 110; and Erin, 36; and jazz, 90, 110, 164; Magdalen laundries, 129, 200n86; Virgin Mary, 32, 33, 35–36, 37, 184n46; and women, 36, 110, 114, 129, 198n47
Cavarero, Adriana, 27, 62, 99–100, 102, 106–7, 179n1
céilí dance, 88–89, 90, 91, 191n32
Ceol as Sliabh Luachra (Music from Sliabh Luachra) (Julia and Billy Clifford album), 125, 133
Ceoltóirí Chualann, 190n5

chain migration, 16, 181n36
Chakrabarty, Dipesh, 32
Cheever, Susan, 196n7
Cherish the Ladies (Shanachie Records), 182n42
Chieftains, 121, 190n5
citizenship in Ireland, 9, 10, 13, 14
Clancy, Martin, 74, 75–76, 192n55
Clan-na-Gael, 8, 69
Clare Champion, 40, 48
class distinctions, 8, 48, 67, 70–74, 126, 165, 187n98, 192n54
classical music/art music, 66–82; and Asian musicians, 169; and class, 67, 70–72; as contaminant, 67; as effeminate, 65–69, 95, 99; and Feis Ceoil, 69–70; as foreign, 65–69, 99; Gaelic League on, 69; and imperialism, 169; and Ó Riada, 190n5; stereotypes of musicians, 71, 160; and *Teagosc-Leabhar na Bheidhline*, 83; and trad, 66–67, 95–96; and women, 66–72, 95, 190n19
Clifford, Billy, 101, 109, 110, 117, 121, 197n27; *Ceol as Sliabh Luachra*, 125, 133; on Clifford, Julia, 126, 198n56; Star of Munster Céilí Band, 116, 118–19
Clifford, Catherine, 121, 199n70
Clifford, James, 196n4
Clifford, John, 101, 115–18, 121–23, 124, 133, 198n53
Clifford, Julia, 7, 23–24, 44, 97–134, 103, 156, 200n87, 201n98; bassing skill, 119; and biography, 101, 106–7; and Catholic Church, 129–30; *Ceol as Sliabh Luachra*, 125, 133; on Chieftains, 121; childhood, 109–13, 197n28; and Clifford, Billy (*See* Clifford, Billy); and Clifford, John, 101, 115–18, 121–23, 124, 133, 198n53; and Coakley, 111, 117; and Coleman, 116; contest story, 110–13; and "C-supernatural," 123; and dance halls, 117; on "Danny Ab's Slide" *Kerry Fiddles* recording, 119; drink preferences, 126, 200n78; in Falkirk, Scotland, 113, 198n43; fame of, 125; family, 118, 197nn27–28;

and Farr, 111, 117, 125, 133; femininity, performance of, 129; "Freddy Kimmel's/ The Home Brew," 121–24, *122, 124,* 199n73; Hall interview, 110–11, 126, 198n43; hotel maid work, 114, 198n47, 198n49; *Humours of Lisheen, The,* 121–24, *122, 124,* 133, 199n73; and Irish economy, 113; in *Journal of Cumann Luachra,* 107–11, 113, 118–19, 196n15, 198n47; "Julia the Waiver," 197n27; in London, England, 114, 116–17, 118, 125, 131–33, 194n84; McCarthy on, 131, 132; and Murphy (*See* Murphy, Denis); "My Life and Music" autobiography, 107–11, 113, 118–19, 196n15, 198n47; and nationalism, 110; and O'Connell, 122, 129–30, 132; O'Connor on, 130–33, 200n78; and O'Keeffe, 110, 111, 119, 123, 125, 132, 133, 196n9; personality, 129–33, 200n91; playing qualities, 121–23; post-World War II, 118–25; prizes and distinctions, 121, 125; radio performances, 116, 118; and religion, 129–30; in *The Rushy Mountain: Classic Music from Sliabh Luachra 1952–1977* liner notes, 111; and Sliabh Luachra, 103, 115, 122, 133; as soloist, 133; *The Star above the Garter,* 119–21, *120,* 133; Star of Munster Céilí Band, 116, 118–19, 133; *The Star of Munster Trio,* 133; and stereotypes, resistance to, 129–31; and Stroh fiddle, 98, *99,* 196n1; as teacher, 119; Topic recordings, 121–24, *122, 124,* 133, 199n73; transposing skill, 116–17, 119, 199n62; travels, 113, 114, 116–17, 118, 121, 125; as "woman musician," 100, 125–26, 129; and World War II, 117

Coakley, John, 111, 117

code switching, 132

Coimisiún le Rincí Gaelacha, An (Irish Dancing Commission), 81, 88–89, 91–92

Coláiste na Rinne, 73, 82

Coleman, Michael, 19, 81–82, 93, 95–96, 116, 128, 138

College of Ring, 73, 82

colonialism, 15, 17, 18, 26, 28–30, 36

Comhaltas Ceoltóirí Éireann (Society of the Musicians of Ireland), 181n37, 193n66, 205n47; All-Ireland, 17, 64–65, 73, 77, 121, 194n80; and nationalism, 14, 16–17, 173

"commonsense citizenship" referendum, 9, 10, 13

competitions: Feis Ceoil, 68–72, 76–79, 81, 84, 190n15, 192n61, 193n64, 194nn78–79; Fleadh Cheoil na hÉireann, 17, 64–65, 73, 77, 121, 194n80; Oireachtas, 40, 65, 69–73, 80–82, 188n106, 193n66

Connaught Tribune, 80

conservatism, 42, 128

Constitution of Ireland, 9, 10, 108, 129, 180n20

convent schools, 59, 68, 74

Cooley, Joe, 6, 135, 140

copyright laws, 17

counteridentification, 160–61

"craic" term, 202n23

Cranitch, Matt, 83–84, 94, 95

crans (ornamentation), 199n72

Crenshaw, Kimberle, 7

Cronin, Edward, 55, 57

Cronin, Maureen O'Carroll, 196n15

Cronin, Paddy, 108

Crowley, Una, 4, 9, 15, 181n33

Csikszentmihalyi, Mihaly, 141, 202n16

"C-supernatural," 123, 199n73

cultural imperialism, 11

cultural values, Irish, 9, 153, 154, 161, 173, 175, 177, 203n8

Cumann na mBan (Irishwomen's Council), 39, 43, 55, 185n57, 186n78

Curran, Sean (Seán Ó Cuirrín), 82–84, 88, 90, 193nn73–76, 194n78

Curtin, Nancy, 183n18

Cusick, Suzanne, 105, 148–49

cut (ornamentation), 199n72

Daily Sketch, 54, 188n114

dance, 81, 86, 96, 194n86; animal dances, 8; and "authenticity," 88; and Catholic Church, 90, 110; céilí dance, 88–89, 90, 91, 191n32; and class distinctions, 73; and Gaelic League, 73, 90, 91, 96; and gender, 91–92; Irish Dancing Commission (An Coimisiún le Rincí Gaelacha), 81; and Irish Ireland movement, 73; and nationalism, 89–90; Ní Ailpín as dancer, 72–73; quadrilles, 88–89, 91; and "Rogha an Fhile," 89, 93; set dance, 88–89, 91, 96; step dance, 58, 88–89, 191n32

Dance Music of Ireland: 1001 Gems, The (O'Neill), 46

"Danny Ab's Slide" (*Kerry Fiddles*, Clifford, Murphy, O'Keeffe), 119, *120*

"Dark-haired little rose" ("Roisín Dubh"), 34

Dark Rosaleen (personification of Ireland), 34–37, 184n39

"Dark Slender Boy, The" ("An Buachaill Caol Dubh"), 81, 84, 93–96

Darley, Arthur, 76–79, 193n64

dating within trad scene, 115–18, 173, 174, 175

Daughters of Erin (Inghinidhe na hÉireann), 39, 42–43

"Delahunty's" (The Home Brew), 122, *122*, *124*, 199n73

demographics in trad scene, lack of information on, 12–13

"Denis the Waiver" (Denis Murphy). *See* Murphy, Denis

diaspora, Irish, 9, 10, 13, 17, 30, 134, 181n36

disbelief, aggression of, 165–72

disciplinary purity, 21

discrimination, 11, 14; and disidentification, 173; against foreigners, 176; gatekeeping, 163–65; and immigrants, 9, 12, 162–63; against Irish people, 9, 29, 162–63, *163*; moving beyond, 17–18; and nationalism, 7; sexism, 127–29, 143–44, 146–47; and "the music itself," 18, 136, 173; against Traveller community, 49, 164, 187n92. *See also* racism

disidentification, 159–62, 167, 173

diversity discourse, 6

divorce, 10

domestic role, women and, 39, 41

Donnelly, Seán, 91, 195n91

"don't ask, don't tell" messages, 156–59, 162

Doyle, Jimmy, 108

drastic and gnostic, 157–58

Duggan, Mike, 108

Dyer, Richard, 103

education, music, 59, 67–68, 112

1800 Acts of Union, 27, 182n3

Eiré (personification of Ireland), 57

emigration from Ireland, 113, 114, 184n49, 194n84. *See also* immigrants

England: and Ireland, relationship with, 27–30, 70–71, 113; John Bull as personification of, 28, 182n8; London, 114, 116–18, 125, 131–33, 194n84, 199n60

Ennis, Séamus, 51

"Ennistymon Jig, The" (recording, Ní Ailpín), 79–80, 93, 193n64

erasure, 6, 23, 44–45, 66, 95–96, 98–99, 113, 165, 180n11

Erin (personification of Ireland), 26, 29–30, 36, 40, 55–57, *56*, 129

"Erin Go Bragh Series" #177 (Raphael Tuck and Sons), *56*

"Erin Machree," 184n35

Ériu (goddess), 29

eroticism, music and, 149, 150–51, 152

escapism, 105–6, 177

ethnic nationalism, 7, 9, 67, 177; alternatives to, 6, 15, 18, 175; and "authenticity," 11, 66; and Comhaltas Ceoltóirí Éireann, 173; control of bodies and, 10–14; critique of, 3–4, 11, 14–15, 17, 18, 155, 175; cultural nationalism's reinforcement of, 8; and disidentification, 167; and ethnography, 19; inborn talent fallacy, 180n29; and passing, 160; and purity, 11; and racial anxieties, 161–62; reproductive heterosexuality and, 26; and white supremacy, 11, 26. *See also* nationalism

ethnography, 5, 19, 24, 101, 102, 134, 196n4, 201n1

ethnomusicology, 13, 15, 21, 127, 135–36, 148, 182n44, 200n87

eugenics, 180n29
exceptionalism, 24, 44, 137–38

FairPlé initiative, 12
Faithful Companions of Jesus, 74
Falkirk, Scotland, Clifford in, 113, 198n43
Farr, Lucy, 27, 44, 59; and Clifford, 111, 117, 125, 133; family, 38, 60–61; and Irish Ireland movement, 61; Kilcar, comparison with, 60–62; McCarthy on, 132; nursing and, 114, 198n49; as tradition bearer, 61; as "woman musician," 125
Fathers and Daughters (Shanachie Records), 182n42
Feis Ceoil, 68–72, 76–79, 81, 84, 190n15, 192n61, 193n64, 194nn78–79
Feis Ceoil Collection of Irish Airs Hitherto Unpublished (Darley, McCall), 76–79, 193n64
feminism, 43, 102–3
fiddles, 50, 65, 75–77, 84, 98, 99, 187n98, 196n1
"fideogist," term, 188n108
Fitzpatrick, A. J., 184n47
Fleadh Cheoil na hÉireann (Music Festival of Ireland, or the All-Ireland), 17, 64–65, 73, 77, 121, 194n80
Flowing Tides (Ó hAllmhuráin), 16, 181n35, 181n38
flow state, 24, 140–50, 202n16, 203n46
Flow: The Psychology of Optimal Experience (Csikszentmihalyi), 202n16
"foreignness," 8, 90, 144, 176
Foucault, Michel, 10, 12, 162
"Freddy Kimmel's/The Home Brew" (*The Humours of Lisheen* album, John and Julia Clifford), 121–24, *122*, *124*, 199n73
future of trad, 174–78

"Gaelic" language. *See* Irish language
Gaelic League, 26, 39, 41, 185, 188n115; on classical music/art music, 69; and cultural nationalism, 14, 40; and dance, 73, 90, 91, 96; and Kenny, 48, 79; and McCarthy, 54, 55, 57; and Morrissey, 54, 55; and Ní Ailpín, 72, 76, 91, 195n91; Oireachtas, 40, 65, 69–73, 80–82, 188n106, 193n66; and uilleann pipes, 43
Gaeltachtaí (Irish speaking regions), 64, 91
Galway, music education in, 59
gatekeeping, 163–65
gender: and biography, 100; and colonization, 28–30; and dance, 91–92; and differences in ways musicians are remembered, 100, 103–4; erasure of, 100, 127; and Feis Ceoil, 68, 190n15; and instrument choice, 68, 144, 188n106; Irish men's identity, 11, 29–33, 35; and Irish pubs, 125, 126, 129, 144; and name recognition, 91; "neutral gender," 127–34; roles, 10, 25–26, 39, 41–42, 63, 127; and trad scholarship, 5, 45. *See also* women; women trad musicians
genderqueer experience in session, 159, 204n15
genealogy, patriarchy and, 20, 182n42
Gibbons, Luke, 29
Giddens, Rhiannon, 167
"Gile na Gile" (Ó Rathaille), 189n121
Gilmartin, Mary, 4, 9, 15, 181n33
"glocal" term, 181n35
gnostic and drastic, 157–58
Goff, Ivan, 188n108
"Gold Ring, The" origin story, 137
Gonne, Maud, 43
"good man" phrase, 127–29
"Great Time For Ireland!, A" (*Punch*), 163
Grenan, Julia, 185n58
Guinan, Joseph, 37
Gupta, Charu, 32

"Had Wicklow Its Own Michael Coleman?" (Linneen), 193n66
Hall, Reg, 86, 110–11, 121, 126, 191n26, 194n84, 198n43
Hall, S. C., 50
Halpin, Joseph (Seósamh Halpin), 72, 73, 75, 76, 192n54
Halpin, Teresa. *See* Ní Ailpín, Treasa

Halpin, William, 75, 192n54
Halpin Trio, 84–93, 87, 89, 92, 93, 194n84, 194n86
"'Hanging Up Looking Glasses at Odd Corners': Ethnobiographical Prospects" (Clifford, James), 196n4
Hanley, Kitty, 51, 187n104
harassment, 144, 146–47, 200n87, 205n46
Hardebeck, Carl, 70, 80–81
Hayes, Martin, 2, 138
heterosexism, 11, 20, 143, 155, 157–59, 165, 176–77. *See also* homophobia
heterosexual reproduction, 10, 26, 61, 63, 155, 189n131
Hibernia (personification of Ireland), 25, 26, 29–30, 56, 57
hierarchy, 105, 144
historiography, 19–20, 44
History of John Bull, The (Arbuthnot), 182n8
HMV recording company, 88, 194n84
"Home Brew, The" (*The Humours of Lisheen* album, John and Julia Clifford), 122, 122–24, 124, 199n73
homophobia, 156–59, 162, 165. *See also* heterosexism
homosocial interaction in sessions, 127
hornpipes, 85
humanism, 18, 139, 180n23
Humours of Lisheen, The (album, Clifford, John and Julia), 121–24, 122, 124, 133, 199n73
Hyde, Douglas, 39–40

identity, "trad musician" as, 15–16, 23, 26, 63, 106–7, 160–61
immigrants, 9, 12, 113, 114, 184n49, 194n84, 194n87
imperialism, 9, 11, 15, 161, 169
inborn talent, fallacy of, 180n29
inclusivity and "the music itself," 18
Incorporated Society of Musicians, 68, 190n13
independence, Ireland's fight for, 9, 10, 27–28, 39
India, 26, 29, 32
individuality, ambivalence toward, 103

Inghinidhe na hÉireann (Daughters of Erin), 39, 42–43
Innes, Catherine, 36, 183n33
instrument choice, 68, 144, 188n106
interactive responsiveness, 150, 203n43
interpellation, 154–55, 170–72
intersectionality, 7, 22, 146, 166
Ireland and Britain, relationship between, 9, 27–30, 70–71, 113, 162, 183n18, 188n115, 198n40
Ireland as maiden. *See* maiden, Ireland personified as
Ireland as mother. *See* Mother Ireland (personification of Ireland)
Irish, stereotypes of, 9, 29, 42, 81, 162, 163
Irish, The (Kennedy), 184n49
"Irish" as adjective, 10, 21
Irish Catholic Church. *See* Catholic Church
Irish citizenship, 9, 10, 13
Irish Constitution, 9, 10, 108, 129, 180n20
Irish cultural values, 9, 153, 154, 161, 173, 175, 177, 203n8
Irish Dance Music (Hall), 191n26
Irish Dances, Marches and Airs (Roche), 90
Irish Dancing Commission (An Coimisiún le Rincí Gaelacha), 81, 88–89, 91–92
Irish diaspora, 9, 10, 13, 17, 30, 134, 181n36
Irish ethnicity, musicians of color and, 166–67
Irish Examiner, 99
Irish Fiddle Book (Cranitch), 83–84
Irish Historical Statistics (Fitzpatrick, Vaughan), 184n47
Irish independence, fight for, 9, 10, 27–28, 39
Irish Ireland movement, 8, 26, 39, 40, 42, 43, 61, 73, 185n62
Irish language, 14, 39; Gaeltachtaí (Irish-speaking regions), 64, 91; Halpin family and, 72, 90–91, 191n36; hostility toward, 195n90; and IRTRAD-L, 195n90; and Laurel Hill School, 74; names and gender in, 91; Oireachtas competitions, 69; *Teagosc-Leabhar na Bheidhline*, 83, 193n73; women and revival of, 40–41

Irish marriage equality referendum (2015), 10
Irish Melodies (Moore), 68, 80
Irish men's identity, 11, 29–30
Irish Minstrels and Musicians (O'Neill), 45–63; Clancy in, 74–75; Kelly in, 47; Kenny in, 47–50; McCarthy in, 47, 53–55, 57, 57–58; Morrissey in, 47, 53–55, 57, 57–58, 188n107; nationalism and, 47; Ní Ailpín in, 76, 192n49; on pipes/pipers, 50–58, 187nn103–5; reprinted editions, 186n86; women musicians given different treatment in, 52–54, 57, 58, 62–63, 186n87, 197n31
Irish Music: A Fascinating Hobby (O'Neill), 50
Irish portrayed as apes, 9, 29, 162, *163*
Irish pubs, 118, 125, 126, 144
Irish speaking regions (Gaeltachtaí), 64, 91
Irish step dance, 58, 88–89, 191n32
"Irish trad list" (IRTRAD-L) (listserv), 195n90
Irish Volunteers, 185n57, 186n78
Irishwomen's Council (Cumann na mBan), 39, 43, 55, 185n57, 186n78
"Irishwomen's work" ("Máire"), 41
IRTRAD-L ("Irish trad list") (listserv), 195n90

Jankélévitch, Vladimir, 156–58
Japan, trad in, 17, 169
jazz, 90, 110, 164–65
John Bull (personification of England), 28, 182n8
"John O'Dwyer of the Glen" ("Seán O'Duibhir a' Ghleanna") (poem/air), 55
Journal of Cumann Luachra, 107–11, 113, 118–19, 196n15, 197n23, 198n47

Kathaleen Ny-Houlahan (personification of Ireland), 30, 34–37, 184n42
"Kathleen Ny-Houlahan" (Mangan), 35–36
Katz, Mark, 93, 195n103
Kavana, Ron, 111
Kearney, Richard, 32, 181n32
Kearns, Gerry, 30
Kelly, Luke, 193n66
"Kelly the Piper" (Hall), 50

Kennedy, Robert E., 184n49
Kenny, Bridget: and "authenticity," 49; and class, 48, 71–72, 187n98; concerts, 48–49, 54, 73; daughters, 50, 70; at Feis Ceoil, 78; and fiddle, 187n98; and Gaelic League, 48, 79; in *Irish Minstrels and Musicians*, 47–50; and nationalism, 48, 79; and Ní Ailpín, 65, 81; as Oireachtas judge, 81; playing qualities of, 81, 138; and poverty, 48; public appearances, 48–49, 54, 73; and Traveller community, 49; and wax cylinder recordings, 49
Kerry Fiddles (Clifford, Murphy, O'Keeffe), 112, 133, 197n37
Kerryman (newspaper), 7–8, 51, 69
Kilcar, Mary, 23, 27, 45, 59–62, 63, 189n131
Kimball, Solon, 110
Kimmel, John, 85, 121
Kitchin, Rob, 4, 9, 15, 181n33
knowledge transmission, 20, 194n87
Kreisler, Fritz, 96

Ladies' Pictorial, 52–53, 58, 188n108
Land of Spices, The (O'Brien), 74
Latour, Bruno, 139
Laurel Hill School, 74, 75, 192n49
Left Hand of Darkness, The (Le Guin), 135, 140
Le Guin, Elisabeth, 150, 203n43
Le Guin, Ursula K., 135, 140
Leys, Ruth, 149
LGBTQ+ musicians, 134, 143, 147, 161–65, 173–74, 176–77, 204n19
liberal humanism, 18, 139, 180n23
lilting, 42, 78, 109, 185n72
Limerick, Ireland, 64–65, 68, 72, 190n16
Limerick Echo, 68
Linehan, Johnny, 112
Linneen, Tony, 193n66
London, England, 114, 116–17, 118, 125, 131–33, 194n84, 199n60
love, 9–10, 32–34, 108
Luddy, Maria, 37, 184n49
Lutz, Catherine, 188n107

Index **231**

"machree" term, 34, 184n35
Magdalen laundries, 129, 200n86
magic, 20, 53–54, 104, 150, 157, 201n8. *See also* magical nationalism
magical nationalism, 24, 31, 53–54, 137–39, 188n111
maiden, Ireland personified as: Dark Rosaleen, 34–37, 184n39; Eiré, 57; Erin, 26, 29–30, 36, 40, 55–57, 56, 129; Hibernia, 25, 26, 29–30, 56, 57; Kathaleen Ny-Houlahan/Cathleen Ní Houlihan, 30, 34–37, 184n42; and Mangan, 57; and McCarthy, 52, 57; and Morrissey, 52, 57; Mother Ireland, similarities with, 35. *See also* personification, nation-as-woman
"Máire" (Mary Butler), 41, 185n68
Making of Irish Traditional Music, The (O'Shea, Helen), 200n87
Mangan, James Clarence, 35–36, 57, 184n42
Margeson, Bill, 138
Marianne (personification of France), 29, 57
marriage bar (1932), 10, 197n21
marriage equality referendum, Irish (2015), 10
Marry, Tom, 90, 91
Mary, Virgin, 32, 33, 35–36, 37, 183n33, 184n46
McCall, Patrick Joseph, 76–79, 193n64
McCann, Anthony, 17
McCarthy, Bernadette, 58, 131, 132
McCarthy, May, 45, 47, 52, 53–55, 57, 57–58, 63, 137
McClintock, Anne, 29
McDonough surname, 49, 187n91
McIntosh, Peggy, 102–3
McMahon, Timothy G., 40–41, 185n66
McNaughton, Ian, 203n36
melodic ornamentation *vs.* vibrato, 95
men's identity, Irish, 11, 29–33, 35, 106
Mitchell-Ingoldsby, Mary, 55
mixed race musicians, 166–67. *See also* musicians of color
"mo chroí" term, 34, 184n35
Moloney, Mick, 13, 16, 196n104, 204n21
Montagne, Renee, 167
Monty Python's Flying Circus, 203n36

Moore, Thomas, 68, 80
Moran, David P., 40, 185n62
"Morning Star, The" (Halpin Trio recording), 85, 92
Morrissey, Mollie, 45, 47, 52–55, 57, 57–58, 63, 188n107
Morrissey, Molly, 186n82
Mostov, Julie, 31–32
mother-as-home metaphor, 30–32, 34
Mother India (personification of India), 26, 29
Mother Ireland (personification of Ireland), 26, 29–35, 41, 129, 183n28, 183n33, 184n36
"Mother Machree" (song, Tin Pan Alley), 34
mothers and tune transmission, 185n72, 197n23
Moylan, Terry, 195n91
Muñoz, José Esteban, 154, 160, 174
Murphy, Bill, 28, 197n27
Murphy, Denis, 98, 103, 109, 111–13, 115, 125–26, 130, 132–33, 197n25; on Clifford, Julia, 117, 199n62; "Danny Ab's Slide," 119; "Denis the Waiver" name, 197n27; and ornamentation, 123; radio performances, 116; *The Star above the Garter*, 119–21, 120
music competitions. *See* competitions
music education, 59, 67–68, 112
Music Festival of Ireland (Fleadh Cheoil na hÉireann), 17, 73, 77, 121, 194, 194n80
Music from Sliabh Luachra *(Ceol as Sliabh Luachra)* (Julia and Billy Clifford album), 125, 133
"Music from Sliabh Luachra" (Ward), 197n27
musicians of color, 22, 134, 143, 164, 166–72, 174, 180n11, 204n27. *See also* racism
"music itself, the," 7, 18, 24, 106, 134–40, 148–52, 158, 172–73, 203n46
"musicking" concept, 179n5
musicology, 21, 136, 182n44
music teachers, 73, 82, 107, 110–11, 119
music tourists, 181n38
"My Dark Rosaleen" (Mangan), 35
"My Life and Music" autobiographies, *Journal of Cumann Luachra*, 107–11, 113, 118–19, 196n15, 198n47

name recognition, gender and, 91
'Nance the Piper,' 51, 187n105
natalism, 180n29
National Folklore Collection at University College Dublin, 192n62
nationalism, 27, 31–32, 63, 76–77, 193n67; and activism, 42–43; and bodies, 10, 81; and class distinctions, 70–71; and classical music/art music, 66–67, 96; and Clifford, 110; critiques of, 7, 15, 18, 23, 26; cultural nationalism, 8, 10, 14, 16–17, 40, 47–48, 52–53, 74, 164; and dance, 89–90; and emigration, 114; and feminism, 43; and fiddlers, 65; and Gaelic League, 14, 40; and "glocal" term, 181n35; and *Irish Melodies*, 68; and *Irish Minstrels and Musicians*, 47; and Kenny, 48, 79; and Laurel Hill School, 74; magical nationalism, 24, 53–54, 137–39, 188n111; and masculine identity, 106; and McCarthy, 54–55; and Morrissey, 54–55; and motherhood, 9–10, 41; and Ní Ailpín, 79; and Ó Cuirrín, 193n76; and Oireachtas, 65, 81; and O'Neill, 47; and pipes, 51–54; and song topics, 9–10, 34; and *Teagosc-Leabhar na Bheidhline*, 83; and trad, ideals for, 49–50, 65; and women, 25–26, 28, 39, 41, 42, 62. *See also* ethnic nationalism; personification, nation-as-woman
National Public Radio, 2, 167
National Schools, music education in, 59, 67–68
Ní Ailpín, Treasa (Teresa Halpin), 64–97, 99; and "authenticity," 96–97; as child star, 72–82; and Clancy, 74, 75, 76; and class, 73, 192n54; at Coláiste na Rinne, 73; and Coleman, 65; and competitions, 65, 78; concerts, 54, 73; dance creation, 89–90; as dancer, 72–73; education of, 73–74; "Ennistymon Jig," 79–80, 93, 193n64; erasure of, 23, 95–96; family, 72, 73, 191nn35–36; in *Feis Ceoil Collection of Irish Airs Hitherto Unpublished*, 77–79; Gaelic League and, 72, 76, 91, 195n91; Halpin Trio, 84–93, 87, 194n84,

194n86; and Irish language, 72, 90–91, 191n36; in *Irish Minstrels and Musicians*, 76, 192n49; on Kelly, 193n66; and Kenny, 65, 81; and Laurel Hill School, 74, 75, 192n49; name, 90–91, 189n1, 195n91; and nationalism, 79; and Ó Canainn, 94; and Ó Cuirrín, 88, 90; O'Donovan on, 90; at Oireachtas, 73, 80–82, 193n66; prizes and distinctions, 76, 77, 78, 80, 81; recordings, wax cylinder, 74, 77, 79–80, 93, 193n64; repertoire, 75, 76, 192n49; Roche on, 89–90; "Rogha an Fhile," 84–93, 87, 194n84, 194n86; 78 rpm album recordings, 82–96, 87, 194n84, 194n86; as teacher, 73, 82; *Teagosc-Leabhar na Bheidhline*, 82–84, 193nn73–74, 194n78; "The Siege of Ennis," 90, 91; as traditional musician, 74–76, 82–96; vibrato and, 23, 79, 81, 85, 86, 93–94; *Violin School*, 84; "Walls of Limerick, The," 90, 91; wax cylinder recordings, 74, 77, 79–80, 93, 193n64
Ní Chonghaile, Deirdre, 193n73
"nonnormative" term, 22
"nonwhite" term, 22, 205n32
"normative" term, 22
NPR (National Public Radio), 2, 167

Obama, Barack, 205n30
O'Brien, Kate, 74
O'Brien, Paddy, 138
O'Callaghan, Margaret, 186n82
Ó Canainn, Tomás, 94–95
O'Connell, Connie, 113, 129–30, 132, 133, 201n98
O'Connell, Molly (Molly Morrissey), 186n82
O'Connor, Donal, 130–33, 200n78
Ó Cuirrín, Seán, 82–84, 88, 90, 193nn73–74, 193n76, 194n78
O'Donnell, Eugene, 95, 196n104
O'Donovan, Joe, 90
O'Farrell, Elizabeth, 39, 185n58
O'Farrelly, Agnes, 43
Ó hAllmhuráin, Gearóid, 16, 45, 181n35, 181n38
Oireachtas, 40, 65, 69–73, 80–82, 188n106, 193n66

O'Keeffe, Maurice, 108, 112, 186n82

O'Keeffe, Pádraig, 75–76, 186n82, 197n21; Clifford and, 110, 111, 119, 123, 125, 132, 133, 196n9; in "My Life and Music" autobiographies, 107; personality, 103; as teacher, 107, 110, 111

Ó Murchú, Labhrás, 205n47

On Being Included (Ahmed), 180n10

O'Neill, Barry, 70

O'Neill, Francis, 27, 77, 188n114. *See also Irish Minstrels and Musicians* (O'Neill)

"On the Outskirts of Milan" (Cavarero), 62

Ó Rathaille, Aogán, 189n121

Ó Riada, Seán, 190n5

Orientalism (Said), 206n54

origin narratives, 1–2, 75

ornamentation, 92–93, 95, 123, 195n96, 199nn72–73

O'Shannon, Cathal, 135

O'Shea, Helen, 13, 15, 127, 148, 200n87

O'Shea, John Augustus, 54

"Over the Moor to Maggie" (Halpin Trio recording), 84–93, 87, 194n84, 194n86

Owens, Rosemary Cullen, 37, 184n46

Oxford Handbook of Queerness and Music, The, "Queer as Trad" (Slominski), 204n19

Parlophone Records, 82–96, 87, 184n86, 194n84, 194n86, 195n103

passing as Irish, 1, 9, 26, 159–61, 166

Past Masters of Irish Fiddle Music (Hall), 194n84

patriarchy, genealogy and, 20, 182n42

Pearse, Pádraig, 33, 39, 185

people of color. *See* musicians of color; racism

personification, nation-as-woman, 28, 183n12, 188n119; Curtin on, 183n18; Dark Rosaleen, 34–37, 184n39; Eiré, 57; Erin, 26, 29–30, 36, 40, 55–57, 56, 129; Ériu, 29; Hibernia, 25, 26, 29–30, 56, 57; Kathaleen Ny-Houlahan/Cathleen Ní Houlihan, 30, 34–37, 184n42; "Máire" on, 41; and Mangan, 57; Marianne, 29, 57; and McCarthy, 55, 57; men, impact on, 30, 31–33, 35; and Morrissey, 55, 57; Mother Ireland, 26, 29–35, 41, 129, 183n28, 183n33, 184n36; passivity, 30, 37; Shan Van Vocht, 26, 30–32, 183n22; women, effects on, 30, 39, 43–44, 46, 62, 99, 129. *See also* maiden, Ireland personified as

piano girls, 67–69

"Pipers' Competition at the Feis Ceoil, The" (Young), 192n61

pipes and pipers, 43, 50–58, 84, 186n78, 187n99, 187–88nn103–106

"Poet's Choice, The" ("Rogha an Fhile") (Halpin Trio recording), 84–93, 87, 194n84, 194n86

postcolonialism, 3, 11

posthumanism, 18, 180n23

postnationalism, 11–12, 14–19, 174–78, 181n32, 181n35

Postnationalist Ireland (Kearney), 181n32

Potts, Tommy, 191n26

poverty, 37–38, 48, 50–51

Povinelli, Elizabeth, 189n136

printed notation, lack of, 83

Public Dance Halls Act (1935), 164

public performance, women and, 23, 26, 48, 58, 98–99, 101, 109, 165. *See also* individual musicians' names

pubs, 118, 125, 126, 144, 147–48

Punch, 56, 57, 163

punters (audience members), 144, 146

"pure drop," 20, 67

purity, 11, 20, 21, 37, 67, 91, 110

quadrilles, 88–89, 91

"Queer as Trad" (Slominski), 204n19

queer musicians, 22, 134, 143, 147, 159, 161–65, 173–74, 176–77, 204n19

race and trad, lack of scholarship on, 5

racism: anti-Asian racism, 146–47, 166, 169; disbelief as, 166–68; elimination of, 176–77; flow state, prevention of, 143–44; and gatekeeping, 163–65; and interpellation, 170–72;

"jazzy" term and, 164–65; and nationalism, 11, 18, 146–47, 161–62, 166, 169; of police and immigration officials, 170–71; and silence/silencing, 157–59; slavery, 3, 9, 163, 167, 203n46; stereotyping, 110, 146, 164, 169, 206n54; white supremacy, 26, 163–64, 168
radio performances, 116, 118
Ramayana, 29
Raphael Tuck and Sons, 56
Rebellion of 1798, 31
recognition, Butler on, 176
recording and transcription of tunes, 46, 69, 78, 124, 195n103, 196n1; 78 rpm album recordings, 82–96, 87, 194n84, 194n86; wax cylinder recordings, 49, 70, 74, 77, 79–80, 93, 193n64. *See also* individual tune names
reel playing, 84–93, 87, 194n84, 194n86
reproductive heterosexuality, 10, 26, 61, 63, 155, 189n131
responsiveness, interactive, 150, 203n43
restraint/understatement, 14, 123, 128, 150, 155–59
Riordan, Sonny, 108
"rising step, the" term, 191n32
Riverdance, 190n5, 200n85
Roche, Frank, 79, 89–90
"Rogha an Fhile" ("The Poet's Choice") (Halpin Trio recording), 84–93, 87, 194n84, 194n86
"Roisín Dubh" ("Dark-haired little rose"), 34
roll (ornamentation), 199n72
romantic relationships within trad scene, 115–18, 173, 174, 175
rose, symbolism of, 35–36
Rubin, Gayle, 61
Rushy Mountain: Classic Music from Sliabh Luachra 1952–1977, The, liner notes (Kavana), 111
Ryan, Louise, 114

Saariaho, Kaija, 126
Said, Edward, 206n54
same-sex marriage referendum (2015), 205n47
saxophones, 199n60
Scabbia, Cristina, 126
scholarship gaps, 5, 19
schoolteachers, trad musicians as, 197n21
Scoil a Leanbh, Coláiste na Rinne (Children's School at College of Ring), 82
Scotland, Clifford in, 113, 198n43
Scott, Joan, 44
seanbhean bhocht ("poor old woman"), 26, 30–32, 183n22
sean-nós singing, 94–95
"Seán O'Duibhir a' Ghleanna" ("John O'Dwyer of the Glen") (poem/air), 55
sessions, 62, 104–6, 127, 144, 146–48, 159, 201n98
set dance, 88–89, 91, 96
78 rpm album recordings, 82–96, 87, 194n84, 194n86
sex/eroticism, comparisons of music with, 149, 150–51, 152
sexism, 11, 44, 127–29, 143–47, 157–59, 176–77
sexual harassment at sessions, 144, 146–47
sexuality and trad, scholarship gap, 5
Shanachie Records, 182n42
Shan Van Vocht (Poor Old Woman) (personification of Ireland), 26, 30–32, 183n22
"Shan Van Vocht, The" ("The Poor Old Woman") (song), 30–31, 32
Sheridan, Christina, 50, 70, 81, 191n26
short roll (ornamentation), 93, 195n96
Shouse, Eric, 150
Siamsa Gaedheal Ceilidh Band, 50, 70
"Siege of Ennis, The" (dance, Ní Ailpín), 90, 91
silence and silencing, 18, 24, 136, 156–59, 173, 204n12, 205n46
singing, 94–95, 198n60
slavery, 3, 9, 163, 167, 203n46
Sliabh Luachra, 98, 105, 123, 160, 186n82, 198n60; Clifford and, 103, 115, 122, 133; *Journal of Cumann Luachra,* 107–11, 113, 118–19, 196n15, 197n23, 198n47
Slobin, Mark, 204n19
Slominski, Tes, 1–3, 5, 11–12, 135, 160, 179n1,

182n44, 204n19. *See also Trad Nation* (Slominski)
slow airs, 81, 85, 93, 95, 133
Slow Airs and Set Dances from Ireland (Moloney, O'Donnell), 196n104
Small, Christopher, 179n5
Society of the Musicians of Ireland. *See* Comhaltas Ceoltóirí Éireann
"soul" term, 164, 204n27
"Speaking Out" (Ahmed), 205n46
Speak it Louder (Wong), 204n12
spéirbhean (sky-woman), 31, 54, 55, 137
spinsters/single women, 37–38, 59, 60, 62, 101, 189n131
Star above the Garter, The (album, Clifford, Murphy), 120–21, *120*
Star of Munster Céilí Band, 116, 118–19, 133
Star of Munster Trio, The (Topic recording, Clifford), 133
step dancing, 58, 88–89, 191n32
stereotypes: of classical musicians, 71; Clifford's resistance to, 129–31; of gay people, 71; of Irish people, 8–9, 22, 29, 81, 162, *163*; of people of color, 146, 169; of women, 129
"Stick to the Craythur," 140
Stroh violin/fiddle, 98, *99*, 196n1
stylistic individuality, ambivalence toward, 103
Subcultural Sounds (Slobin), 204n19
subject-object binary, 203n46
subtlety, 123, 128, 156–59
suffragists, 39, 42, 62
Sullivan, A. M., 31
symbolism: of nation-as-woman (*See* personification, nation-as-woman); of rose, 35–36

tableaux vivants, 43, 186n75
talent, inborn, fallacy of, 180n29
teachers, music, 73, 82, 107, 110–11, 119
teaching school as trad musician career, 197n21
Teagosc-Leabhar na Bheidhline (Instructional Book for the Violin) (Ní Ailpín, Ó Cuirrín), 82–84, 193nn73–74, 194n78

Teahan, Terry, 181n36
temperance societies, 59, 65, 68, 81, 189n128
Tenniel, John, 56, 57
terminology choices in *Trad Nation*, 6, 21–22, 196n9
Texas trad scene, 143, 145
The Cunning of Recognition (Povinelli), 189n136
"The Necessity for De-Anglicizing Ireland" (lecture, Hyde), 39
"Three Tunes, The" (tune), 88
Tin Pan Alley, 34
Topic recordings, 121–24, *122*, *124*, 133, 199n73
Toss the Feathers: Irish Set Dancing (Moylan), 195n91
Tourish, Martin, 199n72
tourists, 181n38
trad, appeal of, 104–6, 140, 141, 172, 177–78
"traddie," term, 6, 22
trad flow, 24, 140–50, 202n16
Traditional Music in Ireland (Ó Canainn), 94–95
traditional *vs.* non-traditional music, 80
tradition bearers, musicians as, 20, 45, 48, 55, 61, 182n43
Trad Nation (Slominski): goals, 4–7, 14–15, 134, 153, 155, 157; methodologies, 5, 19–21, 24, 65–66; structure, 22–24; terminology choices, 6, 21–22, 196n9
"trad" term, 21
"Traffic in Women, The" (Rubin), 61
transgender people, negativity toward, 145–46
transmission of tunes, 20, 61, 185n75, 194n87, 197n23
transnationalism, 16, 27, 33–34, 47
transphobia, 146
Traveller community, 38, 45, 49, 164, 187nn91–92, 205n29
trebles, 199n72
Treoir, 193n66
triplets, 199n72
tunes, age and value of, 90, 195n92
tune structure, 79, 86, 194n83

236 *Index*

tune transmission, 20, 61, 185n75, 194n87, 197n23
"Two Forces" (Tenniel), 56, 57

uilleann pipes, 43, 50–58, 186n79, 187n99, 188n106
understatement, 14, 123, 128, 150, 155–59
Undoing Gender (Butler), 63
union pipes, 50–58, 186n79, 187n99, 188n106
United Irishman, 41
United States, 11, 15
University College Dublin, National Folklore Collection, 192n62

value of tunes, age and, 90, 195n92
Vaughan, W. E., 184n47
vibrato, 23, 79, 81, 85, 86, 93–95, 96, 195n103
violin, 50, 77, 84. *See also* fiddle
"Violin Class for Ballinasloe," 189n128
Violin School (Ni Ailpin), 84
Virgin Mary, 32, 33, 35–36, 37, 183n33, 184n46
"'Vote Yes for Common Sense Citizenship': Immigration and the Paradoxes at the Heart of Ireland's 'Céad Míle Fáilte'" (Crowley, Gilmartin, Kitchin), 4, 9, 15, 181n33

"Walls of Limerick, The" (dance, Ní Ailpín), 90, 91
Ward, Alan, 197n27
Ward, Margaret, 43
Warner, Marina, 36
warpipes, 52, 53, 188n106
wax cylinder recordings, 49, 70, 74, 77, 79–80, 93, 193n64
Weheliye, Alexander, 180n23
Whelan, Bill, 190n5
Whelan, Josephine, 50, 70, 81, 191n26
White (Dyer), 103
White, Harry, 67, 95, 136, 193n67
whiteness: and colonialism, 26; passing as Irish and, 1, 9, 26, 159–61, 166; and purity, 20; white ethnic musics, 6, 11; white nationalism, 4, 5, 6, 11, 15; white privilege, 171–72; white supremacy, 26, 163–64, 168; white womanhood, idealization of, 36
"Wicklow Hornpipe, The" (The Home Brew), 122, 122–24, *124*, 199n73
Woman's Life, A (Cheever), 196n7
women: Catholic Church's control of, 36, 110, 114, 129, 198n47; and class distinctions, 37–38, 126; classical musicians, 66–72, 95, 190n19; domestic roles, 39, 41, 42, 108–9; and factory work, 185n69; and Gaelic League, 40–41; Inghinidhe na hÉireann (Daughters of Erin), 39, 42–43; and Irish constitution, 10, 108, 180n20; and Irish Ireland movement, 40, 42; and Irish language, 40–41; and motherhood, 9–10, 33–34, 41; and nationalism, 25–26, 28, 34, 39, 41, 42; and poverty, 37–38; and reproductive heterosexuality, 10, 26, 28, 34, 61, 63, 155, 189n131; respectability of, 33; and sexism, 11, 44, 127–29, 143–47, 157–59, 176–77; spinsters/single women, 37–38, 59, 60, 62, 101, 189n131; statistics on, 37, 184n47; stereotyping of, 129; suffragists, 42; Travellers, 38; and Virgin Mary, 37, 184n46; and whiteness, 36; and writing, 183n28, 188n107. *See also* personification, nation-as-woman; women trad musicians
women trad musicians, 44–62, 71, 134, 191n30; abilities as supernatural, 53–54; and age, 131, 200n95; amateurs, 67; and classical/art music, 67; conservative approach required for acceptance, 128, 200n85; diminishing phrases used to describe, 53, 54, 58, 176; and disbelief, aggression of, 165; erasure of, 23, 44–45, 66, 98–99, 113, 165; and family responsibilities, 108; in *Feis Ceoil Collection of Irish Airs Hitherto Unpublished*, 76–79; harassment of, 144, 146–47, 200n87; in *Irish Minstrels and Musicians*, 52–54, 57, 58, 62–63, 186n87, 197n31; and lilting, 42, 78, 109, 185n72; and motherhood, 45, 48, 185n75, 197n23; music education for, 67–68;

and nationalism, 63; O'Shea on, 148; and personification of nation-as-woman, 43–44, 46, 66, 99, 129; pipers, 51–58, 187n105; and public performance, 23, 26, 48, 58, 98–99, 101, 109, 165; and pub sessions, 147–48; and representation, desire for, 174; safety concerns of, 166; scholarship on, lack of, 19; sexualization of, 131; and Sliabh Luachra, 109; and trad flow, 143; as tradition bearers, 45, 48, 61; tune transmission between, 20. *See also* women; individual women's names

Wong, Deborah, 204n12
Wu, Frank H., 206n54

Yeats, William Butler, 137, 184n42
Young, Robert, 78, 192n61
Yuval-Davis, Nira, 28

Zimmermann, Georges Denis, 31, 34

MUSIC / CULTURE

A series from Wesleyan University Press
Edited by Deborah Wong, Sherrie Tucker, and Jeremy Wallach
Originating editors: George Lipsitz, Susan McClary, and Robert Walser

Marié Abe
Resonances of Chindon-ya: Sounding Space and Sociality in Contemporary Japan

Frances Aparicio
Listening to Salsa: Gender, Latin Popular Music, and Puerto Rican Cultures

Paul Austerlitz
Jazz Consciousness: Music, Race, and Humanity

Harris M. Berger
Metal, Rock, and Jazz: Perception and the Phenomenology of Musical Experience

Harris M. Berger
Stance: Ideas about Emotion, Style, and Meaning for the Study of Expressive Culture

Harris M. Berger and Giovanna P. Del Negro
Identity and Everyday Life: Essays in the Study of Folklore, Music, and Popular Culture

Franya J. Berkman
Monument Eternal: The Music of Alice Coltrane

Dick Blau, Angeliki Vellou Keil, and Charles Keil
Bright Balkan Morning: Romani Lives and the Power of Music in Greek Macedonia

Susan Boynton and Roe-Min Kok, editors
Musical Childhoods and the Cultures of Youth

James Buhler, Caryl Flinn, and David Neumeyer, editors
Music and Cinema

Thomas Burkhalter, Kay Dickinson, and Benjamin J. Harbert, editors
The Arab Avant-Garde: Music, Politics, Modernity

Patrick Burkart
Music and Cyberliberties

Julia Byl
Antiphonal Histories: Resonant Pasts in the Toba Batak Musical Present

Corinna Campbell
Parameters and Peripheries of Culture: Interpreting Maroon Music and Dance in Paramaribo, Suriname

Daniel Cavicchi
Listening and Longing: Music Lovers in the Age of Barnum

Susan D. Crafts, Daniel Cavicchi, Charles Keil, and the Music in Daily Life Project
My Music: Explorations of Music in Daily Life

Jim Cullen
Born in the USA: Bruce Springsteen and the American Tradition

Anne Danielsen
Presence and Pleasure: The Funk Grooves of James Brown and Parliament

Peter Doyle
Echo and Reverb: Fabricating Space in Popular Music Recording, 1900–1960

Ron Emoff
Recollecting from the Past: Musical Practice and Spirit Possession on the East Coast of Madagascar

Yayoi Uno Everett and Frederick Lau, editors
Locating East Asia in Western Art Music

Susan Fast and Kip Pegley, editors
Music, Politics, and Violence

Heidi Feldman
Black Rhythms of Peru: Reviving African Musical Heritage in the Black Pacific

Kai Fikentscher
"You Better Work!" Underground Dance Music in New York City

Ruth Finnegan
The Hidden Musicians: Music-Making in an English Town

Daniel Fischlin and Ajay Heble, editors
The Other Side of Nowhere: Jazz, Improvisation, and Communities in Dialogue

Wendy Fonarow
Empire of Dirt: The Aesthetics and Rituals of British "Indie" Music

Murray Forman
The 'Hood Comes First: Race, Space, and Place in Rap and Hip-Hop

Lisa Gilman
My Music, My War: The Listening Habits of U.S. Troops in Iraq and Afghanistan

Paul D. Greene and Thomas Porcello, editors
Wired for Sound: Engineering and Technologies in Sonic Cultures

Tomie Hahn
Sensational Knowledge: Embodying Culture through Japanese Dance

Edward Herbst
Voices in Bali: Energies and Perceptions in Vocal Music and Dance Theater

Deborah Kapchan
Traveling Spirit Masters: Moroccan Gnawa Trance and Music in the Global Marketplace

Deborah Kapchan, editor
Theorizing Sound Writing

Max Katz
Lineage of Loss: Counternarratives of North Indian Music

Raymond Knapp
Symphonic Metamorphoses: Subjectivity and Alienation in Mahler's Re-Cycled Songs

Victoria Lindsay Levine and Dylan Robinson, editors
Music and Modernity among First Peoples of North America

Laura Lohman
Umm Kulthūm: Artistic Agency and the Shaping of an Arab Legend, 1967–2007

Preston Love
A Thousand Honey Creeks Later: My Life in Music from Basie to Motown—and Beyond

René T. A. Lysloff and Leslie C. Gay Jr., editors
Music and Technoculture

]Ian MacMillen
Playing It Dangerously: Tambura Bands, Race, and Affective Block in Croatia and Its Intimates

Allan Marett
Songs, Dreamings, and Ghosts: The Wangga of North Australia

Ian Maxwell
Phat Beats, Dope Rhymes: Hip Hop Down Under Comin' Upper

Kristin A. McGee
Some Liked It Hot: Jazz Women in Film and Television, 1928–1959

Tracy McMullen
Haunthenticity: Musical Replay and the Fear of the Real

Rebecca S. Miller
Carriacou String Band Serenade: Performing Identity in the Eastern Caribbean

Tony Mitchell, editor
Global Noise: Rap and Hip-Hop Outside the USA

Christopher Moore and Philip Purvis, editors
Music & Camp

Rachel Mundy
Animal Musicalities: Birds, Beasts, and Evolutionary Listening

Keith Negus
Popular Music in Theory: An Introduction

Johnny Otis
Upside Your Head: Rhythm and Blues on Central Avenue

Kip Pegley
Coming to You Wherever You Are: MuchMusic, MTV, and Youth Identities

Jonathan Pieslak
Radicalism and Music: An Introduction to the Music Cultures of al-Qa'ida, Racist Skinheads, Christian-Affiliated Radicals, and Eco-Animal Rights Militants

Lorraine Plourde
Tokyo Listening: Sound and Sense in a Contemporary City

Matthew Rahaim
Musicking Bodies: Gesture and Voice in Hindustani Music

John Richardson
*Singing Archaeology:
Philip Glass's Akhnaten*

Tricia Rose
*Black Noise: Rap Music and Black Culture
in Contemporary America*

David Rothenberg and
Marta Ulvaeus, editors
The Book of Music and Nature: An Anthology of Sounds, Words, Thoughts

Nichole Rustin-Paschal
*The Kind of Man I Am: Jazzmasculinity
and the World of Charles Mingus Jr.*

Marta Elena Savigliano
*Angora Matta: Fatal Acts
of North-South Translation*

Joseph G. Schloss
Making Beats: The Art of Sample-Based Hip-Hop

Barry Shank
*Dissonant Identities: The Rock 'n' Roll
Scene in Austin, Texas*

Jonathan Holt Shannon
*Among the Jasmine Trees: Music and
Modernity in Contemporary Syria*

Daniel B. Sharp
Between Nostalgia and Apocalypse: Popular Music and the Staging of Brazil

Helena Simonett
*Banda: Mexican Musical Life
across Borders*

Mark Slobin
*Subcultural Sounds: Micromusics
of the West*

Mark Slobin, editor
Global Soundtracks: Worlds of Film Music

Tes Slominski
*Trad Nation: Gender, Sexuality, and Race
in Irish Traditional Music*

Christopher Small
The Christopher Small Reader

Christopher Small
*Music of the Common Tongue:
Survival and Celebration
in African American Music*

Christopher Small
Music, Society, Education

Christopher Small
*Musicking: The Meanings
of Performing and Listening*

Maria Sonevytsky
*Wild Music: Sound and
Sovereignty in Ukraine*

Regina M. Sweeney
*Singing Our Way to Victory:
French Cultural Politics and Music
during the Great War*

Colin Symes
*Setting the Record Straight: A Material
History of Classical Recording*

Steven Taylor
*False Prophet: Field Notes
from the Punk Underground*

Paul Théberge
*Any Sound You Can Imagine:
Making Music/Consuming Technology*

Sarah Thornton
Club Cultures: Music, Media, and Subcultural Capital

Michael E. Veal
Dub: Songscape and Shattered Songs in Jamaican Reggae

Michael E. Veal and
E. Tammy Kim, editors
Punk Ethnography: Artists and Scholars Listen to Sublime Frequencies

Robert Walser
Running with the Devil: Power, Gender, and Madness in Heavy Metal Music

Dennis Waring
Manufacturing the Muse: Estey Organs and Consumer Culture in Victorian America

Lise A. Waxer
The City of Musical Memory: Salsa, Record Grooves, and Popular Culture in Cali, Colombia

Mina Yang
Planet Beethoven: Classical Music at the Turn of the Millennium

ABOUT THE AUTHOR

Tes Slominski is a music/sound scholar and a fiddle player in the Irish tradition. In addition to her scholarly work, Tes is an active performer who specializes in the regional repertoire and style of Sliabh Luachra, an area at the border of Counties Kerry and Cork. She founded the still-thriving Blue Ridge Irish Music School in Charlottesville, Virginia, in 1999 and taught ethnomusicology at Beloit College. Tes is the recipient of the American Musicological Society's Alvin H. Johnson AMS 50 Dissertation Fellowship, an ACLS Recent Doctoral Recipients fellowship, and a Woodrow Wilson Women's Studies Fellowship.